THE ALBIGENSIAN HERESY

VOLUME II

The Albigensian Heresy

VOL. II

(Its Suppression by Crusade and Inquisition)

BY THE REV.

H. J. WARNER. M.A.

NEW YORK / RUSSELL & RUSSELL

FOREWORD

In vol. I an attempt was made to trace the Sources of the Albigensian Heresy, and to describe its tenets and system.

In the present volume we endeavour to give an account of its Suppression by Crusade and Inquisition, the former an adaptation of military measures originally taken against enemies outside the Church ; the latter, a development of legal measures against enemies within the State.

BIBLIOGRAPHY

Mansi, *Concilia.*

Hefele, *Councils.*

Migne, *Patrol. Lat.* (Pearson's Index to Regesta of Innocent facilitates references).

Ripoll, *Bullarium* (For Preaching Friars).

Quetif and Echard, vol. 1.

Acta Sanctorum (August 4, pp. 358 foll.)

Martene and Durand, vol. 5.

Bernard Gui, *Practica*, 1321 (published by Douais, 1886, with valuable preface. Four copies exist, of which one is at Carcassonne, one at Toulouse, one at St. Roche, and one in the British Museum. B. Gui was born 1261, and was Inquisitor of Toulouse from 1307–23. Died 1331. His sentences were published by Limborch in his Amsterdam edition of his ' Inquisition.')

Eymeric, *Directorium*, 1358 (late for our purpose, but useful for precedents quoted).

Peter de Vaux-Sarnai, *Hist. Albig.*, 1203–18, (Nephew of Guy, Abbot of Citeaux, and later Bishop of Carcassonne. Bouquet, *Recueil*, xix).

William de Tudela, *La Chanson de la Croisade Albig.* (unfinished, possibly by two authors ; published by Fauriel, translation in modern French by Lafon).

William de Puy-Laurent. *Hist. Albig.* (1145–1272). (Notary of the Bishop of Toulouse, 1241, and Chaplain to Raymond VII, Count of Toulouse, 1242–49, Bouquet, Recueil xix).

Anon. Hist. de la Guerre des Albig. en Languedoc. (Vaissete vol. viii).

Bibliography

Cæsarius d'Heisterback (Cistercian).

William Pelhisse, *Chronicon* (born at Toulouse and died there 1268. Earliest authority for Inquis. at Toulouse. A Preaching Friar, eye-witness of and participant in many events he records).

Stephen de Bourbon (Lecoy, *Anecdotes Hist.*, 1877).

Belhomme. *Mémoires de la Soc. Archaeol. du midi*, vol. vi., containing Documents inédits sur l'Hist. des Albig. (' badly done ' Molinier).

Doat, *Coilection*, 1669 (largest collection of documents relative to the Inquisition. In the National Library, Paris, and consists of copies of the muniments of the Midi made by Jean de Doat, King's Counsel, who, under royal commission, investigated all the title deeds concerning the rights of the French Crown in Provence and Languedoc. Of the 258 volumes, volumes 21–37 deal with the Inquisition and have been published by Mahul in *Cartulaire et Archives des Communes de Carcassonne*).

Percin, *Monumenta conventus Tolosani*, 1693 (but without B. Gui's *Practica*, which Percin thought lost, although there was a copy in Toulouse itself).

Potthast.

Teulet, *Layettes au Trésor des Chartres*.

Pertz, *Leges*, vol. ii.

Compayré, *Etudes Historiques*.

Douais, *Les Albigeois*, 1879, *les Sources*, 1881.

" *Les hérétiques du Comté de Toulouse*, 1891.

" *Les Albig. et les Fr. Prêch. à Narbonne*, 1894.

        ,,   ,,   *en Gascogne*, 1895

" *Documents*, 1900, 2 vols.

" *Acta Capitulorum Ordinis Fratr. Pred.*, 1894.

" *L'Inquis. ses origines et sa procédure*, 1906.

Molinier, *Etude sur les sources*, 1880.

Döllinger, *Sektengeschichte*, 1890, 2 vols.

Limborch, *Inquisition, 1692 (Amsterdam)*

Bibliography

Schmidt, C., *Hist. et Doc. des Cathares*, 1849, 2 vols.

Mahul, *Cartulaire et Archives de Carcassonne.*

T. de Cauzons, *Hist. de l'Inq. en France*, 2 vols.

Guiraud, *L'Albig. Languedocien* (Introduction to *la Cartulaire de Prouille*, 2 vols.)

D'Achery, Spicelegium.

Balme et Ledidiére, *Cartulaire de S. Dominique.*

Bede Jarrett, *Life of St. Dominic.*

O'Leary, *Life and Times of Dominic.*

Tanon, *Hist. des Tribunaux de l'Inquis.*, 1893.

Luchaire, *Innocent III*, 6 vols. (of which vol. 2 deals more particularly with the Albigenses.)

Lea, *The Inquisition*, 3 vols. (Also the French edition with Frédéricq's criticisms ; also Acton in *Essays on Liberty*.)

Vacandard, *The Inquisition.*

Vernet, (*Dictionary of Catholic Theology*, ' Cathares ').

Hauréau, *Bernard Délicieux.*

Vaissete et C. Devic, *Histoire Générale de Languedoc*, 15 vols.

Peyrat, *Hist. des Albig.* (2 vols. unfinished).

Tardif, *Nouv. Revue Hist.*, 1883 (earliest manual for guidance of Inquisitors).

Mélanges de Littérature et d'Hist. religieuse, vol. i, 1899.

Nickerson, *The Inquisition.*

Turberville, *Mediæval Heresy and Inquisition*, 1920.

Coulton, *The Death Penalty for Heresy* (*Mediæval Studies*, No. 18).

THE ALBIGENSIAN HERESY

Its Suppression by Crusade and Inquisition

PART I.—THE CRUSADE

CHAPTER I

NOT until a century and a half had elapsed could the Roman Church claim that it had succeeded in conquering and extirpating that religious movement known in history as the Albigensian Heresy.[1] To this day members of that Church refuse to regard those over whom it triumphed as, in any sense, Christians. Luchaire, the second volume of whose work on Innocent III deals with that Pope's measures against the Albigenses, wrote : ' Innocent III is the first Pope who invoked frequently the secular arm and invented this unheard-of thing, a home crusade, a war made upon a *Christian* people, because it had ceased to be Catholic.' But his reviewer observes that if

[1] Why Albi should have given its name to the Heresy, in preference to all the other names, will probably never be satisfactorily settled. It is, as we have said (vol. i, Preface), ' a mere accident of history ' Vaissete (*Hist. de Lang.*, vol. vii, note xiii) discusses the question, and after rightly dismissing several suggestions, concludes that the name was given to the heretics by the Crusaders from the North because they first met with them at Albi on crossing the Tarn. To this we may add that when the whole country fell to Alfonso, Count of Poitiers, he had one seneschal for both Toulouse and Albi (Correspondence, passim). Usually it was more convenient to name a heresy after its founder or chief exponent (Arian, Pelagian, etc.). But *this* heresy had not one founder or exponent but many ; and hence recourse was had to the *place* where the army of the Church first encountered it, and where it lingered longest and strongest.

M. Luchaire had gone to original sources for his information
as to the creed, rites, manners and organization of the
Albigenses, he would have found that what with their
dualism, their docetism, their grimly pessimistic ethics and
their anarchist doctrines, the Catharists were no more
Christians than the worshippers of Ormuz and Ahriman, the
fakirs of India, or the fatalists of Islam.[1]   Well, we have in
vol. i done what Luchaire is charged with having failed to
do ; we have gone to the original sources, and we decline to
place those who were persecuted by the Roman Church in
the same class as fire-worshippers, fakirs, and fatalists.
There was, we submit, no relationship between the dualism
of the Parsees and that of the Albigenses.   There was as
much resemblance between the asceticism of the Catharists
and fakirs as between the latter and Franciscans ; and
Dominicans were as much fatalists as Moslems.

That the military operations launched against them were
given the holy name of Crusades did not make them pagans.
We are astonished that their resistance was so strong and
long.   And if we search for the secret source of that
strength we shall find it in their conviction, that it was a
Struggle for Freedom—in the earlier stages for freedom of
thought, and in the latter for freedom of country.   Many of
the nobles were tainted with heresy, but gave it only luke-
warm support until the struggle assumed a territorial aspect.
At first they used it rather as a means to flout prelates than
as an assertion of religious convictions.   Though varying
among themselves, the one danger welded the heretics into
one body.   By means of messengers (*nuntii*) and guides
(*ductores*) they secretly apprised one another of the plans
and movements of crusader and inquisitor, and fugitives
could always depend upon all possible shelter and support
from the ' faithful,' while the proximity of the mountains

[1] *Revue des Quest. Hist.*, 1906.

always afforded avenues of escape, from which they could issue for further propaganda when the tyranny was overpast.

The blameless lives of the heretics, contrasting with the luxury of the clergy,[1] commended heresy itself to the reception of the people. The Catharists were the Puritans of the time. The preaching of Dominic was at first, at any rate, as much a protest against the corruption of the Church as a preaching against the doctrines of the heretics.[2] Moreover the clergy were not preachers but ceremonialists, and were not able to withstand the wisdom and the spirit with which the heretics spake.

[1] Bernard of Clairvaux : 'Certe vinearum demolitio testatur vulpem . . . Clerici et sacerdotes, populis ecclesiisque relictis, intonsi et barbati apud eos inter textores et textrices plerumque inventi sunt. An non gravis demolitio ista ? An non opera vulpium haec ? ' *Serm. in Cantica*, lxvii. Migne *P. L.* t. 183, coll. 1093, 1094.

[2] For the general looseness of the age, see Peyrat, *Hist. des Albi.*, vol. i, pp. 140 ff, and in dramatic form, ' I. S (timson) of Dale' ' The Light of Provence.'

NEARLY a century before the invasion of the Crusaders, heretics, probably Petrobrusians, were condemned at the Council of Toulouse (1119) and ordered to be expelled from the Church and 'coerced by outside powers' (Canon iii). The second Lateran Council (1139) repeated [1] the sentence (Canon xxiii), and the Council of Rheims (1148) was more explicit in describing them as 'men dwelling in Gascony, Provence, and elsewhere.' A year previously Bernard of Clairvaux had been sent by Eugenius III to preach against the heretics ; but even if we accept it as no exaggeration that, whereas the legate could only attract thirty, 'so great was the multitude that assembled to hear the word of God that the vast Church (of Albi) could not hold them' when Bernard preached, they remained hearers of the word and not doers.[2] Another Council at Rheims (1157) condemned 'Majors'[3] to perpetual imprisonment, 'unless a severer punishment ought to be inflicted,' and their followers were to be branded on forehead and cheek with a hot iron. The option of 'the ordeal' was, however, offered them. Again : the Council of Tours (1163) plainly refers to the Albigensian heretics :[4] 'In the parts of Toulouse a damnable heresy has lately come to light, which

---

[1] Lea (*Inquis.* vol. i, p. 117) says the Council of Toulouse 'was forced to content itself with sentencing the heretics to expulsion from the Church. . . . Innocent II when restored to Rome seems to have awakened to the necessity of action, and in the second Lateran Council in 1139 issued a decisive decree which is interesting as the *earliest* example of the interpellation of the secular arm.' This is wrong. Canto iii of the Council of Toulouse and Canto xxiii of the second Lateran Council are *verbatim* the same, and both contain the expression ' per potestates exteras coerceri.'

[2] *Bernardi Vita*, lib. vi, 3, ch. xvii § 10 (Migne P.L.t. 185, col. 414), Will. de Puy, L. ch. i.

[3] See vol. i, p. 77.   [4] Can. iv.

little by little like a cancer has spread into the neighbouring
localities through Gascony and other provinces, and has
already infected a good many. . . . Wherefore we direct
that the bishops and all the priests residing in those parts
be on their guard against them ; that no one give them
shelter under pain of anathema ; that no one trade with
them ; that, when arrested, they are to be handed over to
the custody of Catholic nobles, and their goods confiscated ;
their meetings to be strictly forbidden.' This Council was
attended by seventeen cardinals, one hundred and twenty
archbishops—of whom Becket was the most famous and
honoured—and bishops, besides hundreds of abbots and
influential laymen ; but the heretics pursued their course as
if the Council had never met or passed such a decree.
Equally ineffective was the council of Lombers, *two*[1] years
later, for immediately after it the heretics responded with a
Council of their own at St. Felix de Servian.[2] This may
account for Roger Hoveden's '*re*vixerat' in his account of
another Council at Toulouse in 1165. ' The Arian heresy
which had been condemned in the province of Toulouse had
just broken out *again*.'[3]

Certainly something more drastic than conciliar decrees
was required ; and the King of France and the King of
England both promised to send military assistance to
Raymond V, Count of Toulouse, but in the end contented
themselves with the Church Militant, as represented by
Peter Chrysogonus, Cardinal and Legate, Garin, Archbishop of Bourges (formerly Abbot of the Cistercian
Monastery of Pontigny), Reginald, Abbot of Bath, Henry
of Clairvaux (afterwards Cardinal Bishop of Albano) and
several other prelates ' converting the heretics to the

---

[1] Vol. i, p. 42.
[2] Caraman is a mistake, but a significant mistake of a copyist
vol. i, p. 15.
[3] Roger Hoveden, vol. ii, pp. 105, 150 (Stubbs)

Christian faith by preaching' (1177).[1] The secular pressure was assigned to Raymond, Count of Toulouse, his namesake, Count of Castelnau and others. Henry of Clairvaux declared in an open letter to the Catholic world that ' if they had deferred their visit for three years, scarcely anyone would have remained orthodox.' Imposing as was the personnel of this commission, it was likewise unsuccessful. Such, at least, is the opinion of Robert de St. Marien of Auxerre, a contemporary chronicler. Roger Hoveden, however, avers that it was not without fruit. At first, Chrysogonus and his colleagues were hooted through the streets with cries of ' Apostates! Heretics! Hypocrites!' and other opprobrious names. But at last, partly by menaces, partly by flattery, they secured the attendance before them of a ringleader, named Peter Mauran, a man of wealth, who, feigning himself, as it was alleged, to be John the Evangelist, held nightly meetings, clothed in a sort of dalmatic, 'like a king.'[2] Being condemned, he was deprived of his property and ordered to present himself during eight days at different churches in Toulouse, there to be scourged on the bare back, and afterwards to go to the Holy Land for three years. On the completion of his penance his property was to be restored to him on a payment of five hundred silver pounds to the court. A hard sentence for an old man, but the contract was faithfully observed on both sides. Mauran, however, on his return was hailed as a hero, and three times elected capitoul. Raymond took an oath in the presence of the people that he would not, either by prayer or bribe (*sive prece sive pretio*) favour the heretics. According to the missioners other

---

[1] Migne, *P. L.t.*, cciv, col. 223. Mansi, xxii. pp. 109 ff. Heresy infected, ' non solum vulgus simplex, sed et ecclesiam Dei, sacerdotes et episcopos cum principibus laicis.

[2] He owned two fortified houses, one in and one outside Toulouse, where he received heretics. Migne, *Patrol. Lat.*, t. cciv, pp. 235 ff.

notable heretics were reconciled, though secretly. From Toulouse the mission visited Albi, Carcassonne, Béziers and Castres. Roger Trenceval, Viscount of Béziers, who had imprisoned the Bishop of Albi, retired before them, leaving his wife and children in the Castle of Castres. In their presence the Abbot of Clairvaux pronounced husband and father a heretic and perjurer, declared war against him in the names of the King of England and the King of France, and excommunicated him.[1] Two other distinguished sectaries now surrendered, Raymond de Baimiac, and Bernard Raymond, complaining that they had been driven away by the Count of Toulouse. Safe-conduct having been granted them, they presented themselves in the Church of St. Stephen, Toulouse, where before more than three hundred prelates and nobles they read a long denial of their alleged errors, and a profession of their faith.[2] They were then conducted to the larger Church of St. James, in the presence of a great congregation. ' Do you believe in your heart what you affirm with your mouth ? ' ' We have never held any other doctrine.' ' You lie,' shouted the count and others, ' we swear we have heard you preach against the Faith.' ' Will you affirm *on oath* the creed you have just read ? ' demanded Peter Chrysogonus. This they declined to do, and their refusal to take the oath was regarded as evidence of their heresy.[3] They were condemned as heretics, but the safe-conduct was respected, and they withdrew to Béziers. And this was all the mission accomplished, although composed of prelates of the highest rank, French and English, and with the direct authority of the pope and the two most powerful monarchs of Europe, Henry II and Louis VII. On their departure, the heretics rose up like rocks from a receding tide. *Parturiunt montes, nascetur ridiculus mus.*

---

[1] Vaissete, *Hist. de Lang.*, vi. 79, 85.   [2] Vol. i, p. 46.
[3] See vol. i, under ' Oaths '.

Alexander III, now triumphant over his antipopes, summoned a great Council at Rome, called the Third Lateran (1179), which condemned the heretics ' of Gascony, Albi, the parts about Toulouse and elsewhere, whom some called Cathari, others Publicani, others Paterini, others by other names.' [1] ' As saith blessed Leo, although ecclesiastical discipline is content with priestly sentences, and does not proceed with blood-penalties (*cruentas ultiones*), it is nevertheless in accordance with the constitutions of catholic princes that a wholesome cure is often effected by the mere fear of corporal punishment.' Against heretics and routiers alike was the sentence given. They were to be denounced publicly in all churches on Sundays and other holy days, and not received into communion ; no one was to receive them or deal with them or keep any contract with them ; no Mass was to be offered for them when dead, nor were they to be buried with Christians ; they were to be opposed with armed force. The Council itself confessed the failure of previous efforts. The heretics practised their *pravitas* quite openly. Denunciation could be met with denunciation ; boycotting with boycotting. They cared for nothing, for no shrift when dying, no Mass when dead, no service when buried. Why should they ? They had their own rites and ceremonies.

Hardly had the Peace of Constance been signed than the Pope, Lucius III, at the instance of the Emperor Frederick Barbarossa issued from Verona the Bull, ' *Ad abolendam* ' against the ' Cathari, Paterini, and those who falsely call themselves Humiliati or the Poor Men of Lyons, Passagnini, Josepini, Arnaldistae ' (1184). This decree was more drastic and detailed than any before. Receivers and defenders of heretics were to be treated as actual heretics. Tainted clergy were to be deprived of all the privileges of their

---

[1] Mansi, xxii, Can. xxvii.

order and handed over to the secular arm, unless immediately after arrest they returned freely and fully to the
unity of the Catholic Church, publicly recanted and made
full satisfaction. The same penalties, *mutatis mutandis*,
awaited laymen. This decree was to be published by all
patriarchs, archbishops and bishops under pain of suspension for three years. ' Every bishop in person or by his
archdeacon shall twice or thrice in the year go through
every parish in which it is reported that heretics reside ; he
shall summon to him three or four good men and true, or,
if expedient, all the people, and make them swear that they
will report to him or his archdeacon any heretics and those
who frequent secret assemblies and sever themselves from
the society of the faithful and differ from them in life and
manners. All counts, barons, governors and consuls are
to give all possible aid, acting under the advice of the archbishops and bishops. All who favour heretics are to be
debarred from pleading or giving evidence in a court of
law, and from all public offices.' Such was the plan of
campaign, and a plan it remained. It is true that Henry of
Clairvaux, now promoted Bishop of Albano and Cardinal,
was appointed legate to carry it out. Not daunted by
previous failures, he collected a small army, placed himself
at its head, and forced his way into Lavaur (1184). The two
Catharist ' Bishops ', Baimiac and Raymond, were captured
and recanted, and Roger, Viscount of Béziers, promised to
withdraw his protection from heresy. In three months the
legate went everywhere, even to the confines of Spain,
wielding the sword of steel as well as that of the spirit, a
harbinger of the Crusade, the people fleeing before him to
the valleys of the Pyrenees. He deprived Pons d'Arsac,
Archbishop of Narbonne, for official slackness.[1] But nothing
more came of this thunder and lightning. The pope once

[1] Steph., Torn. *Epp.*, 73–75.

more had his hands full in his struggle with Barbarossa, while the counts in southern France, themselves not untainted with heresy, had no inclination to use up their military resources in the quarrels of the Church. Raymond V declared himself impotent to stem the tide. 'Families were divided by heresy, priests were corrupt, churches were deserted and had fallen into ruins.' [1] Protests were uttered by the Council of Montpellier (1195)—the year that Raymond died—but the protests were laughed to scorn. For twenty years heresy had a luxuriant growth. William de Puy-Laurent, who in his *Chronicle* avers his purpose to relate only those things which he has seen and heard, in the Preface remarks : 'Chaplains were held in such contempt that their name was as much a by-word as that of a Jew. Thus, just as it used to be said, " I would rather be a Jew than do it," so it is now said, " I would rather be a chaplain." Clergy had to hide their tonsure.[2] Nobles no longer presented their sons for ordination, but the sons of menials. ' The heretics have filled the land, as if the Lord had ordained now as He did in the primitive Church, " not many wise after the flesh, not many mighty, not many noble are called." ' Heretics were no longer put on their trial, but held disputations with legates as with equals. At Pamiers, Esclarmonde, the sister of Bernard Roger, Count of Foix, daughter of Philippa of Aragon, wife of the Lord of Lille-Jordan, openly defended heresy, and Stephen, a Cistercian monk, dared only to scold, telling her that such speech ill became her, and that she would be better employed in minding her distaff. She was only twelve when Nicetas, the Paulician Bishop of Constantinople, visited the Catharists at Pamiers.[3] On the death of

---

[1] *Rec. des Hist. de France*, vol. xiii, p. 140.
[2] That this contempt was not undeserved, see Innocent's *Regesta*, xiii. 86, 88 ; xiv. 32–34 ; xvi. 5.
[3] See vol. i, p. 15.

Jordan, her husband (1200), she returned to her native mountains and took up her abode in the Castle of Pamiers which her father had given her as her dowry. Here she became the most powerful patroness of heresy. Her brother, the Count of Foix, besides the Castle, had made for her a great establishment, consisting of workshops, schools and hostels for heretics. A mile and a half away was the Abbey of St. Antonine, and the rivals eyed one another with a vigilant jealousy that sometimes developed into actual conflict. Faïs de Durfort, an old lady who had renounced all her worldly possessions, had decided to spend the rest of her days in the Catharist cloister as the colleague of Esclarmonde. But as the train approached the gates, the monks of St. Antonine dashed out, captured the lady and took their prize into their monastery. News of the outrage was brought to Pamiers. Her two sons, the consuls of Pamiers and some knights assaulted the monastery, broke open its gates, and brought the old lady in triumph to the castle.[1] But heretics must be not only clothed and fed; they must be protected. Hence Esclarmonde repaired and fortified Mont-segur, near the Pyrenees, which, true to its name (Mons securus), became the fortress, sanctuary and tomb of the last of the Albigenses.[2]

Without let or hindrance the sectaries preached their doctrines and practised their ritual. The rich and powerful, even in the families of the clergy, submitted to the Consolamentum,[3] and preferred the ministrations of heretics at their death-bed to those of the clergy. They showed their gratitude by leaving them large sums of money and valuable property. Impecunious nobles sent their daughters to be educated in the schools conducted by

---

[1] Peter de Vaux-Sarnai, ch. 2. Vaissete, *Hist. de Lang.*, vol. v p. 535. The story is given with much detail, Peyrat vol. i, p. 332 ff.
[2] Peyrat, vol. i, p. 282.   [3] Vol. i, p. 83.

heretics.[1] Free education was offered by heretics to all
children, who were attracted, it was said, by little presents,
e.g., at Linans, near Fanjeaux. [2]   Sometimes they were
accused of kidnapping, as Pons of Avignonet declared
had been the fate of his son in 1215. [3]   Heretics were of
every trade, profession and social rank, and used the
influence of social superiority or the opportunities of em-
ployment for the propagation of their tenets.   Doctors and
herbalists gave their services often for no fees, but left their
patients in the lurch when they refused their doctrine.[4]
They were money-lenders, shop-keepers, farmers, wool-
combers. [5]   They had apprentices of both sexes to whom
they taught their tenets at the same time as they taught their
trades.   So numerous were they that ' tesserand ' (weaver)
became   synonymous   with   Catharist. [6]   Women   were
especially active, and Esclarmonde had many, if humbler,
imitators.   Blanche de Mort and her daughter were
perfects, and kept open house for all heretics, and meetings
were held there daily, with no attempt at concealment.
Disputations were indulged in by all classes ; even tramps
discussed the mystery of the Eucharist, sometimes in a
grossly irreverent manner. [7]

On the other hand, the nobles were wild and violent,
committing acts of refined or coarse brutality against the
clergy.   When Roger, the Viscount of Béziers (1178), im
prisoned the Bishop of Albi, he appointed a heretic his
gaoler.   Twenty years later his successor, objecting to
the election of a certain abbot to the Abbey of Alet, burnt
part of the Abbey, killed some of the monks and imprisoned

[1] Humbert, ch. 12. Quetif and Echard, vol. i, p. 6.
[2] Ms. 609 f. 30. Libr. of Toulouse, *Balme et Ledidier*, p. 132.
[3] Ms. 609 f. 81.   [4] *Ibid*. ff. 65, 130, 135, 247.
[5] *Ibid*. ff. 121, 190, Doat, xxiii, 166, 231.
[6] Ms. 609 f. 237 Libr. of Toulouse. See also Ducange s.v.
' pifle.'
[7] Doat, xxiv, p. 83.   Also Jarrett's *Dominic*, p. 37.

the new abbot, following this up by the gruesome joke of exhuming the late abbot and seating the corpse in the abbot's chair. Presenting his nominee to the corpse, he called upon it to appoint him his successor, and as silence gives consent, he declared him duly elected, and forced the surviving monks to accept him. Simony was rampant, and bishoprics were sold to the highest bidder.

The practice of the counts of employing routiers or military adventurers for marauding, for self-defence or for punishing defaulting vassals, opened the way to every excess, which was regarded as their wage or recreation. For this any church was a ready scene and easy prey. Horses were stalled therein, the furniture was broken up for fuel, vestments and hangings were used for bedding, images were decked out in armour and then tilted at, as in the game of quintain. Luchaire [1] gives several other examples of a lawlessness which heresy incited and clerical worthlessness invited. Disputes between temporal and spiritual lords were frequent. There was no common law ; local precedent, actual possession and force were the basis of settlement. Such a dispute, for instance, of seventeen years' standing, between the Viscount of Albi and its Bishop was settled by arbitration, the terms being that the fortress of Castelviel should be the property of the viscount, together with one-third of the revenues of the town, the other two-thirds to go to the bishop. [2]

Many of these disputes had nothing to do with heresy, and were merely quarrels between secular and ecclesiastical barons. Hence their transformation by Catholic historians, e.g., Peter de Vaux-Sarnai, into offences against Catholicism must be viewed with suspicion by the impartial student.

---

[1] *Innocent III*, vol ii, ch. 1.
[2] Compayré *Etudes historiques sur les Albigeois*. See also Vaissete, *Hist. de Lang.*, v, 1334. Moline, *Hist. des Contes de Toulouse*, vol. ii, p. 511.

CHAPTER III

ON January 8, 1198, Giovanni Lothario Conti, a man of ancient and distinguished lineage, in the prime of life, was elected to the papacy and took the name of Innocent III, perhaps the most remarkable of all popes. Of blameless life, of immense capacity for work, great intellectual ability, and nephew of a pope (Clement III), he had conceived the most exalted views of the power which a pope possessed of divine right. In his inauguration sermon he exclaimed : ' Ye see what manner of servant that is whom the Lord hath set over His people ; no other than the vicegerent of Christ, the successor of Peter. He is the mediator between God and man, below God, above man, less than God, more than man. He judges all, is judged of none.' He was not one, therefore, from whom heresy could expect the slightest toleration or clemency. Yet so enormous was the pressure of business from Spain to Palestine which confronted him that even Innocent's immense energy could give but a casual attention to the affairs of the Albigenses. Three months after his elevation (April) he wrote to the Archbishop of Auch,[1] pointing out that ' if it were necessary, the heretics must be coerced by princes and people by the sword of steel (*materialis*) ; ' and this letter was, three weeks later, followed by one to all the prelates of south France, to all princes, barons, counts, and all Christian people. He appointed, as commissioners, first Rainer and Guy, who were succeeded by the more celebrated Peter de Castelnau and Ralph, all Cistercian monks.[2] For the present these saw that a frontal attack upon heresy was futile. It drew its strength largely from

[1] *Regesta*, i. 81, 94.
[2] Potthast, 764, 785.   Vaissete, *Hist. de Lang*. vi, 223.

the corruptions of the Church itself ; and accordingly they
set themselves to purge the Temple and make it a house of
prayer instead of a den of thieves. A scandalous example
was the Archbishop of Narbonne. He refused to join the
legates in their insistence upon the Count of Toulouse
actively co-operating with them in suppressing the heretics.
Not once in thirteen years had he held a visitation of his
province—a scandal of which the heretics had made capital,
declaring that it was a characteristic of the whole episcopate.
He was given over to avarice but had given up teaching,
and thought simony no wrong. Nicholas, Duke of Aragon,
a plunderer of churches and monasteries, the Archbishop
had warmly welcomed and had given him two castles which
he had furnished by robbing the castle of a catholic. He
was neither hospitable nor charitable ; in fact he was
strongly suspected of being a heretic himself. Many
benefices he retained in his own hands and appropriated
their revenues. Monks had abandoned their religious habit
and had publicly taken concubines, some of whom had been
enticed from their husbands. They had become money-
lenders, huntsmen, lawyers, paid judges in secular matters,
companions of jesters.[1] For these offences the Archbishop
was suspended, his clergy were released from their obedience
to him, and the diocese put under the charge of the Bishop
of Agen (May 1204). The Pope strengthened the hands
of Peter and Ralph by sending to them the 'abbot of
abbots,' Arnauld of Citeaux, with enlarged, almost
absolute powers (January 26, 1205). The suspension of
the Archbishop of Narbonne was not only confirmed ; he
was deposed and excommunicated. The Bishop of Béziers,
because he refused to take any part in the inquiry into the
orthodoxy of the consuls of the city, was also deposed.[2]

[1] *Regesta*, vii. 75, also vol. i, p. 27.
[2] He was treacherously killed the following year. *Regesta*, vi. 242,
243.

The Bishop of Viviers shared a similar fate, but was restored after due submission. Raymond de Rabasteins, Bishop of Toulouse, was also deposed, and Fulk, the ex-troubadour, succeeded him. The Bishop of Carcassonne was found incapable of managing his diocese and was forced to resign, yet when his successor endeavoured to drive his erring and straying sheep into the fold, the sheep attacked the shepherd and drove him out of the city, and all who had sided with him were heavily fined.

A clean sweep was thus made of most of the principal bishops in the southern part of the infected area ; yet these heroic measures only gave greater publicity to the corrupt condition of the Church and strengthened, for a time at least, the hands of its enemies. The appeals which Innocent issued from time to time to the secular powers were unheeded. Peter, King of Aragon, did indeed summon some Waldensians to a conference at Carcassonne with the Bishop of Carcassonne (who had returned to his see) and the two Legates, Peter and Ralph. After hearing both sides he condemned the Waldensians for heretics. ' But on the morrow on the petition of the vicar of the Viscount of Carcassonne I gave audience to other heretics, having thirteen heretics and thirteen catholics as assessors. When Bernard de Simorra the " Bishop " of the heretics, and his companions were questioned, I asked if there was one God. After much quibbling they publicly confessed with sacrilegious mouth that there were three gods or even more ; also that Jesus Christ had human parents.'[1] For these opinions they were condemned, but the powerlessness of the *Church* to stem the tide of heresy is seen in the fact that a layman presides and gives judgment on matters of doctrine, and no punishment was inflicted. The

---

[1] Compayré, *Etudes Hist.*, liv. Recorded in a MS. of the thirteenth century belonging to M. Cavilié.

only practical result of Peter's assistance was that he turned some Catharists out of a castle belonging to the pope, and then kept it for himself.[1] So discouraged were the legates that they entreated the pope to recall them.

But Innocent was not of the nature to admit defeat, and the despair of his nuncios stirred him into direct action. He forced Raymond's vassals to stop their petty wars and unite in a league for the object of exterminating heresy. Then he adroitly invited Raymond to join it ; but, as the latter saw that the league was aimed against himself and his subjects, he refused. ' No man can serve two masters ' ; and as Raymond had refused to serve the Church, he had virtually, so the legates interpreted, declared himself the servant of heretics. On May 29, 1207, by order of Innocent his excommunication was to be published in all the churches of the Archbishoprics of Vienne, Embrun, Arles and Narbonne. His offences were that : he had hired routiers to ravage the country ; broken the peace of Lent, Feast Days and Ember Days ; placed Jews in public offices ; persecuted abbeys ; armed churches as fortresses ; imposed exorbitant tolls ; robbed the Bishop of Carpentoracte ; refused to sign the League ; protected heretics ; received them into his house ; and by repeated breach of his oath had become a heretic himself. Therefore all his vassals were released from their feudal obligations. All, from prince to farmer, who aided him, were placed under the same anathema.[2] To the Count himself the pope wrote a letter in which the dignity of a reprimand is lost in the violence of the language. ' You are not made of brass, your body is like that of other people, you can be struck with fever, leprosy, paralysis, madness, and all kinds of incurable diseases. You can be changed into a beast like

---

[1] *Regesta*, viii. 94, 97. He was allowed to retain it as a fief of St. Peter's on payment of an annual rent.
[2] *Regesta*, vii. 76, 77, 79, 165, 210, 212.

the King of Babylon. That illustrious Prince, the King of
Aragon, and nearly all your neighbours have joined the
League, and sworn to obey the apostolic legates. But
you! you alone refuse and seek filthy lucre in war like a
crow its carrion. You have shamelessly broken your oath
to drive the heretics out of your coasts. And when our
legate charged you with this, you dared to tell him that
you could easily find a heresiarch, a Cathar bishop, who
would prove that his religion was superior to the Catholic.
That alone furnishes ground for strong suspicion that you
favour heresy and belong to it yourself. What folly! Do
you suppose that you are wiser than all the faithful of the
Church? How can you think that all who keep the Catholic
Faith are damned, and the partisans of these mad and false
people saved?' [1] Nor was this 'mere sound and fury
signifying nothing.' The fief, which, it was claimed, he
held by direct tenure of the Roman Church, the pope
would take away. He would urge all the neighbouring
princes to attack him and take all they could snatch from
him. There is one expression, however, in this letter
which explains the vacillation later of papal policy—he
suspected Raymond of heresy, he was not certain of it.

Before the tempest Raymond cowered, made new
promises and was absolved. For since the advent of
Arnauld and the consecration of Fulk, as Bishop of
Toulouse in place of Raymond de Rabasteins, the count
had felt the ground slipping beneath his feet. Arnauld,
Fulk and Simon de Montfort were the triumvirate to whom
the success of the Crusade against the Albigenses may be
chiefly ascribed. Fulk, the troubadour [2] of Marseilles, saw
that success must ultimately rest with the Church, and in
that way lay honours and wealth. He became a zealous
catholic and was made Abbot of Thoronet, and from

---

[1] *Regesta*, x. 69.   [2] Nineteen of his songs survive.

Thoronet he passed to Toulouse as its Bishop (February, 1206). But ' all that glitters is not gold,' and Fulk found more glitter in the dignity than gold in its coffers ; for his predecessor had depleted them to pay for his wars. Fulk, as Bishop of Toulouse, unlike his predecessor, was a thorn in the side of its count. He kept ceaseless watch upon all his words and works, gathered the fragments of the Catholic Church together and united and inspired them to resist and attack heresy in its strongest citadel—his own diocese.

CHAPTER IV

A T this juncture there came upon the scene a mission which had nothing to do with heresy, but from which, nevertheless, sprang the organization which eventually exterminated it.

In 1203, Diego, Bishop of Ozma, was sent by Alfonse IX, King of Castile, to negotiate a marriage between his son Ferdinand, and a daughter of ' the Lord of the Marches ' (? Denmark [1]), and he must needs pass through France. The Bishop took with him Prior Dominic who, although of noble birth,[2] had been all his life under clerical influence. At seven years of age Dominic was sent to an uncle, a priest, to be educated ; at fourteen he went to Pallenzia,[3] where he remained ten years. A Bishop of Ozma, Martin de Bazan, wishing to convert his clergy from seculars to regulars, sent to Pallenzia for help. Diego was there and offered his services, which the bishop accepted, appointing him prior of the new regulars. Dominic, his fellow-student, accompanied him, and, on Diego being made Bishop of Ozma, succeeded him as prior. It was the association of these two men that wrought a profound and permanent change in the policy of the Church towards heresy. When about thirty years of age, Dominic left the seclusion of the cloister for public preaching, ' giving up,' as Jordan of Saxony observes, ' Rachel for Leah,' i.e. the contemplative for the practical life.

The proposed marriage between Ferdinand of Spain and the daughter of ' the Lord of the Marches,' required two

[1] Quetif and Echard, vol. i, p. 4, note 1.
[2] Bremond ' de Guzmani stirpe Sti Dominici.' But this is questioned by the Bollandists.
[3] Pallenzia received its charter as the first University of Spain in 1209. Denifle, ' *Universities of the Middle Ages*.'

embassies; one to make the marriage settlement, and another to bring back the bride. On the first journey through the Midi Diego and Dominic lodged one night at a house in Toulouse, and there for the first time came in contact with the Albigensian heresy, for their host, unabashed, declared himself a Catharist. Not until the dawn did Dominic recover the erring sheep. The second journey proved abortive, owing to the sudden death of the bride ; but the passage through France only impressed bishop and prior more deeply with the strength of heresy and the feebleness of the Church. The embassy was recalled, but instead of returning at once to his diocese Diego met the legates at a council, either at Narbonne or Montpellier,[1] at a time of deepest discouragement. But so far from receiving any sympathy they were severely rebuked for their sumptuousness and splendour. Let them do what the Master said and commanded : let them travel on foot, live as poor men, have no money, no costly apparel, and so drive out the false sanctity by the true. If they claimed to be the Apostles' successors in preaching, let them also be in practice.[2] The twelve Cistercians and the three legates consented only if some one would lead the way. This Diego promised if he could obtain the pope's permission to resign his see ; he would provide preachers at his

---

[1] Place and date uncertain. Vincent ' *Gesta*,' places the Council at Narbonne 1207, but gives no details : ' only by a true exhibition of holiness and religion could they recall to the faith souls deluded by the heretics.' Jordan says : ' At that time Innocent had directed twelve abbots of the Cistercian Order with one legate to preach against the Albigensian heretics who held a Council with the archbishops, bishops, and other prelates of that country. . . . Meanwhile, while they were consulting, the aforesaid Bishop of Ozma happened to pass through Montpellier where the Council was being held.' Now Diego died in 1207, as his epitaph shows, and Jordan says expressly that he continued after that Council preaching for two years, and, returning to Ozma, died in a few days. This gives 1205 as the date of the Council.

[2] *Acta SS.*, p. 544. Quetif and Echard, vol. i, p. 4. ' Clavum clavo retundite, fictam sanctitatem vera religione fugare.'

own expense.[1]   Resignation was refused, but the pope allowed him to return to the Midi for a time.   Gathering around him a company of thirty monks of the Cistercian order, whose habit he had adopted, Bishop Diego and ' brother' Dominic, as he was now called, visited the chief seats of heresy, poorly clad, bare of foot, begging their bread, like the ' Perfects.'   Their first meeting was at Servian,[2] near Béziers.   Here the heretics under the protection of Stephen, the castellan, had had free scope, holding schools, preaching and disputing publicly and privately under the leadership of Baldwin and Theodoric.   The former was of noble birth and had been Canon of Nevers.   His uncle had been condemned for heresy in Paris, but had escaped to Narbonne, where he was held in the highest repute by heretics ; and his nephew embraced his uncle's opinions and succeeded to his influence.   Theodoric, like Baldwin, had been Dean of Nevers, and was nephew of Eudes of Castelnau (the same town as the legate's) who only five years before had been burnt for heresy.   For eight days the discussion was continued, but neither party could convert the other, and at its close Peter and Ralph ordered the two heresiarchs to be expelled—a mild sentence compared with that passed upon their uncles—but even that Stephen refused to execute.[3]   Baffled but not disheartened, the champions of the Church moved on to Béziers itself, a city notorious for its turbulence.   Thirty years before, the people had killed its viscount and bishop ; and now, for reasons not connected with religion, Catholics and

[1] Peter de V.S., ch. vi.

[2] By copyists' error ' Caramanum ' for ' Servianum,' the latter is correct.   Balme et Ledidier, vol. i, p. 93.

[3] His property was confiscated, but on his abjuration it was restored to him as a fief from Simon de Montfort in February 1210.   Vaisette, viii. 150, 584, 587.   But whether the castellan was heretic or catholic, heresy flourished, for in 1215 few died there without heretication. (Ms. 609 f. 213 Libr. of Toulouse) ; v. also p. 123.

Catharists were so hostile to Rome, and particularly to its legate, Peter de Castelnau, that Diego advised him to withdraw. The Conference lasted fifteen days, but so stormy were the meetings, that Diego and his company effected nothing, and left for Carcassonne. Here the ' Bishop' Bernard de Simorra had disputed with the legates in the presence of the King of Aragon (1204), but of the discussion we have no details. From Carcassonne they passed to Montréal where they were rejoined by Peter de Castelnau, and here the most celebrated of these conferences took place. It is symptomatic of the inroads which Catharism had made into the Church that the exposition of its doctrine was entrusted to four *clergy*, Gilbert de Castres, Archdeacon of Fanjeaux, Benedict de Termes, Deacon of Limoux, Pons Jordan, Deacon of Verfeuil, and Arnauld Hot, Deacon of Cabaret. Four arbitrators were appointed, of whom two were knights and two burgesses. Each side drew up a list of the points it proposed for discussion. The arguments advanced by either side were reduced to writing and presented to the judges—again laymen all—each evening of the fifteen days of the Conference. The debate was held in public, but the judges, who were said by Peter de Vaux-Sarnai to be favourable to the heretics, refused to give the heretics' papers to the Catholics, although they gave the Catholics' papers to the heretics.[1]

To the acute mind of Dominic it soon became clear that these disputations were not only fruitless but impolitic. They but emboldened the enemy to further defiance. Church authority, personal austerity, religious zeal were all in vain. The direct attack upon heresy must give way to siege and sap.

---

[1] A ' miracle ' on this occasion proved the indestructibility of the Catholic creed. Dominic's schedule was given to the Catharists who promptly threw it on the fire. But it was miraculously ejected. Three times this happened. The ' miracle ' was related to Peter de V.S. (ch. 3) by Dominic himself.

One summer evening, being the Feast of St. Mary Magdalene (July 22, 1206)[1], Dominic sat brooding over their failures outside Fanjeaux.[2] The condition of that town was worse than it had been a thousand years before, for what had been the fane of Jove had become a Christian church, and the Christian church was now a Catharist conventicle. *Corruptio optimi pessima.* All the people were heretics except Nar-Cavers, co-seigneur with William de Durfort.[3] Its archdeacon was that heresiarch, Gilbert de Castres whom he had encountered at Montréal. ' Below him the ground sloped away into that wide and fertile valley which had become the home and the support of the southern heretics, the vast pasture-lands of Lauragnais and, beyond, the Toulousain, with the Black Mountain range, guarding all the rich corn-lands to the north and east, standing out against the sky and just touched by the setting sun. From that high place he could have marked the citadel of Carcassonne and Castelnaudary . . . nearer stood up Montréal.'[4] It was this smiling country that he was to deluge with blood and blacken with fire. As he gazed, his gloomy thoughts dissolved into a vision—like that of St. Peter at Joppa—thrice repeated, but unlike the Apostle's, in that there was no message from Heaven of inclusive love, but of destruction—a globe of fire hovering over, and then descending upon the deserted Church of Prouille, a little village between Fanjeaux and Montréal, in the very heart of heresy. This was to be, so he interpreted the vision, the starting-point of his life-work. Dominic communicated his thrice-given vision to Diego who accepted it as a divine commission. Through the Bishop of Toulouse, in whose diocese Prouille was, he secured from Nar-Cavers, the

---

[1] Cf. p. 51.
[2] At a spot called Signadou, or ' the sign of God,' now marked by a cross.
[3] Cf. p. 11.   [4] Jarrett, *Life of St. Dominic*, p. 33.

patroness, the Church of St. Mary of Prouille, and thirty
feet of land around it, without tithe or first-fruits, ' for those
converted by preachers delegated to preach against heretics,
and drive back pestiferous heresy, and for those living
there a religious life, both now and in the future, but so that
tithes and first-fruits, which appear to have belonged by
parochial right to the said church, shall be paid in full to the
Church of Fanjeaux; they shall, however, possess the Church
itself without any dues or services or suit hereafter, unless
the said tithes and first-fruits are granted by the bishop to
the said Church of Prouille.' [1]   It is generally stated that
Prouille was intended by Dominic only for nuns ; but that
he intended to admit men as well as women from the first
is clear not only from the above Charter, but also from
the deeds of conveyance of the endowments. [2]   Thus
' Ermengard Godolin and her husband, Sanche Gasc, gave
to God and the blessed Mary of Prouille and all the saints
of God, and for the holy preaching, and for Master Dominic
of Ozma and to all the *brothers* and sisters who are here
to-day and shall be in future, our house in the castle of
Vilari with all its buildings.' [3]   This gift was extended four
years later by Raymond de Vilari when he gave all his
honours, lands tilled and untilled, orchards, vineyards,
waters, etc., to the same person mentioned in the preceding
deed, including ' all the *brothers* and sisters in Prouille.' [4]

[1] The original deed has disappeared, but Percin gives a copy after
an old MS. in the Monastery of Toulouse (*Monumenta*, p. 5.)

[2] Even Jarrett, a Dominican prior and dedicating his book, published
with authority, to Dominican sisters, has made this serious mistake
(p. 39).   The whole chapter dealing with the foundation of Prouille
is called ' The Nuns.'   He also makes several errors in translating
the Charter but the most misleading is his interpolation of the word
' women.'

[3] Vaissete, *Hist., de Lang*, viii. 137.

[4] *Ibid.* See also the gift of the Church of Brom and its appurte-
nances by the bishop of Toulouse, with the advice and consent of the
provost of St. Stephen's the same year for ' the converts of the Church
of Prouille living the religious life.'   Their sex is not mentioned,

In the following year three more gifts are recorded, but in each case for ' the *brothers* and sisters of Prouille.' (i) Fremis the Frenchman gave half his land, and if he died there he promised to give half of his goods (*mobilia*) to the same community, for ' Simon de Montfort had given it him. ' [1] (ii) Bernard Catolica de Barssa bequeathed all his goods, real and personal, to ' the *brothers* and sisters of Prouille.' While living, as a guarantee, he promised to pay every All Saints' Day two pounds (Melgor) for himself and for his sons. When he took the habit of the Order he paid one hundred pounds in alms. Dominic, on his part, for himself and the monastery of Prouille declared : ' I receive thee, Bernard Catolica de Barssa for a brother, and your sons, Peter and Bernard, and all your goods, real and personal, now and for the future, and will maintain and keep you and yours fairly and include you in our benefits and prayers and in those of the Abbey of St. Mary of Prouille.' [2] (iii) William del Essart, a French knight, gave two acres of land in the tithing of Fanjeaux to ' the *brothers* and sisters of Prouille.' ' And this gift I have made from the manor which the Count de Montfort gave me.' [3]

Even the document which Dominic brought back from the Lateran Council, given him by Innocent III, is addressed ' to the prior, *brothers* and sisters of the Monastery of Prouille.' This association of men and women in one religious community was an innovation for the Church, but not for the Catharists, and it looks as if Dominic deliberately copied their methods in order to counter their activities. Not until the founding of the Monastery of Preachers at Toulouse in 1216 was Prouille devoted exclusively to women. The fact is that Dominic founded at Prouille a double monastery, part for sisters, and part for brothers.

although the thirteen names of such (*all* feminine) are added, perhaps later. Also Ripoll, vol. i, p. 1, note 4.
  [1] Vaissete, viii. 137.   [2] *Ibid.*   [3] *Ibid.*

The former, of which we hear most, consisted, according to Humbert de Romans, of nine women of noble birth who had been heretics more or less, and who themselves suggested to Dominic some organization by which they might receive enlightenment. [1] But Prouille had this weakness as compared with the establishment of the Catharists, that while its rule allowed women and children to come to the convent for instruction, the nuns could not themselves go out into the highways and hedges and streets and lanes and ' compel them to come in,' as did the Catharist ' Perfect ' women. Hence Dominican nunneries were few in number, small in membership and weak in propaganda. Membership was increased by those who sought refuge from the world, like the ' Homes of the Converted,' set up by the Jews. [2]

[1] Ch. xliv.
[2] Jarrett, *Life of St. Dominic*, p. 48 ; also v. *infra* p. 38.

CHAPTER V

FOR nearly ten years our information of Dominic and his work is singularly meagre. This may be accounted for partly by the nature of the work itself, and partly by the Crusades. Mountain and hill must be made low, crooked straight, and rough places plain. In other words the protection which the heretics found behind the walls of city and castle must be battered down before Dominic could reach them. Hence we find Dominic, not at Prouille, but at the side of Simon de Montfort at Lavaur, La Penne and Muret.[1] He officiated at the marriage of Simon's son Amauri, and the Count rewarded his 'dear brother, Dominic' with the spoils of war, e.g. Casseneuil, a gift which was confirmed to him by Innocent III and Honorius III.[2] In the next year (1215) after receiving this gift, his friend, the Bishop of Toulouse, presented him with the benefice of Fanjeaux, with one-sixth of its endowments, but these latter he withdrew when he found them to be more valuable than he estimated.[3] Once Dominic deputized, as far as one not a bishop could, for the Bishop of Carcassonne while absent in the north recruiting for the Crusade (February 1213).

Up to the Lateran Council the numbers of preaching Friars remained unchanged, viz. about fifteen. In April 1215 an important recruit was found in Peter de Cella or Seila, a wealthy citizen of Toulouse, who gave Dominic some large plain houses [4] where they began their work, so

---

[1] He did not carry a cross in battle although the very cross is alleged to be at Toulouse (Quetif and Echard, vol. i, p. 10 note).
[2] *Cartulaire*, i, pp. 480–83.   [3] *Ibid.*, 515–16, iii, p. 270.
[4] Balme et Ledidier, vol. i, p. 510 gives a facsimile of the original deed.

that it became a joke, of which Peter never tired, that ' he received the Order and not the Order him.' But Dominic would not accept the gift without the sanction of the bishop. In obtaining this there was no difficulty. Indeed, Fulk went further as the following instrument shows : ' For extirpating heresy and expelling wickedness, and for teaching the rule of faith and instructing men in sound morals, we institute as Preachers in our Diocese brother Dominic and his companions who have religiously offered to go afoot and preach the Gospel. And . . . we will that when they go preaching they have from the Diocese necessary food, and with the consent of the Chapter of the Church of the blessed Stephen and the clergy of the Diocese of Toulouse we assign in perpetuity to the afore-said Preachers and others, whom zeal for God and love for the salvation of souls in the same way have stirred up for this office of preaching, a sixth part of the tithes which are allotted for the ornaments and upkeep of all the parochial churches, which are in our authority, for clothing and other necessaries for their infirmities, and when they wish at any time to rest. Any surplus is to be given back to the said churches for their ornaments and upkeep, or given to the poor. Given 1215, Philip being King of France and the Count de Montfort holding the principality of Toulouse.' [1] But Dominic was not satisfied with an episcopal sanction for his work which made it local and precarious. He aimed at making it commensurate with the Church, and this could only be effected through the authority of the pope. In the approaching General Council he saw his opportunity. He had already disclosed his project to the Bishop of Toulouse, and with him went to Rome where they obtained an interview with Innocent before the Council began. Dominic first of all obtained his sanction for all

---

[1] Jordan xxiii, Humbert xxi, Quetif and Echard, vol. i, p. 12.

that had been done at Prouille,[1] and then opened up the wider question of a definite and distinct Order of Preachers. But in this he was only partially successful. The zeal of the reformer encountered the discretion of the statesman. The project was an absolutely new one. ' It was possibly the first time that recognition not of a particular Convent, but of an Order had been solicited. No doubt there had existed centuries before the time of St. Dominic the two great Rules of St. Benedict and St. Augustine; but if there had been monasteries following the observances of one or the other, there had never been, to speak accurately, a Benedictine or an Augustinian Order, if by this is meant a collection of monasteries grouped together, not only under the obedience of the same Rule, but, above all, under the authority of a single head. . . . The Holy See had been asked to give confirmation to each separate convent; to no one had it occurred to demand a general license for a collection of monasteries forming an indivisible whole.'[2] The nearest analogy was the Hospitallers and Templars under a Grand Master, but these were in the East, and had never sought confirmation of their Order. In the second place, the Lateran Council by its thirteenth canon had prohibited the founding of any further Orders. Setting itself against all disruptive tendencies, its aim was towards amalgamation of existing Orders, not the introduction of fresh ones, ' Whoever wishes to become a religious must adopt one of the Rules already sanctioned, and whoever wishes to found a religious house may do so provided he accepts the Rule and the Constitutions of some authorized congregation.'

But order within was not the only need of the Church; there must be growth, enlargement; she must recover the

---

[1] *Cartulaire*, i, p. 526.

[2] Balme et Ledidier, *Cartulaire*, vol. i, pp. 80 ff. See also Jarrett, *Life of St. Dominic*, pp. 65 ff.

ground lost through the apathy of her members and the encroachments of heresy. Hence the Council enacted by Canon : ' Since it often happens that bishops, on account of their many occupations or infirmities or hostile attacks [1] or other obstacles (not to say lack of knowledge which is most reprehensible in them, and not to be tolerated in future), are not able themselves to minister the word of God to the people, especially in large and scattered dioceses, we by a general order (*constitutione*) sanction that the bishops choose men fit to undertake properly the office of sacred preaching, men of power in deed and speech, who, when they (the bishops) cannot do so, shall diligently visit the flock entrusted to them instead of the bishops, and edify them by word and example. For such let adequate provision be made, so that they may not be compelled through lack of necessaries to abandon their undertaking. Wherefore we order that both in Cathedral and other Conventional Churches fit men be ordained whom the bishops shall have as coadjutors and fellow-workers not only in the office of preaching but also in hearing confessions and enjoining penances and other things which pertain to the salvation of souls.' [2]

If these two canons were suggested by Dominic's petition they were very far from satisfying it. They in fact placed him in a dilemma ; on the one hand was the limitation of monastic orders, on the other the extension of episcopal authority. Preachers henceforth were to be regulated, registered. Their appointment rested solely with the bishop ; by him their license was issued, by him withdrawn ; only in his diocese could they officiate, and he was the sole judge as to whether, where, when, and how long they were to function. They might not even be allowed to preach,

---

[1] Not necessarily ' of heresy ', as Jarrett interpolates.
[2] Ripoll, p. 19. Confirmed by Gregory, ix. (1227) *ibid.*, p. 23.

they might be ordered only to administer sacraments. To
the ardent and ambitious spirit of Dominic this was stifling,
and he never rested until he got these canons of a General
Council rescinded.[1] For the time being all he could do
was to return and discuss with his brethren to what Order
they should attach themselves. These—sixteen in number
—he met at Prouille in August 1216. Their names are
given by Bernard Gui, but Balme adds two more, and an
examination of the list shows that they were representative
of France, England, Normandy, the Midi and Spain. The
choice, which must be unanimous,[2] fell upon the Order of
St. Augustine, because upon its Rule of study, preaching
and poverty could more easily be grafted the special
work of preaching by the Dominicans.[3]

But if they could not have a separate organization, they
could, and indeed must, have a separate habitation, and this
was secured for them by the good offices of Fulk by the
grant of the Chapel of St. Romans in Toulouse. ' Let all
men know that we, M., Provost of Toulouse and of the
Convent of the same place, at the suggestion and request of
Fulk, Bishop of Toulouse, give and concede for ever to
Brother Dominic, Prior and Master of the Preachers, and to
his companions present and future the Chapel of St. Romans
with its belongings to be possessed freely and peacefully in
perpetuity, and that they may be able to have and make a

---

[1] Ripoll (p. 5, note 3) himself a Master General of the Preaching
Friars says : ' At that time (of the Council) that name (Preaching
Friars) was given to us, as Stephen Salanac, a contemporary writer
teaches in his treatise '' on the glorious name of Preachers '', chap. i.
When, at the Lateran Council 1216, the Pope was making some rules
for the Faith in Toulouse, deciding to write about these matters to
the blessed Dominic and those with him, he called a notary and said
to him '' Sit down and write to Friar Dominic and his companions in
these words,'' then pausing a little he said : '' Don't write so but thus,
' To Friar Dominic and those preaching with him in the parts of
Toulouse, etc.' But at once considering a little more he said ' Write
so : '' to Master Dominic and the Preaching Friars '' ' and he rose up.'
[2] *Analecta*, vol. iv, p. 306.   [3] Quetif and Echard, vol. i, p. 28.

cemetery for the use of their brothers,[1] canons and converted professed, and no one else, for burial. But if anyone at
the point of death wishes to take there the habit and to be
professed, let them have liberty to accept him, yet so that
if he die from such sickness the Church of St. Stephen shall
have a third of all legacies and gifts bequeathed for that
Chapel; but if he recover he shall remain there with all
such legacies and gifts. No parochial rights may be
exercised there, except by permission asked and obtained
from the provost or steward (*cellario*) of St. Stephen on
payment thereto of three pounds Tolosan at Easter
annually.'[2] Henceforward Toulouse, being exclusively for
men, takes precedence of Prouille, and is regarded as the
parent of all Dominican priories, with Dominic as the first
prior. Among the 'belongings' of the Chapel was a small
hostel into which Dominic gathered his little band. But
almost on the very day that Dominic entered into possession
of St. Romans, Innocent died (July 18, 1216). Perhaps the
greatest of all popes, pre-eminent in vigour, ability and
learning,[3] the Italian never really understood the special
character and conditions of Southern France; he was
entirely dependent upon second-hand and biassed reports.
Had he shown the same energy in authorizing and organizing the *suaviter in modo* of systematic preaching, as planned
by Dominic, there might have been no *fortiter in re* of the
Crusades. 'The successor of St. Peter' drew two swords
—the Crusades in the East, and the Crusades in the West;
and for the latter at least the responsibility is his in proportion to the indisputability of his power. The stain of that
blood—innocent blood, for it was the blood of the patriot
as well as the heretic—remains indelible.

[1] No mention here of sisters.
[2] *Gallia Christiana* xiii (*Instrum. Eccl. Tol.* 42)
[3] E.g., in reply to an inquiry of the Archbishop of Lyons he sent a
scholarly treatise on the Tetragrammaton, *Regesta* vi. 193.

CHAPTER VI

ON the death of Innocent, Dominic repaired again to
Rome in the hope of securing fresh concessions from
the new Pope, Honorius III, as well as the confirmation of
the priory of St. Romans. On December 22, 1216, Honorius
issued a bull[1] addressed to ' our beloved sons Dominic,
prior of St. Romans of Toulouse, and its friars present and
future professing the regular life.' It consists of thirteen
clauses : (1) It takes the Church of St. Romans under the
pope's protection, and the Rule of the blessed Augustine is
to be kept unchanged for ever. (2) All the possessions
present and future of the said Church are given to Dominic
and his successors. (3) More expressly—the aforesaid
Church and all its pertinences, the Church of Prouille, the
town of Casseneuil, the Church of St. Mary of Lescura, the
Hostel of Toulouse, called Arnauld Bernard's, the Church
of Holy Trinity of Lobens, and the tithe which Fulk,
Bishop of Toulouse, with the assent of his Chapter had
given them. (4) No one to demand or extort from them
tithes on land brought under cultivation for the first time
by their own labour or at their own expense, or on the
grazings of their animals. (5) They may receive and
retain anyone, clerical or lay, who is free and absolved,
fleeing from the world. (6) No one to leave the Order
without permission of the prior except for an Order more
austere ; and no one to receive such without his warrant
in writing. (7) In the parish churches which belong to
them they may elect priests and present them to the
bishops ; and if the bishop thinks such a fit and proper
person, he shall commit to him the care of souls. Such

---

[1] *Epp. Hon.* iii, Bk. I, *Ep.* 3 (Horoy's edition, vol. ii, p. 142.)

priest shall be responsible to the bishop in things spiritual, and to them in things temporal. (8) No new or unaccustomed exactions to be imposed upon them, and no excommunications or interdicts to be pronounced upon them without manifest and reasonable grounds. In the time of a general interdict they may perform the offices in their own churches (but not for the persons under excommunication or interdict) with closed doors, silent bells, and in a low voice. (9) Chrisms and holy oils for consecration of altars or basilicas or ordination of clergy they must obtain from the diocesan, if a Catholic, and if the Apostolic See orders such to supply them : but if he refuse, they may apply to any other bishop they may prefer, provided he is in the favour of and communion with the Apostolic See. (10) They may bury in their cemeteries not only the friars but others who piously seek burial therein (provided they are not under excommunication or interdict), and saving the burial rights of other churches. (11) On Dominic's decease all succeeding priors are to be elected by the unanimous consent of the friars, or failing that, by a majority, according to God and the Rule of Augustine. (12) All ancient liberties and immunities granted to this Church to be retained. (13) No one to disturb the Church or deprive it of its possessions.

Thus the cord which bound Dominic to an Order already established was fraying but was not yet severed. The same day [1] Honorius addressed a brief summary to Dominic alone : ' We, regarding the friars of your (singular) Order to be the future champions (*pugiles*) of the Faith and true lights of the world, confirm your (singular) Order with all its castles and possessions and take it under our governance and protection.' [2] Yet their position was still indefinite.

---

[1] Not ' next ' as Jarrett, p. 72.
[2] *Ep.* 112 (Horoy, p. 144); Ripoll, p. 4.

The Bull appeared to bind them closer to the Augustinian Order : the supplement to establish a new one. Neither states what the friars of Dominic were to *do*. So a month later Honorius wrote to the company in Toulouse, addressing them as his ' beloved ones, the prior and friars of St. Romans, preachers of the country of Toulouse.' He calls them ' invincible athletes of Christ ' and gives them authority to preach the word in season and out of season. (January 21, 1217).[1] One thing more was needed—a prior —and he was not elected by the friars but was appointed by the pope, viz., Dominic. To him the friars were to submit by papal order, and no one was to leave the Order without his permission, except for one more severe. In none of these documents do we find the exact title : ' Ordo Praedicatorum,' by which they were subsequently called, but the Order claims December 22, 1216, and not January 21, 1217, as the true date of its foundation. Called into being in a time of local emergency and intended to be disbanded when the crisis was over, the Order of Preachers grew to be a tower of strength to the Roman Church and has rendered it indispensable service throughout the world.[2]

After nearly a year's absence, Dominic returned to France to organize his Order on the new basis. But so far from organizing he disorganized. Never had things been less favourable for preaching. Everywhere was the country up in arms against the Crusaders, and the star of Heresy was in the ascendant. Toulouse was inflammable, and a meeting of the Order at its headquarters would certainly have caused an explosion. Dominic, therefore, prudently summoned his friars to Prouille, and there on the memorable August 15, 1217, he dispersed them. ' We must sow

---

[1] Ripoll, p. 5.
[2] For notes and dates on Monasteries, see Quetif and Echard, p. 1.

the seed, not hoard it.' The brethren were astounded at
the decision, yet none disputed it. He sent some to Spain,
some to Paris, two only to Toulouse ; two remained at
Prouille, and himself and another went to Rome. But
none was to be idle, none to abandon the Order. If
temporary circumstances prevented them from preaching,
they were to study, and so prepare themselves for more
effective preaching when opportunity offered. This pursuit
of knowledge was the Dominican's chief merit and justifies
the highest gratitude from posterity. Its demerit was that
it allied itself with the Inquisition and stimulated all its
horrors. But for several years in that pursuit no knowledge was alien, and Dominic dispersed his companions
to the Universities. Honorius III (February 11, 1218),
addressed a letter of commendation to all archbishops,
bishops, etc., on behalf of the Order of Preaching Friars.
Probably to this commendation we owe the founding of
the Convent of Lyons in 1218 by two friars, Arnauld of
Toulouse and Romeo de Livia,[1] of whom Arnauld acted
as Prior, and was succeeded by Romeo in 1223. At the
Universities we find the friars both learning and teaching.
At Bologna (1220), then the most famous, was held the
first General Chapter, at which by a perpetual constitution
'the Order of Preachers', by abandoning all temporalities
und resigning all present and future revenues, professed
voluntary poverty.[2] A second General Chapter was held
there the following year, at which the final Constitution of
the Order was drawn up. With the details we are not
concerned and need only note generally that its wonderful
balance of autocracy and democracy imparted to the whole
body a living unity in which discipline never frowned on

[1] Romeo became fifth Prior of Provence, of which he was a native
and died at Carcassonne, 1261. Quetif and Echard, p. 161 (*a*), not
160, as Guirard says.
[2] Jordan 38, Bernard Gui, *Chron*. A.D. 1220.

initiative, and produced that massive solidarity which eventually destroyed Albigensianism.

Two months after this second chapter at Bologna, Dominic died there, August 6, 1221, in his fifty-first year. ' He died in brother Moneta's bed because he had none of his own : in brother Moneta's tunic because he had none to replace the one he had long been wearing.'[1] But the foundation of the Order of Preachers was well and truly laid. Nunneries were practically a failure ; for fifty years Prouille was the only one : eighty years after the death of Dominic there were only three.

It has been maintained that Dominic was never a persecutor, and that he attacked heresy only by preaching and example. The following penance, however, which he imposed upon a ' convert ' reveals him in a different light. ' By virtue of the Lord Abbot of Citeaux (Arnauld), Legate of the Apostolic See, who has charged us with this office, we have reconciled the bearer of these presents, Pons Roger, converted from the sect of heresy by the favour of God, commanding in virtue of the High Sacrament that on three Festal Sundays he be led, naked to the thigh, by a priest who shall beat him from the entrance of the village of Treville to the Church. He shall wear the religious habit with distinguishing marks—two small crosses on each breast. All his life, except at Easter, Whitsun and Christmas, he shall eat neither flesh, eggs nor cheese. Three days a week he shall abstain from fish, oil and wine, except in sickness. He shall observe three feasts during the year and hear Mass every day. Once a month he shall show this letter of penance to the curé of Treville, under whose supervision he is placed. If he disobey he shall stand excommunicate.'[2] If it be contended that this is not

---

[1] *Acta SS.*, p. 599, August 4.
[2] See Acton, *Essays on Liberty*, p. 554.

persecution but wholesome discipline, it may be replied that it was extremely irksome and one from which death was the only discharge. But no such defence can be set up against the following, for, as Lord Acton observes : ' Nothing is better authenticated in the life of the saint (Dominic) than the fact that he condemned heretics and exercised the right of deciding which of them should suffer and which of them should be spared.' [1] ' It happened that certain heretics on being captured were convicted by him to be handed over to secular judgment, because they were unwilling to return to the Faith, 1209, and when they were told off (*deputati*) for the fire, he saw among them a man named Raymond de Grossi, and, believing (*intuitus*) that he had in him a ray of divine predestination, said to the officers of the Court : " Keep back that man, and don't let him be burnt with the rest." Then turning to him he said gently : " I know, my son, that you will, though slowly, become a good and holy man." ' [2] The transaction is memorable in Dominican annals as the one link distinctly connecting St. Dominic with the system of executions, and the only security possessed by the Order that the most conspicuous of its acts is sanctioned by the spirit and example of the founder. [3] It is said that Dominic quoted with approval the Spanish proverb : ' ou non valsenhe agols val bagols ' (*where kindness fails, try a stick*). Little fault, indeed, can be found with Dante's summary of Dominic :

' Benignant to his own and terrible to his foes.' [4]

---

[1] See Acton, *Essays on Liberty*, p. 554.

[2] Constantius, *Vita St. Dominici* (Quetif and Echard, vol. i, p. 33.) Bernard Gui, *Vita St Dominici, MS. Tol.* 481 f. 112. *Acta SS.* August 4, p. 410-4. When Simon de Montfort burnt heretics he did so ' haud dubie inquistorem agente sancto Dominico.'

[3] Acton, *Essays on Liberty*, p. 554.

[4] Par. xii. 55.

I T was not, however, by either preaching or penance that the tide turned in favour of Rome, but by a fortunate tragedy, i.e., an incident which Rome knew how to turn to good account. The blood of a ' martyr ', whether in a good or a bad cause is often the seed of his particular ' Church ' ; and so it proved in this case. Arnauld, whose arrival put fresh zeal into the Commission, summoned into the Church of St. Stephen at Toulouse certain representatives of the King of France, the consuls, clergy and people, and received from them the following oath :

' We, Hugo Gerald, Doctor of Laws and Knight of Our Lord, the King of France, holding the position of Seneschal of Toulouse and Albigensium, and Ivo, Doctor of Laws and Judge of our Lord, the King, at Toulouse and John de Turre Esquire of our Lord, the King, and Peter Gouraud, holding the position of Vicar of Toulouse, do swear by the holy Gospels of God that we will hold and cause to be held the faith of our Lord Jesus Christ and of the Holy Roman Church, and will defend the same by force against all ; that we will proceed against (*persequamur*) and seize and cause to be seized the heretics, their credents, aiders and abetters, to the utmost of our power, and we will accuse and denounce them to the Church and the Inquisitors if we know where they are ; that we will not commit any bailiwicks or administrations or public offices to any of the aforesaid pestiferous persons or to those suspected or reported to be heretics, or to anyone who by reason of the crime of heresy has been penalized from performing public offices ; that we will not knowingly receive any of the aforesaid into or have them in our houses or company or in our service or counsel; and if by chance it should happen otherwise, unknown to us, when it shall come to our notice, we will at once drive them out; and in this and in other matters which pertain to the office of the Inquisition we will obey God and the Roman Church and the Inquisition. So help us God and these holy Gospels of God.'

But the ink was scarcely dry on their signatures when Peter de Castelnau, Legate and Inquisitor, was assassinated on the banks of the Rhone (1208), perhaps in revenge for the burning of Eudes of the same town.[1] The horror of the deed seems to have overwhelmed attention to its details. The Chanson[2] says that a routier maintained by Raymond, Count of Toulouse (for which, among other things, he had been excommunicated by Peter), treacherously stabbed him in the back with a hunting spear, while riding on a mule. The ' Anonymous ' historian declares that the fatal blow was struck in a moment of irritation by one of Raymond's suite in a discussion on heresy. William de Puy-Laurent adds that he passed to God ' by the sword of the impious ' (plural), which may mean that one struck the first blow and others completed the murder. Baronius implicates Raymond directly declaring that he ' suborned satellites to kill the legate as he was crossing the Rhone.'

Was Raymond guilty ? Our answer must affect the view we take of the Crusade which followed from it. We should expect Baronius to take the same view as the pope, but the chronicler is more positive than the pontiff. There is nothing whatever in contemporary records to justify the

---

[1] ' Digna recipiens stipendia meritorum.' Martene and Durand, ii. 802 ; v. *supra,* p. 22.

[2] p. 46 (Lafon) ; Peter de V. S. ch. 8.

word ' suborned.' Innocent does not go beyond ' it is *presumed* he is guilty,' and ' as it is asserted.' His guilt is presumed ' not only because he had publicly threatened him with death and laid an ambush for him, but also because, as it is asserted, he had shown the murderer great friendship and liberally rewarded him, not to mention other proofs which had come to our notice.' [1]   Against this we must set the ' Anonymous ' history which says ' the assassin fled to Beaucaire, to his parents and friends ; for if Count Raymond had caught him, he would have punished him to the satisfaction of the legate, for nothing had ever upset and distressed the count more than this murder.' If Raymond's feelings are here correctly described, they were due doubtless less to his reprobation of the murder than his apprehension of the consequences. But this does not prove him accessory to it. And if the murderer fled to Beaucaire, Raymond could not have received him at Toulouse. After four years of investigation, Innocent could not get beyond a ' strong suspicion ' of his guilt (August 1212).[2] The account of the murder in the *History of the Crusade against the Albigenses* by Barrau and Darragon is rightly characterized by Moline in his *History of the Counts of Toulouse* [3] as dramatic but fanciful. The latter also gives a contemporary hymn in rhymed Latin describing the murder, in which the name of Raymond never occurs.[4] But whether Raymond was guilty or not, Innocent reconstructed the case out of the fragmentary reports which reached him as follows : Raymond was angry because Peter had renewed the excommunication, although the count had fallen into line with others against the heretics. When, however, the legates insisted upon him translating promises into performances, and he refused, they threatened

---

[1] *Regesta*, xi. 20–29, 32, 33.   [2] *Ibid*, xv. 102.
[3] Vol. iii, p. 99.   [4] *Ibid.*, pp. 102 *seq.*

to leave Toulouse. The count retorts by threatening them
with death. 'Beware wherever you go, by land or water,
I am watching you.' Neither the prayers of the Abbot of
St. Gilles nor the importunity of the consuls and burghers
could placate him ; and so realizing the danger to which
the legates were exposed, they provided them with an
escort as far as the Rhone, where all unaware, they put up
for the night at a hostelry at which also some of the count's
satellites were lodging. The next morning, very early,
after Mass, the party started to cross the river, when one
of these satellites, brandishing his spear, suddenly struck
Peter from behind,—Peter so-called because his firmness
was built immovably upon Christ the Rock. The legate
said to his murderer, 'May God forgive thee, as I forgive
thee.'[1] He gave his last orders for the conduct of the
mission, and after many prayers fell asleep in the Lord.
He was buried at St. Gilles. The murderer's name is not
known, and he was never caught. Innocent was much
concerned that no miracles attended such a martyrdom,
but ascribed their absence to the prevalence of heresy,
for even Christ Himself could do no miracle because of
unbelief. But the pope wrote to all the archbishops of
France to publish in all churches with the full formalities
the ban of excommunication against the murderer, his
aiders and defenders. All places whither he fled were to
be placed under an interdict. And further, as regards
Raymond : ' Since according to the canonical sanctions of
the Holy Fathers, faith must not be kept with him who
keeps not faith with God, he is removed from the
communion of the faithful. All who are bound by oath to
the said count by any fealty, federation or treaty ye shall
declare absolved by apostolic authority ; and it is allowed

[1] *Regesta,* xi. 26 (to the Archbishops of Narbonne, Arles, Embrun,
Agen and Vienne and their Suffragans) ; 27 (to the Archbishop of
Lyons and his Suffragan) ; Peter de, V.S., ch. 8.

any catholic, saving the right of the suzerain, not only to persecute the same but to occupy and hold his land, since it is fitting that the hands of all should be against him whose hands are against all.'[1]

In this astounding document the pope is making outrageous claims, but less so than he did in the case of King John of England three years later. He is scrambling amongst military adventurers things that were never his. It means that the successful robber must be accepted by the superior lord; he violates the feudal rights of the King of Aragon on one side, and the King of France on the other. These feudal rights he invoked only when it suited his policy. He once more renewed his appeal to Philip[2]— *renewed*, because he had already appealed to him four times, viz. May 28, 1204, January 16 and February 7, 1205, and November 17, 1207. He had begged Philip to bring pressure to bear upon the local barons and the citizens to take action. If they declined, he, Philip, had the right as suzerain to seize their fiefs for himself. He would thus have the King of France usurp[3] the place of the Emperor by making the Pope's quarrel his own. In this fourth letter he joined with the King of France all the dukes, counts and nobles of his kingdom. He now points out that, since the death of Peter de Castelnau, faith and peace had vanished, and heresy increased. Heretics are worse than Saracens. Therefore Philip should drive out the heretics and put catholics in their place.[4] As an inducement he promises the same privileges as those who went to fight the infidel in Palestine. Peace was to be made between

---

[1] *Regesta*, xi. 26 (1208).   [2] *Ibid.* xi. 28.

[3] ' Usurp ' because he exhorts him to do that which according to the strict theory of the Holy Roman Empire was the duty of the Emperor; cf. the more arrogant claims of the Bull ' *Unam Sanctam*,' a century later.

[4] *Regesta*, xi. 29.

England and France, and their forces were to be united against the heretics.[1]

Without the word being actually used, here is the first hint of the campaign being a Crusade. The credit or discredit of the suggestion for a Crusade appears to belong to Arnauld the Legate, and the pope accepted it readily and supported it vigorously. A tempting bait! A crusader was a hero, a saint: a crusader's person was sacred: a crusader received indulgence for his sins: a crusader's family and goods were under the special protection of the pope: a crusader need not pay his debts, and no usurer could recover principal or interest, and the latter did not accumulate during his period of service.[2] But the Holy Land was a long way off. A Crusade there meant absence from home for many months certainly, for many years probably. Here was a Crusade at one's own doors, with greater advantages, at less risk and expense.

But Philip had his hands full, and though he ignored the first three letters, he replied to the fourth. He said he had not got two armies, one for the Albigenses and one to defend his own land. If the pope would ensure a truce between France and England for two years, and would put a levy upon the clergy to cover the expense of the campaign, and, if John broke the truce, relieve him of his undertaking against the heretics, he would have no objection to his barons and knights and the clergy of France rendering help, and he would himself give fifty pounds a day.[3] To the fifth appeal wherein the pope urged and prayed (*monens et deprecans*) Philip, either in person, or by his son Louis, to render the Church immediate help,[4] the king replied that he had 'two great fierce lions on either side'—Otto the Emperor and the King of England, and that therefore he

[1] *Regesta*, xi. 30, 31. [2] *Ibid.*, 159 ; xii. 136, 137.
[3] Vaissete, *Hist. de Lang.*, viii. 138. [4] *Ibid.*

could not come himself or send his son ; but he had no
objection to any of his barons going 'to disturb the disturbers of faith and peace in the province of Narbonne.'
He, however, enters a caveat against Innocent's bait of
disposing of Raymond's lands to those who fought against
the heretics. According to experts whom he had consulted,
Innocent could only do that, after the count had been
condemned for *heresy*. His guilt had not been proved ; and
until then, Innocent could not despoil him of his lands,
which he held of the king.[1] Nor was Philip willing to
leave the response to the pope's summons absolutely
to the discretion of his nobles. A letter [2] has been discovered in the archives of the king, in which he gives
permission to the Duke of Burgundy and the Count of
Nevers to join the Crusade, but limiting the number of
their knights to five hundred. Dissatisfied, the pope issued
a ' general letter to all prelates, counts, and barons and to
all people in the kingdom of France,' urging them to
avenge the insult to the Crucified (Crusade language), as
they knew that all their sins would be remitted by God and
His Vicar, ' provided that they were sufficiently contrite and
confessed.'[3] The Archbishop of Sens and his suffragans
were to give one-tenth of their revenues for one year to
the expenses of the forces from Burgundy, Nevers and St.
Paul.[4] ' What more ? When that indulgence was published in France, a great multitude of the faithful armed
itself with the sign of the cross.' The Chanson puts the
number of Crusaders, Frenchmen, Burgundians, Germans,
Gascons, etc., at 20,000 fully armed knights, 200,000
infantry, and an innumerable company of clergy and
citizens, under the leadership of the Abbot of Citeaux, the
Duke of Narbonne, and the Counts of Nevers, St. Paul,

---

[1] Peter de V.S., ch. 10.
[2] See Luchaire, vol. ii, p. 127 ; Vaissete, viii. 142, 563.
[3] *Regesta*, xi, 156.   [4] *Ibid.*, 158.

Auxerre, Genoa, and Poitiers.　William le Breton more modestly says of Philip :

> Corde pio motus ter millia quinque virorum,[1]
> Ad proprios sumptus instructos rebus et armis,
> Dans exemplum aliis, in Christi proelia misit.[2]

The king's alleged motives may be questioned. It was a speculation in which the King of France would lose nothing, and might gain much, for he was quite willing for his powerful vassals to weaken themselves in the South, himself meanwhile watching for opportunities to intervene and increase his own power.

In the early spring of 1209, the appeal to the king and to all the faithful was repeated : ' Hitherto perhaps you have fought for transitory glory, now fight for eternal.'[3]　Philip was for the former in the name of the latter.

Three immense hosts, one from the north—the largest one from the west, and one—the smallest—from midway between them, converged southwards and met at Montpellier.

There was thus let loose upon some of the fairest and richest provinces of France at the instigation of the Vicar of Christ the bitterest of all wars, a mixture of civil and religious strife, which lasted for nearly a quarter of a century, and left the horrible aftermath of the Inquisition.

---

[1] The figures of the two Williams may be partly harmonised by noting that le Breton refers only to the king's contingent, whereas de Tudela's figures cover the force gathered ' from all parts ' to Carcassonne, after Raymond had made his peace.

[2] *Philippidos*, viii.　　　　　　　　[3] *Regesta*, xii, pp. 229, 230.

CHAPTER VIII

WHILE this imposing army was mobilizing Arnauld was engaged in obtaining reinforcements of another kind. The death of Peter de Castelnau and the departure of Diego and the brothers Peter and Ralph having seriously depleted the preaching power of the Church, he despatched the Bishop of Toulouse and the Bishop of Conserans to Rome for replacements. This request was, strange to say, supported by Raymond himself. His nephew, the Count of Béziers, pressed him to fight it out, but either from policy or piety[1] he threw in his lot with the Crusaders. Following the example of Arnauld, he too sent a deputation to Rome, viz., the Archbishop of Auch, Bernard, Lord of Rabensteins, and, some add, [2] Raymond, the deposed Bishop of Toulouse, to state his case to the pope, declaring himself ready to submit unreservedly to the successor of the murdered legate. When early in the following year (1209) he heard that the pope had chosen Milo, a notary of the Curia, ' a man unmoved by bribes or threats,' and Thédise as his assistant, Raymond professed to be delighted, exclaiming : ' All goes well ; I have a legate after my own heart. It is just as if I were legate myself.' Milo's powers, however, were purely nominal. The pope's instructions to him were : ' Let the Abbot of Citeaux do everything : you are to be merely his instrument. For the Count of Toulouse suspects him : he will not suspect you.'[3]

---

[1] ' Poenitudinem simulans, timens se digne pro meritis puniendum, Peter de V. S. ch. 9.

[2] *Chanson*, p. 50. (Lafon).

[3] Milo died the next year at St. Gilles (*Chanson*, p. 51, Lafon).

While Raymond's envoys were pleading his cause at Rome, he went himself to plead it before the King of France. His reception was friendly but unfruitful. The King advised him to submit to Rome, and obtain peace at any price ; at the same time he extracted a promise from him not to help the emperor in any way whatever. As Marquis of Provence, Raymond was feudatory to the emperor, so that his promise placed him in an awkward position. In fact Philip's promises of help were so vague that he sought something more substantial from the emperor. Here he met with nothing but refusal, and his quest of the emperor only offended the king.

The suspicion to which the pope referred had been deepened, while the missions were at Rome, by the refusal of Arnauld at a Council held at Aubenas to re-open the question of the count's excommunication on the ground that it was *sub judice* at the Papal Court. On the arrival of Milo a great Council was summoned to meet at Montélimart.[1] It had been pre-arranged that each of those summoned should bring with him a written and sealed statement of what he proposed should be done to the Count of Toulouse ; and when these documents were opened, the measures proposed were identical. The Council then moved up the Rhone to St. Gilles to which Raymond was cited. Here, believing, though erroneously, that in Milo he had an *amicus curiæ*, he agreed to carry out whatever conditions might be imposed on him, provided the excommunication were removed. As a security of good faith he promised to give up seven of his strongest castles. Standing naked at the door of St. Gilles' Church, where his alleged victim was interred, he swore, in the presence of Milo and some twenty prelates over the body of Christ and the relics of the Saints, which were exposed before the Church door with great

[1] Peter de V. S. ch. 11.

veneration, that he would obey the commands of Holy
Church in all things at all times, and perform without fraud
or wrong intention all the things for failing in which he
had been and remained at that time excommunicate.
These were (*a*) refusing to swear peace when others did ;
(*b*) not expelling heretics as he had sworn to do ; (*c*) being
suspected of heresy ; (*d*) keeping routiers and brigands ; (*e*)
converting churches into castles ; (*f*) not keeping the holy
days ; (*g*) appointing Jews to public offices ; (*h*) detaining
unjustly the revenues of certain monasteries and churches ;
(*i*) exacting illegal tolls ; (*j*) deposing the Bishop of Carpentoracte ; (*k*) being suspected of complicity in the murder of
Peter de Castelnau, and of receiving the murderer ; (*l*) violence and robbery.   Furthermore he promised to grant full
liberty to all churches and religious houses in Vienne,
Arles, Narbonne, Auch, Bordeaux, and Bourges, and to
surrender or destroy all castellated churches.   He and his
bailiffs were not to question the decision of the bishops as
to who were heretics.[1]   Then the legate placed on him a
long robe, and dragged him by it into the church, beating
him all the time.   The huge crowd prevented him from
retiring by the same door, but compelled him to pass the
tomb of the murdered Peter.   ' O just judgment of God,
never heard of before ! ' exclaims Peter de Vaux-Sarnai.
' Him whom he had despised living he is forced to
reverence dead.'[2]   The corpse was declared to be as fresh
as when first buried and to give out a wonderful
fragrance.

The Count of Toulouse was now committed to the
suppression of heresy, and receiving the cross from Milo
joined the Crusaders at Valence.   They made an imposing
array.   Among them were the Archbishops of Rheims,

---

[1] Collection of documents in Migne after *Regesta*, xii. 85.
[2] ch. 12.

Sens and Rouen, the Bishops of Autun, Clermont, Nevers and other prelates, the Duke of Burgundy, the Counts of Nevers, St. Paul, Auxerre, Genoa, Poitiers, and, one destined to be the most famous of all, Simon, Count de Montfort. Several small places fell at once, and many heretics of both sexes were burnt on refusing to recant. Casseneuil, however, resisted all attempts to capture it.[1] The Crusaders then moved in full force against Béziers. There was a strong Spanish strain in its population, for after the massacre of the inhabitants in 1167, the Spanish soldiers who had come with Alfonse, King of Aragon, were given the women who had been spared.[2] Its viscount, ' no better knight in all the world,' and ' a good Catholic,' [3] had skilfully fortified the city, and then went to Carcassonne [4] to raise reinforcements, but before he could return, the enemy were at the gate. The Bishop of Béziers urged his flock either to leave the city, or to drive out the heretics and open the gates ; but, confident in their fortifications and buoyed up by the hope of succour from Carcassonne, they stoutly refused, and resolved to defend their city. But in vain. Their sorties were driven back, and the city was quickly captured by a general assault of the superior forces of the Crusaders. The people fled into the Cathedral, where the priests recited Masses for the dead. But neither priest nor place protected them. The whole city was given over to fire and sword. The surfeited crusaders were succeeded by rapacious camp-followers. ' From the least to the greatest nearly all were killed.' Many women and children, old men and clergy had taken refuge in the Church of St. Mary Magdalene, and there on St. Mary's Day (July 22, 1209)

[1] *Chanson*, p. 53. (Lafon.)
[2] Peyrat, *Hist. des Albig.* vol. i, p. 26.   For their violent character see Peter de V. S. ch. 16.
[3] *Chanson*, p. 55.
[4] Not ' fled in panic ' as O'Leary, *Life of Dominic*, p. 71.

they were massacred in thousands.[1]   Peter de Vaux-Sarnai remarks that very rightly was the city captured on that day because the heretics had grossly insulted her and Christ. It was on this occasion that Arnauld is reported to have exclaimed : ' Slay all : the Lord will know His own.'[2]   Two reasons, hardly reconcilable, are given for this ruthlessness : (*a*) that the utter destruction of this, the first important conquest, was deliberately carried out by the crusaders as a warning to other nests of heresy, thus saving further bloodshed ; and (*b*) that it was due to the riff-raff (*ribaud, orlotz*), whose spoils the knights appropriated, and who in revenge set fire to the city.[3]   In their report to the pope, Arnauld and Milo give yet another account : the citizens killed their leader, whom the viscount had left in command : but while terms of surrender were being considered, the camp-followers attacked and captured the city.   Then the army, sparing neither rank, sex nor age, burnt it, massacring about 20,000.[4]   Whatever were the facts, terror seized the country, and nearly a hundred castles fell into the hands of the invaders.   Flushed with so easy a conquest, the crusaders

---

[1] *Regesta* xii   108,   Wm.   le   Breton   exaggerates : . . .

' Ingressi sexus utriusque trucidant

Millia bis triplicata decem ; (Philip. Lib. viii ; v. p. 24)

[2] Its genuineness has been questioned. It is given by Cæsar of Heisterbach (i. 301), who, like Arnauld, was a Cistercian, and a contemporary, but only as a report ('*fertur* dixisse, Cædite eos, novit enim Dominus qui sunt ejus ') .   Manrique, historian of the same Order, quotes it, both, no doubt, to the credit of their fellow-monk.   But Peter de V. S. knows nothing of it, neither does any historian of Languedoc.   The Chanson also is silent, although so dramatic an utterance would have suited its theme admirably. See also Acton, *Essays on Liberty*, p. 567, who rejects it.   Coulton thinks it ' perfectly consistent.'   In this Church the people had killed their Viscount Trenceval and broken the teeth of their Bishop who came to his rescue.   Matthew Paris says that the people threw a copy of the four Gospels over the walls, exclaiming : ' This is your law : we care nothing for it.' (p. 203, W. Wats' edition).   The reverence of Catharists for the Scriptures makes this highly improbable. (See vol. i, Index ' Bible.')

[3] Peter de V.S., ch. 16.   [4] *Regesta*, xii. 108.

after three days' rest marched upon Carcassonne, the bishops and abbots singing the *Veni, Sancte Spiritus* with the greatest fervour. Grieved but undismayed at the fate of Béziers, the men of Carcassonne, under the inspiration of Raymond-Roger, the Viscount of Béziers offered a most stubborn resistance. Two suburbs were soon taken, but only the burning ruins were left in the hands of the crusaders. The leaders decided to reduce the city by siege and not by assault, as they had already seized the water supply, and its fall could only be a matter of days, seeing it was August and the weather very hot. At this point, the crusaders were joined by Peter, King of Aragon, not as a combatant, but as a mediator.[1] At first the only terms the king was allowed to offer were that Raymond-Roger with a dozen knights might leave the city, but that all others within it must surrender unconditionally. Peter muttered between his teeth : ' Asses will fly to heaven first,' [2] and, in view of the massacre of Béziers, was not surprised at the viscount's reply : ' I would rather be burnt alive.' But the heat was as pitiless as the foe, and the besieged suffered intensely from thirst. On the other hand, while the city seemed impregnable, the supplies were running short for the besiegers in consequence of their having ravaged the country. Hence a relaxation on both sides. The inhabitants were allowed to go out ' carrying only their sins,' while the viscount was made prisoner.[3] This further success was acclaimed as a fulfilment of a threat of the bishop whom his flock had driven away : 'You will not hear me now, but, believe me, I will bellow so loudly against you that from the uttermost parts of the earth will come

---

[1] *Chanson*, p. 64 (Lafon.)   [2] *Ibid.*, p.66.
[3] He never recovered his liberty. He died, five months later, of consumption, according to Chanson (p. 73), although, according to others, he was assassinated or poisoned. His funeral, carried out with all due ceremony and attended by Simon de Montfort, testified to his being regarded as a Catholic.

those that will destroy your town.' Meagre as was this clemency, the reason for it was not pity but prudence. Only by plenty of food and booty could the nobles keep their followers under discipline, yet this wholesale devastation and pillage denuded the country of the means whereby they alone could subsist.

A RNAULD, assuming that the conquered territory was the property of the Church, offered it to several leaders of the crusaders, but all refused on the ground that they had sufficient domains in France, and had come to destroy heresy, not to despoil a peer of his lands. As a matter of fact the proffered honour had but little security either by feudal right or military force ; and no doubt the Duke of Burgundy and others who declined it saw that they were playing with edged tools. To assume that excommunication *by* the Church implied confiscation of property *to* the Church was a weapon that might strike any of them. The legates took it for granted that the estates of the Viscount of Béziers were forfeited to the Church, and did not revert to his liege lord, the King of Aragon.[1] At length Simon de Montfort, whose zeal and courage had been most conspicuous in the campaign, accepted the position, but only after it had been offered to him twice, and then almost under compulsion, the abbot ' exercising his official authority,' and on condition that the other leaders would come to his aid whenever he required them.[2] From this time Simon de Montfort became the central military figure, and Peter de Vaux-Sarnai seizes the opportunity to indulge in a rhapsody of his virtues finishing with a pun, ' *totus divinis*

[1] Alfonse II had extended his sway over Béziers, Carcassonne, Nîmes, Albi, etc. Peter II, perhaps to give greater dignity to his kingdom, had had himself crowned by the pope, but at the price of swearing fealty and paying an annual tribute. Hence the papacy may have claimed vassalage for *all* his possessions, and not for Aragon only. But the Spanish lords repudiated the bargain, and it was abandoned.

[2] Peter de V. S., ch. 18, 19. *Chanson*, p. 72 (Lafon).

servitiis nuncupatus—de Monte, immo de Mente, oriundus. Simon filled two offices in one ; (*a*) he was the pope's vassal. Said the legate to him : 'From God Almighty receive the land ; for God and the pope guarantee it to you, and we after them, and all the crusaders.' So a month later Simon wrote to the pope, begging him to confirm it to him and his heirs, for he formally acknowledged his duty to God and the pope only ; (*b*) he was the official military leader of a new kind of Crusade, viz., against the infidels of the West. In return for his investiture by the Church he gave to Arnauld's Abbey of Citeaux three houses—the house of Bernard de Levin in Carcassonne, the house of Améli in Béziers, and the house of Felise in Narbonne, all heretics.[1] Also he promised that the tithes and the first-fruits of the lands which fell to him should be paid to the churches therein, and any objector he would attack as his and the Church's enemy.[2]

A hearth tax of threepence and a fixed annual pension from himself[3] should be paid to the Roman Church, saving the rights of his superior lord. (So irregularly, however, were these dues paid that the pope appointed Peter Mark, a sub-deacon and 'corrector of our letters' to collect these and other dues on the spot and forward them to Rome).[4]

The legates were most optimistic in their report to the pope of the campaign. Many indeed had returned to France,[5] but Simon had still sufficient forces, they said, to occupy the whole of the infested country, except Toulouse ; over two hundred of the best castles were in his hands, and

---

[1] Vaissete, *Hist. de Lang.* viii. 145, 571. This is the first instance of Simon de Montfort taking the titles of Viscount of Béziers and Carcassonne.

[2] *Regesta*, xii. 108, Vaissete, *Hist. de Lang*, v. 53.   [3] £1,000.

[4] October 12, 1212. *Regesta*, xv. 167.

[5] e.g. the Count of Nevers, but the Duke of Burgundy remained. Peter de V.S., ch. 20.

the count of Béziers was a prisoner.[1] But the legates
were ecclesiastics, not soldiers, and de Montfort describes
the situation to the pope in very different terms. The
policy of ' frightfulness ' had backfired, and he found himself in a devastated land. The heretics had dismantled
their castles before deserting them, yet they were by no
means crushed, and still held many strong positions.
Many crusaders had left him, and those who remained
demanded double pay, on the ground that an unusual war
called for unusual wages.[2] The pope, in his reply, making
the obvious pun upon his name—that he was ' the strong
mountain for the Church ', confirmed him in his appointment and promised to aid him to the utmost of his power.
This promise he fulfilled by writing to the Emperor Otto,
the Kings of Castile and Aragon, and to several counts,
archbishops and bishops to send him men and money.
Property confiscated from heretics was to be put to pious
uses in the country where the property was situated.[3]
Peter de Vaux-Sarnai is very bitter against the retiring
crusaders. ' Had these remained, they would have been
irresistible.' He is not quite certain whether to attribute
the prolongation of strife to the malice of the Devil or to
the mercy of God, who so designed it that as many different soldiers of Christ as possible might share in the
honour and thus obtain forgiveness of their sins and
eternal life.

But Simon had difficulties other than military. What
was he to do with the Count of Toulouse ? What with
Toulouse itself ? The city was declared to be *fons et origo*
of heresy, but the count a crusader. The pope wanted to

---

[1] *Regesta*, xii. 108.   [2] *Ibid*. 109.
[3] *Ibid* 122, 124, 125, 126, 129. Yet Simon gives the Castle of
Cazouls to the Bishop of Béziers for the salvation and cure of his sins,
and those of his wife and children. Vaissete, viii. 599. v. also
p. 56.

spare him, the legates to crush him. They noped by
haughtiness and harshness so to exasperate him as to drive
him into the arms of heresy. But Raymond was too
astute to play into their hands. In spite of all provocation
he acted as a loyal catholic. Nay, he did more. Their
overbearing conduct drove him not into the arms of the
heretics but to the feet of the pope. For when the legates
laid Toulouse under an interdict, because its consuls
would not admit them within the gates or deliver up the
alleged heretics therein, protesting that there were none,
Raymond determined to lay the whole situation in person
before the pope, and sent ambassadors to prepare the way.
The legates retaliated, first, by demurring to the pope
receiving such an enemy of peace and righteousness ;
secondly, by begging the pope not to restore the seven
castles, as they were invaluable for the destruction of
heresy ; and thirdly by summoning a Council at Avignonet
(September 1209) at which the count's excommunication
was renewed. Twenty-one canons were drawn up ; barons
were ordered to exterminate the heretics : fines were inflicted
on the excommunicated ; Jews were excluded from all
public offices : the people were compelled to keep the
peace ; the descendants of the assassins of Peter de
Castelnau and all other murderers of the faithful were
excluded from ecclesiastical benefices unto the third genera-
tion ; the fortress of William de Porcelet, who had
sheltered the assassin, was to be destroyed. The grounds
upon which the excommunication of Raymond was revived
were : (*a*) he had not given up the heretics ; (*b*) he had not
dismantled the castellated churches ; (*c*) he had not paid
his fines ; (*d*) he had attempted to force the pope's hand in
the matter of the seven castles by appealing to the
Emperor and the King of France. [1]   But they were willing

[1] *Regesta*, xii. 106.

to suspend the sentence until All Saints' Day in the hope that the count would prove his innocence. [1] They deplored any weakening on the part of the pope at this juncture, for the last error would be worse than the first.

Before Raymond's departure for Rome he made his will, making his son, aged eleven, his heir. Baldwin, the count's brother, was appointed executor together with the Count of Comminges and the Consuls of Toulouse. If his son died in childhood, Baldwin was to succeed him. He placed his son under the protection of the Emperor and the King of France. If his race became extinct, they were to share his lands, the King taking that on the right bank of the Rhone, and the Emperor that on the left. [2]

The count took with him to Rome testimonials from several churches in support of his petition for absolution. He had, he declared, as far as possible, carried out the mandates of the legates, and was prepared to fulfil the others. He professed himself ready to purge himself of all heresy in the pope's presence, and pointed out that the retention of the seven castles could no longer be justified. [3] His reception was more than favourable : it was cordial. The pope allowed him to see the very face of the Veronica[4]—a privilege certainly not extended to one excommunicate, gave him the usual absolution on confession, and dismissed him with valuable presents. He also wrote to the legates ordering them (January 25, 1210) to summon a council at some convenient centre within three months of receiving his letter. They were not to act as accusers as well as judges. They were to be a Court of Inquiry only. If any lawful accuser appeared they were to send his evidence and their comments to the Curia. If no accuser appeared, the count was to purge himself before them of the charges previously laid against him, and to be reinstated

[1] Vaissete, *Hist. de Lang.*, v. 134. [2] Vaissete, viii. 573.
[3] *Regesta*, xii, 152. [4] *Chanson*, xliii. 989–91.

in the seven castles. If he objected to these terms, the
legates were to retain the castles and send full particulars
to the pope. The interdict on Toulouse was to be
raised. [1]

Obviously the time was not yet come for crushing the
count and seizing his domains. Simon de Montfort
retained but few of his conquests and was beset on all sides
by enemies. [2] Accordingly a sort of peace was patched
up on Raymond's return ; the abbot was allowed to enter
Toulouse and was even put into possession of the strong
castle of Narbonne. But amity between the leaders did
not carry with it concord in the city. The inhabitants were
suspicious of Montfort's party, all and sundry, and saw no
distinction between conversion and conquest ; hence
disturbances were frequent.

---

[1] *Regesta*, xii. 152, 153, 156. Moline (*Hist. des C. de Toulouse*, vol.
iii) describes these instructions as ' the tactics of a general and the
subtlety of a statesman.'

[2] Peter de V. S., ch. 34. Agnes, Countess of Béziers, ceded all her
possessions and rights to Simon de Montfort, November, 1209.
Vaissete, viii. 579.

THE return of Spring brought the return of the crusaders, among them being the Bishop of Paris. The new campaign opened with an attack on Minerba, at the instigation of the Narbonnese, 'more for their personal advantage than from religious zeal, because Minerba had made raids upon the Narbonnese.'[1] Perched on its lofty crags, it was regarded as almost the strongest fortress in Southern France, yet it fell before the powerful artillery and superior numbers of the invaders. Mangonels[2] and catapults bombarded it day and night. One, '*magna et optima*', directed by Simon himself, did so much mischief that one Sunday night the defenders issued forth with oakum, grease and firewood, and tried to burn it. But the attempt failed, and the besieged sued for peace. At that moment Arnauld and Thédise arrived, and the conditions of capitulation were left to them. Personally Arnauld was for another massacre, but professionally he dare not condemn to death, 'as he was a monk and a priest.' So he compromised between natural cruelty and ecclesiastical propriety by offering them their lives on condition that they accepted the Catholic faith. Against this, however, a certain Robert, 'a stalwart in the Catholic faith' protested. Crusaders had come not to spare but to destroy heretics. 'Never fear' answered the monk, 'very few will turn.' He was right: one hundred and forty 'perfects' refused to save their bodies and lose their souls, and were burnt in

[1] Peter de V. S., ch. 38.
[2] These engines of war were nicknamed 'the bad neighbour', 'the queen', etc. Cf. 'Big Bertha', 'Jack Johnson', etc. in the Great War.

one holocaust, some leaping into the fire of their own accord[1] (July, 1210).

Termes was the next place to fall, but only after a three months' siege (although Simon's army had been increased by reinforcements led by the redoubtable Archdeacon of Paris), and then owing to dysentery. Its fall impressed other places, such as Albi, with the uselessness of resistance.[2] At Bram, which opened its gates after a three days' siege, Simon gouged out the eyes of over a hundred prisoners, slit their noses, and sent them to Cabaret, led by one to whom he had spared one eye. This wholesale and horrible mutilation was a reprisal for similar treatment of *two* of his knights by Gerard de Pepieux.

The more successful the Crusade, the less ready would the legates be to take the measures ordered by the Pope whereby Raymond might be possibly released from the net in which he was entangled. They called a council at St. Gilles in September, 1210, and therefore not within the three months specified, but the legates so manœuvred matters that it dispersed without settling anything. Peter de Vaux-Sarnai admits with refreshing náïveté that this was intentional : ' If the Count were allowed to prove his innocence, all the work of the Church would be ruined.' The Council was purposely delayed in order that it might *not* be said it was the Council ordered by the Pope. Hence, when the Council, instead of granting him absolution, renewed his excommunication, Raymond burst into tears, ' with a wickedness natural to him.' And Thédise ' knowing that these tears were not tears of piety and repentance but of wickedness and deceit exclaimed " You will not reach God by a flood of waters." ' [3]

---

[1] Peter de V. S., ch. 38. At this siege R. Trenceval, younger son of the late Viscount of Béziers, ceded all his rights to the Count de Montfort in the presence of the legate, the Bishop of Toulouse and others. Vaissete viii. 609.

[2] Peter de V. S., ch. 40.   [3] *Ibid.* reading *doli* for *doloris*.

The winter once more brought a cessation of hostilities, and at the beginning of the New Year (January, 1211) another council was held at Narbonne, at which were present, among others, the King of Aragon and Simon de Montfort. Raymond was denied admittance, as being excommunicate, and was kept outside in the biting wind. He was at length handed a document which he was requested to sign, offering him the restitution of all his domains, as well as a third or fourth of all the castles of heretics, on the following conditions : he must expel all the heretics from his dominions ; restore to the clergy all their rights, and banish all Jews, to the satisfaction of the legates, before the end of the year ; eat not more than two kinds of food ; wear only a thick brown cloak, and discard all rich clothing ; dismantle all castles and fortresses ; remove all toll houses ; dismiss all routiers ; receive only the accustomed revenues ; pay fourpence a year hearth tax to the guardians of the peace whom the Church should place in the country ; all knights were to quit the towns and live in the country ; all usurers were to be suppressed and disgorge their gains ; if the crusaders took anything on their march necessary for the war, they were not to be opposed. The count was to go to Palestine and stay there until permitted to return by the legates, when he was to enter the Order of the Templars or of St. John. The legates were to hold his land as a security for the fulfilment of these terms. If he failed to fulfil the covenants, his lands would be forfeited.[1] When these astounding conditions were read to the count, he received them with derisive laughter, and called the King of Aragon to hear them, who hotly remarked, ' By God Almighty this shall be corrected.'[2] Quitting the Council without saluting

[1] Peter de V.S., ch. 43. Vaissete, v. 94.
[2] *Chanson*, p. 92 (Lafon).

it,[1] Raymond took the document to Toulouse, Montauban, Moissac, Agen and other places. Wherever read, it kindled the hottest indignation, knights, burgesses, the common people, even prelates (e.g. the Archbishop of Auch and the Bishops of Carcassonne and Rodez) declaring they would die first. The legates realized that they had gone too far. Particularly were they alarmed at the anger of the king. Casting themselves at his feet they begged him to accept the homage of Simon de Montfort, the latter undertaking of his conquests to retain only Pamiers, and for the rest to acknowledge the suzerainty of the King of Aragon. Peter in turn made himself responsible for the good behaviour of the Count of Foix (the most formidable opponent of the crusaders), and promised that if he broke the bond (to which, however, he had never been a consenting party), he would deliver the Castle of Foix into the hands of the legates.[2] It was 'Hobson's choice' with the king, for Simon de Montfort was in military possession, and it would have been difficult for the king to eject him. In order however, that the land which Simon had conquered might not go out of his family, the king married his eldest son, James, to Simon's daughter, and at the same time, 'hedged' by marrying his sister, Sancia, to Raymond's son, which latter alliance, says Peter de Vaux-Sarnai, 'rendered him infamous and suspected among us.' During the late winter, Fulk, Bishop of Toulouse, and the Bishop of Carcassonne (who entrusted the care of his Diocese to Dominic during his absence)[3] visited France and Normandy, preaching the Albigensian Crusade.

---

[1] This, according to Peter de V.S. (ch. 47), was due not to bad manners but superstition, because he had seen a martin flying on his left hand. 'Ipse enim, more Saracenorum, in volatu et cantu avium et ceteris auguriis spem habebat.'

[2] *Ibid.*

[3] Peter de V.S., ch. 49.

Their fervent zeal and graphic oratory were rewarded when, in the spring, great numbers set themselves on the march for the south. The first place of real importance to fall was Lavaur, after a siege of five or six weeks. Peter de Vaux-Sarnai describes it as ' the spring of the whole heresy, though it did not belong to the Count of Toulouse.' Its citizens were shameless dogs, howling and barking.[1] All the bravery of Aimeric who had left the crusaders and went to the aid of his sister, Giraude, the chatelaine, was of no avail. The crusaders from the north were joined by the forces of Simon, besides those who had been enrolled by Fulk under the name of ' The Brotherhood of Toulouse,' and whom he sent forth to the war with the cross on their breast and his blessing on their head. The Count of Foix endeavoured in conjunction with some Tolosans to ra'se the siege by a daring flank attack on a body of German and Frisian crusaders, five thousand strong, and did cut off a thousand of them. But all in vain. Lavaur fell on the night of May 3. Aimeric and eighty knights were hanged ; but, the gallows breaking with the weight, Simon ordered the rest of the prisoners—about four hundred—to be burnt—' an order which the pilgrims (*peregrini*) most gladly and speedily carried out on the spot.' The sex of Giraude did not save her. Weeping, imploring, shrieking, she was hurled from the castle into the moat and crushed to death with stones.[2]

Montferrand next fell, Baldwin, brother of the Count of Toulouse, making but a feeble resistance and saving his neck by going over to the enemy.[3] The rest of the garrison were allowed to go with their arms, but they were never to use them against the crusaders, or in any way to help the heretics. The submission of other castles put Simon into

---

[1] Peter de V.S., ch. 50. [2] *Ibid.*, ch. 52.
[3] *Ibid.*, ch. 54, *Chanson*, p. 103 (Lafon).

possession of the whole County of Albi within a month of
the capture of Lavaur.[1]

This rapid success emboldened the crusaders to attack
Toulouse itself, ' of all towns, the queen and flower.' The
provost and the clergy, at the advice of the bishop, had
already quitted the city and come out to Simon de Montfort,
with bare feet and ' bearing the Body of Christ.' Not only,
however, did the assault fail, but the crusaders were
themselves attacked and driven off. The summer too, was
drawing to a close, and the forty days of service were
ended. Simon was satisfied for a time with the harvest
and retired to Carcassonne, while the legate went north to
Albi. But no sooner did Raymond hear that Simon had
broken up his camp and that his forces were dispersed, than,
for the first time he took the offensive, and assembled a
huge host, estimated at 200,000.[2] The Counts of Comminges
and Foix, who had joined him when Toulouse was
threatened, still remained with him. Simon took up the
challenge; messengers were despatched in all directions, and
with the forces thus hastily gathered he threw himself into
Castelnau.[3] Bouchard, Governor of Lavaur, hastened to his
aid with food supplies, but the fiery Foix fell upon the
convoy and destroyed it with great slaughter, the spoils
falling to the routiers. But Simon showed his military
ability by seizing on this diversion to issue from the city
with his knights, leaving his infantry on guard within, and
in turn attacked Foix, who, taken by surprise, was compelled to retreat in the night. Raymond, moreover, had
such respect for Simon as a strategist that he did not dare

[1] Most of the booty was given to Raymond de Salvanac, a rich
merchant, who was financing the Crusade ; *Chanson*, p. 101.

[2] *Chanson*, p. 113.

[3] A Cistercian, believing the situation to be desperate, was praying
for Simon, when he heard a divine voice saying to him ' Why do you
pray for him ? So many are doing the same that your prayers are
not wanted.' Peter de V.S., ch. 57.

to meet him in open battle, and withdrew westward, to form a great entrenched camp at Toulouse. Here he recovered most of the castles which had fallen to the crusaders. On the other hand, Simon, relieved of the menace of Raymond, ravaged the whole country about the Tarn. This year winter brought no cessation to military operations. At Castres over eighty heretics were burnt, on refusing to kill an animal.[1] Simon had been reinforced by the arrival of his brother, Guy, from the Holy Land, and on the Feast of the Epiphany (1212), the brothers crossed the Tarn and besieged St. Marcel. Had Raymond marched out of his winter quarters to its assistance, the crusaders, says the Chanson,[2] would have been annihilated, but a demonstration from Montauban kept him in check. On the other hand, the winter rendered it difficult for the crusaders to obtain supplies from a country which they had already devastated ; and so stoutly did the garrison, under the Count of Foix, defend the city, that on Holy Thursday, Simon was compelled to raise the siege. With the exception of Toulouse, St. Marcel was the first city to have the honour of repulsing the invader, and it was a humiliation which was neither forgotten nor forgiven.

[1] Peter de V.S., ch. 60.   [2] p. 127 (Lafon).

CHAPTER XI

THE spring brought reinforcements from the north, the south and the east, Germany, Lombardy and Slavonia. Those from Germany had been raised and were led by the warlike William, Archdeacon of Paris. 'One scarcely knew whether he was a man at all.' He never seemed to sleep or eat. He enlisted, equipped, and supported crusaders. He invented new artillery and improved the old. He lent a hand to carpenters, engineers, woodmen. He led forlorn hopes. At Termes, seeing the batteries ineffective, he proposed to fill up the deep moat which rendered the town inaccessible. The military council said : 'It can't be done.' He did it.[1]

The attack on St. Marcel was resumed, and the second attempt was successful. In revenge for the previous failure the city was given over to massacre and pillage. Some were drowned ; others were caught in the Cathedral and executed ; others tortured to death. Many fled to Cordes, then a mere hunting-box for the Counts of Toulouse, but which henceforth became a hotbed of heresy, and dates its history as a town from this accession of refugees. St. Antonin was the next to be captured, ' in less time than it takes to cook an egg.' [2] The Bishop of Albi had offered it favourable terms of capitulation, but they had been contemptuously refused. From St. Antonin the crusaders marched north-west to Penne, the key of the country of Agen, which had been given by Richard I to his sister on her marriage with Raymond VI. Commanding

---

[1] Langlois, *Hist. de Crois*. Peter de V.S. ch. 63. He was offered the Bishopric of Béziers, but refused it, Peter de V.S., ch. 65.
[2] *Chanson*, p. 129.

two rivers, its importance had been recognized by Cœur de Lion, and by him had been strongly fortified. It had been further strengthened by its present governor, Hugo. Its fortifications proved too strong even for the engineer-archdeacon, but once more hunger and thirst overcame where artillery failed. After a siege lasting from Ascension Day to the end of July, it fell. During the siege Guy attacked Mont-segur, but, true to its name, the attack failed, and Guy drew off his force to help his brother at Penne. From Penne Simon went to Biron in the north, which gave no trouble. Its castellan, Martin Algai, who had deserted Simon for Raymond, was drawn along the road at the horse's tail and then hanged. Returning to the Tarn Simon had reached Moissac when he was reinforced by an army of 15,000 raised by his wife Alise. In the operations Simon was unhorsed, and would have been captured but for the timely aid of William d'Encontre and other knights ; [1] but the nephew of the Archbishop of Rheims was less fortunate. He was killed and his body carried off by the enemy. They put it into a mangonel and hurled it back to the besiegers. But at length, by a large part of the wall falling into the moat, the city was rendered defenceless, and on its surrender, three hundred routiers were executed, and a heavy fine imposed, but the city and its inhabitants were spared. The crusaders now overran the whole of the Marquisate, according to Peter de Vaux-Sarnai, but, as a matter of fact, there still remained to Raymond Toulouse, Foix, Montauban, and Mont-segur. But once more winter rings down the curtain upon the tragedy, and the summer crusaders retire to France.

Casting our eyes back over the year's campaign it is clear that Raymond's position grew more and more desperate. As resolute as ever in his refusal to yield his

[1] *Chanson*, p. 135.

domains into the hands of the legates as a security for the fulfilment of the conditions of his absolution, he nevertheless found it impossible to prevent their partial conquest by Simon. He therefore endeavoured to secure through a mutual interest something more practical than the mere verbal support or neutrality he had so far received from Peter, King of Aragon, viz., by a voluntary acknowledgment of what had hitherto been vague and undefined—the King's suzerainty. On the day before the siege of St. Marcel began, Raymond wrote to the king : ' I, Raymond, by the grace of God, Count of Toulouse, Duke of Narbonne, Marquis of Provence, and I, Raymond his son, of our own free will and in all sincerity, commit unto you, Lord Peter, by the grace of God, King of Aragon and Count of Barcelona, ourselves personally and the state of Toulouse and the suburbs and town of Montauban with all that pertains thereto, all the lands which we have and ought to have with all present and future soldiers and inhabitants and all our rights and prerogatives which we have and ought to have. We transfer to you and your proxies the corporal possession of all these things with full power and jurisdiction as a pledge and security that we are ready to obey and satisfy any command which the Lord Pope or you for him may lay upon us, as far as in us lies, without deceit or fraud.' By significantly omitting all reference to the legates, Raymond not only countered their hostility but interpreted Peter's cryptic remark : ' by God Almighty this shall be corrected.' This undertaking was forwarded to the pope, who wrote to the legates, Arnauld, now Archbishop-elect of Narbonne, and the Bishop of Uzès that although Raymond had been excommunicated and deprived of his lands, still, as his condemnation for heresy and for the death of Peter of Castelnau, although strongly suspected of both, had not been confirmed, he did not see on what grounds he could at present grant his lands to another. He had therefore delegated the Bishop of Rièz and Master Thédise, Canon of Genoa, to proceed in accordance with his previous instructions, and not fail to inform him of the truth.[1] The King of France also had complained to the pope of Simon infringing his overlordship—a complaint which Innocent, inasmuch as the Crusade was largely dependent upon the passive, if not active, good-will of Philip, could not ignore.[2] His reply to the king, as to the legates, shows that he was doubtful whether the truth, the whole truth and nothing but the truth had been told him. He wrote to Philip that he had instructed the legates to remove the bar from Raymond if no lawful accuser within a certain time appeared. ' We do know that he did not discharge his purgation, but we do not know whether it was his own fault, although it is universally declared that in those parts he is regarded as a heretic.' [3]

The time was now considered ripe for the consolidation of the conquests ; and accordingly a council met in November (1212) at Pamiers,[4] of which the Archbishop of Bordeaux was President, Arnauld being conspicuously absent, owing to his quarrel with Simon de Montfort over the right to the Dukedom of Narbonne. By the forty-six articles which were drawn up and sworn to on the four Gospels by Simon and others, it was enacted *inter alia* that all must attend Mass and hour sermons on Sundays and Festivals, when all work was to cease under a penalty of 6*d.* for each default, to be divided equally between the priest and the lord ; no fair or market was to be held on Sunday ; the threepenny hearth tax was to be collected between Ash Wednesday and Easter ; in places where there was no church or priest's house, the best house of the heretics was to be sold and the proceeds to be used for providing such a

---

[1] *Regesta*, xv. 102.   [2] *Ibid*, xiv. 163.   [3] *Ibid*.
[4] Vaissete, *Hist. de Lang*. viii. 625—more correct than Martene or Doat.

church or house ; all goods of enemies of Church and State
were to be confiscated and their persons to be at the
disposal of their lord; the wives of such enemies, even if
themselves catholics, were to quit their estates; no widow
of a noble having property could remarry for ten years
except with a noble of France, and then only with the
count's permission ; [1] no fortress was to be rebuilt without
his consent; every subject of the count was to regard an
enemy of the Faith as his own, on pain of confiscation of his
property and arrest.   In order to give the new régime which
had been thrust upon them *vi et armis* the air of democratic
liberty, the people were allowed to elect a council of twelve
consisting of four ecclesiastics (two of whom were the
Bishop of Toulouse and the Bishop of Carcassonne
ex officio), four knights from northern France, and two
knights and two burghers from southern France,—an
equitable representation of north and south, clerical and
lay, which would allay all suspicion and enable the Church
to enjoy her liberties, and the country peace and prosperity. [2]

Why did Peter render no assistance to Raymond ?
Because of the critical position of Spain itself. The Saracen
Almohads or ' Unitarians,' 400,000 strong, had crossed
the Straits of Gibraltar, and only after a decisive victory at
Las Navas de Tolosa, in which 160,000 of the enemy
perished, could Spain breathe freely. For this deliverance
Innocent was most grateful, and it may account for the tone
of his letters both to Raymond and Simon respectively.

---

[1] These unions prepared the way for the extension of the French
kingdom.
[2] Peter de V S., ch. 65. ; Vaissete, viii. 165. 625.

CHAPTER XII

THE Council of Pamiers had deliberated and decided without the slightest reference to the King of France and the King of Aragon, and it was not to be expected that either monarch would accept these high-handed proceedings without comment. Philip wrote a curt letter to the pope pointing out that, as sole sovereign of France, he was quite capable of settling the assignment of its lands without outside help ; and he asked the pope to assure him that he had given proper instructions to his legates for safeguarding the honour and interests of the kingdom.[1]

The offer of vassalage which Raymond had made to the King of Aragon was followed by an appeal from the Tolosans themselves, in which they recapitulated the course of events since the advent of Arnauld as legate. He had ordered all those whom his messengers had named as heretics to be handed over to the leaders of the crusaders and to purge themselves of the charge under pain of excommunication. They (the Tolosans) had denied that these *were* heretics, for they had examined them themselves. Their present count and his father before him had punished any heretics they could discover, and they, the citizens, had burnt many, and would continue to do so. Yet the sentence of excommunication and interdict had not been removed. They therefore had appealed to the pope, who, on January 19, 1211, wrote to the Bishop of Rièz, the Abbot of Citeaux and Master Thédise, directing that, if the city would give satisfactory guarantees of its orthodoxy, they were to

---

[1] *Regesta*, xiv. 163.

absolve it ; if all three could not act, two would be sufficient. But of the three, only the Abbot of Citeaux was willing, and on the city offering to pay a certain sum of money to the Church, he, together with the Bishop of Toulouse and other good men, had been ready to recognize them and the whole of Toulouse and its suburbs as truly catholic. But as the others had refused, the crusaders had attacked their city, killed poor men and women and children in the country, pillaging and burning everywhere, and had pitched their tents before their gates. These aggressions had provoked collisions, and prisoners had been taken on both sides, but had since been exchanged. Not until the end of June did the crusaders depart, but threatened to come again. They therefore reminded the king that a man must needs stir himself when his neighbour's house is on fire.[1] To this appeal the King of Aragon responded by sending letters and representatives to Rome, pointing out that he had purposely refused to help his vassal, the Viscount of Béziers, although implored to do so, so as to avoid even appearing to be mixed up with heretics ; and this abstention had cost the viscount his country and his life. Yet his suzerain rights had been trampled on by the seizing of Foix, Comminges and other places, whose counts had never been heretics, but, on the contrary, active antagonists. He declared that the Count of Toulouse was prepared to do penance and fight against the infidels in either Palestine or Spain. He therefore asked that the count's excommunication should be lifted, and that his son, the younger Raymond, who had never given any sign whatever of heresy, should be committed to him for instruction in the Catholic Faith, and that he, the king, should hold the province in trust for him. In this way would the

[1] ' Nam tua res agitur, paries cum proximus ardet.' Vaissete, viii. 161, 612.

country be purged from heresy, never to return.[1] This
letter reached the pope on January 16, 1213, and so urgent
did he regard the matter that two days later he sent a sharp
reprimand to the three legates, the Archbishop of
Narbonne, Bishop of Rièz and Canon Thédise, and to
Simon de Montfort. ' You have laid hands on countries
which were never branded with heresy. The king's representatives report that you have left scarcely anything to the
Count of Toulouse beyond Toulouse and Montauban. The
king also expressly mentions Foix, Comminges and Béarn,
the counts of which are his vassals, as well as lands which
Richard, King of England,[2] of glorious memory had given
to the Count of Toulouse as the marriage dowry of his
sister. Not only have you invaded these countries, but you
have exacted from them oaths of fealty, and thus robbed
the king who gained such a splendid victory for the Church
over the Saracens. You must therefore summon a council
of archbishops, bishops, abbots, counts, barons, consuls,
rectors, and other prudent persons in a safe and convenient
place within three months to consider the king's proposals,
and send the report of the proceedings to me that I may
determine what shall be done.'[3] As for Simon himself, the
pope did not wait even a couple of days, but sent a brief
note the very next day after receiving the king's complaint,
reproving him sharply for having taken advantage of the
king's absence in the Saracenic war by warring not only
against heretics but against catholics, and seizing their

[1] *Regesta*, xv. 212.
[2] *Chron. Epis. Albig. et Abbat. Castr. Guillabertus, xxii Abbas*,
ann. 1176 (last ode)—

> ' Inter Raimundum Comitem concordia facta est
> Et Regem Anglorum connubiis stabilis.
> Tuncque Tolosani Legati munere functus
> Est Abbas, nomen cui Guillabertus erat.
> Fitque Johanna uxor Comitis, pro dote Cadurcam
> Dat, Regi Comitis sic stabilita fides.'

[3] *Regesta*, xv. 212.

land. He must restore it at once, and also do homage to the King of Aragon for Carcassonne.[1]

At the same time the king interceded with the legates on behalf of the Counts of Toulouse, Foix, Comminges and Béarn. The legates summoned a meeting of prelates numbering about twenty, two days after the receipt of the king's letter (January 18, 1213). They absolutely refused to reconsider their attitude towards the Count of Toulouse, but were willing to do so for the Counts of Foix and Comminges. As for Gaston de Béarn, he was a notorious persecutor of catholics. He had harboured the assassin of Peter de Castelnau; had in the past year introduced routiers into the Cathedral of Olorun where one of them had cut the cord by which the pyx was suspended, so that it fell to the ground, and the Body of the Lord was thrown out; another had arrayed himself in the priest's Mass vestments, sung Mass, preached a sermon and received the offerings from the routiers; the count had also laid violent hands on the clergy. Still, if he made satisfaction, he would be heard. The council ordered by the pope was duly called, first at Avignon, and then, owing to sickness preventing many of them attending, it was removed to Lavaur. The report which was drawn up by the two legates, the Bishop of Riéz and Canon Thédise, and sealed by Arnauld, Archbishop of Narbonne, and the Bishops of Albi, Toulouse and Comminges, pointed out that at the previous council which the legates had called by order of the pontiff, Raymond had failed to clear himself of the charges brought against him, and fulfil the commands laid upon him, as all the council agreed; that, as his excommunication therefore could not be removed, he left in great anger and added iniquity to iniquity. They had often cited him to appear before them,

---

[1] *Regesta.*, xv. 213, 214. The Abbot of Moissac complained to the King of France of the wholesale exactions of de Montfort from the town. Vaissete, viii. 621. 635.

but he had refused to come. All this was old news to the pope, but it was necessary to refer to it as justifying their present unanimous opinion that the ban should remain. [1] The King of Aragon had asked that he might appear in person and support his proposals ; he was told that he might put them in writing, and that the document must bear his seal. He had also urged that until after the council there should be an armistice, and that the crusaders should cease to do evil ; Simon retorted that he considered that to stop the war would be doing evil, but he was willing for a week to abstain from doing good. The king pleaded for unity ; he reminded churchmen of the real danger at their door, and called upon Simon and all true soldiers of the Cross to come to his aid against the Saracens in Spain. He pointed out that the Church had *ubera* as well as *verbera*, and pleaded on Raymond's behalf for charity instead of chastisement. But his advances were met with cold disdain from those who were determined to destroy the count. What alarmed them most, however, was the softened attitude of Innocent. At the instigation of the legates the pope was bombarded with manifestoes from all the catholic prelates of the South protesting against any weakening towards heresy. ' The Crusade was nearly over and the Christian Faith all but established ; why stop now ? Only let Toulouse be captured, and heresy would be stamped out for ever.' The hopelessness of Raymond's condition was shown in his appeal to the enemies of the Church—John of England, Otto the Emperor, and even the Sultan of Morocco. The pope himself had decreed the Crusade : how could he consistently veto it ? ' Before this unanimity so cleverly engineered, Innocent yielded. *Presto mature, presto marcio.* Changing his tone he wrote to the king reproaching him for doing the very things which he, the pope, had approved.

---

[1] *Regesta*, xvi. 39 ; Mansi, *Concil.* xxii, 863 ; Peter de V. S. ch. 66.

He charged him with obtaining papal support by lies. He ordered him to make peace at once with Simon. If the Tolosans any longer defended the heretics he would start a new Crusade, for defenders of heretics were worse than heretics themselves. He was sending a cardinal or plenipotentiary who would take proper measures for the benefit of the Church.

So little did Peter expect such a *volte face* that he took steps to materialize his proposals. His proclamation to his subjects that he was going to Toulouse, not to fight for or against heretics but to deliver it from destruction, was enthusiastically received. So, when confronted with the pope's and the legates' later letters, he ignored them and led his forces to Toulouse where he was joyfully welcomed by the count and the citizens. Their first object of attack was Muret, which had a garrison of only seven hundred men with little food, whereas Peter's forces numbered three thousand cavalry and thirty thousand infantry. The town was easily captured, and the defenders were driven into its huge castle. De Montfort, who was at Fanjeaux with his wife, hastened to the help of Muret with a picked force of about 800 knights, and a few infantry, sending the countess to Carcassonne for reinforcements. Peter allowed them to pass through his lines into the town, hoping by one blow to capture them all and finish the war. So great was the disparity of the forces that Fulk and other prelates were for appealing to the King's clemency. But Simon 'the athlete of the Lord,' with whom was Dominic, another 'athlete', determined to fight it out. Mass was being said as Simon led his men out of the castle. Throwing himself upon his knees he cried : ' O God, to Thee I offer myself, soul and body.' Fulk had with him, it was alleged, a relic of the true Cross. Taking this in his hands, and in full pontificals, he blessed all the army and declared that all who fell in that combat would die as martyrs and would receive eternal happiness without passing through purgatory. The shock as the knights met is likened by William de Puy-Laurent to the crash of falling trees. Peter was cut down and mortally wounded at the first onslaught.[1] Simon was unhorsed but quickly remounted. The allies retreated, but Simon instead of pursuing them, returned to the castle which had been attacked by the infantry. With his knights he flung himself upon them with the utmost fury. At the same time, the garrison made a sortie, so that being attacked from the front and rear, and deprived of all support from the cavalry, they fled to the river where hundreds were drowned.[2] The battle of Muret dealt a staggering blow to the Albigensian cause from which it never recovered. Peter de Vaux-Sarnai estimated the losses of the allies at 20,000 and was overjoyed at the victory ; ' Glory to God in the highest, and in earth peace to men who love Holy Church with good will.' William de Puy-Laurent puts the casualties at 15,000 and declares that only nine crusaders (knights ?) were killed. The sight of the king's body stripped and bruised by hoofs of horses as they swept over him, deeply moved the knightly heart of de Montfort who wept over him ' as David over Saul.' *De mortuis nil nisi bonum* ; yet when Peter's own son admits that his father had not recovered from the excesses of the night before,[3] we can understand why the whole action was so grossly mismanaged by the victor of Las Navas. Raymond withdrew to the stronghold of Montauban. Baldwin, his brother, who had deserted him for Simon and

---

[1] Two knights, Alain de Roncy, and Florent de Ville had vowed to kill Peter. He had exchanged his armour with one of his bravest knights, whom the two at once attacked, mistaking him for the king. But when he broke both their lances they cried, ' This is not the king, he is a better knight.' ' No, he is here,' shouted the king himself, and was at once overpowered and slain.
[2] Peter de V. S., ch. 71, 72. *Chanson*, 147 *seq.*
[3] Chronicle written by himself, ix (Forster).

had received from the latter many favours, went in pursuit of the Count of Foix, but was himself captured by routiers and handed over to Raymond, who promptly hanged him. ' O a second Cain ! far worse than Cain ! ' (September 12, 1213.)[1]

The conqueror now overran the whole of Southern France, except the city of Toulouse, and by raids and executions terrorized the people. At Causia, whose lord, Bernard, was, according to Peter de Vaux-Sarnai, ' the most cruel person imaginable, and his wife a second Jezebel, yea, and far more cruel then Jezebel,' the crusaders found in a monastery of black monks the bodies of one hundred and fifty men and women horribly mutilated by Bernard and his wife.

Simon's sway now extended from the Bay of Biscay to the confines of Italy, and from the Pyrenees to Dauphinè. Raymond took refuge with King John of England, and did homage to him for the Marquisate of Toulouse. Foix, Comminges and Béarn, had fled to their mountain fastnesses. Many others found safety in Mount-segur which had been specially fortified to meet such emergencies. From a simple adventurer de Montfort had become a peer of the great Dukes of France, nay, of the king himself. Thus the papal Frankenstein grew alarmed at the monster of his own creation. He must be kept from presumptuous sins lest they get the dominion over him. The Cardinal-Legate, Peter de Benevento, whom Innocent had promised to send, received instructions differing materially from those first intended. The war was to stop ; Raymond's absolution was to be granted, contingent upon certain guarantees ; Simon was not master but administrator, and that provisionally, of the land and its revenues : all towns not actually captured were to be handed over to the legates, viz.,

[1] Peter de V. S., ch. 72.

Toulouse, Foix, Comminges and Béarn. The Counts of
Comminges and Béarn were to be reconciled, as also the
citizens of Toulouse. Simon must give up the son of the
King of Aragon whom he held at Carcassonne as a hostage,
though nominally as a friend, and send him to Narbonne :[1]
the homage of Raymond to an excommunicated king (i.e.
John) was null and void, and he was to be reconciled to the
Church on submitting himself and his son and their domains
to the will of the Church, and going into exile when and where
the Church ordered.[2] (January 1214.)

To Peter de Benevento fell the task of taking home the
son of the dead king of Aragon and of arranging for a
regency during his minority. During his absence, affairs
were entrusted to Cardinal Robert de Courcon, an Englishman, who had been sent to Philip, after his victory at
Bouvines, to preach a Crusade for Palestine. Affecting
to be ignorant of the papal instructions to Benevento he,
as the king's representative, confirmed his fellow-country-
man, Simon, in possession of all the lands he had conquered
from the heretics. The Counts of Comminges and Foix
submitted to the Church and vowed not to render any help
to the Count of Toulouse until reconciled, and gave the
Castle of Foix as a security. The citizens of Narbonne
and the Consuls of Toulouse took a similar oath. The
Viscountess of Nîmes and Agde surrendered to Simon
all her possessions.[3] On Benevento's return a council
met at Montpellier, January 8, 1215, at which five
archbishops, twenty-eight bishops and many barons
met.[4] But although the city enjoyed special religious

[1] The more galling to Simon because between him and the Archbishop of Narbonne there was no little friction, first, because Simon
had demanded and the archbishop had resisted the dismantling of
the city walls ; and secondly, because the archbishop claimed *ex
officio* the Dukedom of Narbonne, ' a title which from ancient times
the Count of Toulouse had held.'

[2] Peter de V. S., ch. 77.   [3] Vaissete, viii. 643–53.

[4] Peter de V. S., ch. 82.

privileges,[1] it absolutely refused admittance to Simon
himself; the council had to send out members daily to
consult him.   Once he attempted to steal in, but pickets
were on the watch, and he was glad to get back to his
lodging in the house of the Templars.   The chief matter
the council had to decide was the assignment of the lands
conquered by the crusaders.   The council was unanimous
that they should be given to Simon with the title of Lord
and Suzerain (*monarcha*).   The council's decision was
announced to the count, who entered Montpellier amid the
acclamations of the crusaders; but the inhabitants, who
had already refused the suzerainty of the new King of
Aragon and had placed themselves under the King of
France, drove him out again.   Nor was it a decision which
the cardinal would accept, yet he feared to exercise his
powers as plenipotentiary.   The difference was adjusted
by a letter from the pope, authorizing de Montfort to
administer the land temporarily until the whole question
was adjudicated upon at the great Council at Rome in
November.

But now, quite unexpectedly and to the agitation of all
parties there came upon the scene, Louis, son of Philip, no
longer to the displeasure,[2] but with the full consent of the
king.   Whatever were the prince's motives and the Count
de Montfort's misgivings, he was received with acclamation[3]
(April, 1215).   Probably his instructions were to see and
report the actual position of affairs, for Philip now had,
instead of his peace-loving and innocuous cousin, a
foreigner of great military genius and determination and
a protégé of the pope, master of Aquitaine.   The prince's

---

[1] William, Lord of Montpellier, had been placed under the immediate protection of the Holy See (1201), and the town during an
interdict was allowed to celebrate the divine offices with closed doors,
subdued voices and silent bells, provided no excommunicated person
were present (Supplement to *Regesta*, 1, 1)

[2] Peter de V. S. ch. 66.   [3] *Ibid*, ch. 82; *Chanson*, p. 157.

progress was one triumph. All the cities, including Toulouse, opened their gates to him, for ' *Ludovico præsente*' they had no fear of Simon. The dispute over the Dukedom of Narbonne[1] between Simon and Arnauld was submitted to him; he decided in favour of the former, but only provisionally, until the great Council. But to weaken the province in view of the policy of encroachments of the Kingdom of France, he seized on the opportunity to order that the walls of Narbonne and Toulouse should be demolished. ' The Narbonnese therefore *began* to pull down the walls of Jericho, i.e. of Narbonne.'[2] But it appears that the work was only begun, and at Toulouse, not even that. Louis remained only forty days—enough to earn the indulgence, though the Crusade was over for the year! The archbishop however, was not the man to accept an adverse decision, even temporarily, and appealed to Rome, which reversed the prince's verdict three months afterwards. It is a remarkable judgment ; *mutatis mutandis* it would apply equally to the soldier. Thus the Pope reproached Simon with ingratitude to the archbishop for his services to the Crusade—as if Simon himself had rendered none ! Simon owed his elevation to the archbishop—but would the archbishop have been at Narbonne without the services of Simon ? The General Council was near : its decision would be weighty and final ; let him beware how he persecuted the zealous servants of the Church.

---

[1] A title which carried with it the supreme power over the viscounty and town of Narbonne.

[2] Peter de V. S. *Ibid.*

CHAPTER XIII

THE Fourth Lateran Council, the greatest Church Council for centuries, opened on November 11, 1215 and held two other grand sessions at intervals of ten days. The attendance was estimated at twelve hundred. The *Narratiuncula* says that there were present ninety-two prelates, including the patriarchs of Constantinople and Jerusalem. The patriarch of Alexandria was a prisoner in the hands of the Saracens, but sent his archdeacon. So great was the crush in the Church of St. John Lateran that the Archbishop of Amalfi and three bishops were suffocated to death.

All our *dramatis personæ* appeared upon its stage, except Simon, who, however, was represented by his brother Guy, ' and other faithful and discreet nuncios.' Between the grand sessions select committees, so to speak, were held, whose function it was to investigate and report upon the several important matters for which the General Council had been convened. The most important for our purpose was the Albigensian problem. It was to be expected that a Council in Rome, composed largely of ecclesiastics, would uphold the crusaders in every particular. But Raymond and his party were not without friends, and amongst them were, strange to say, Innocent and Arnauld, although such friendship proved worthless in the end. We are prepared for the former's pusillanimity, but the latter's attitude can be explained not by love of Raymond, but hatred of Simon. For there are natures who hate more bitterly those who were once their friends than those who have always been their foes. The demolition of the walls of Narbonne and

the attempts to filch the dukedom rankled in the ambitious
heart of the archbishop, and in revenge he appears to have
been prepared to condone even that very heresy which he
had been appointed to destroy. ' It is a fact that there were
some there, even prelates, who, opposing the Faith, laboured for the restoration of the said counts, but the counsel
of Ahithophel did not prevail.'[1] The second part of the
Chanson, which is far less ultramontane than the first, gives
a vivid account of the debates, and probably the writer has
availed himself of a poet's license to dramatize the actual
facts. But after making due allowance many an angry
scene was witnessed, now in the pope's apartments, now in
his garden.[2] The orator of the Albigensian interests was
the fearless Raymond—Roger, Count of Foix, who declared
that he was neither heretic nor miscreant, but a loyal servant
of the Church. His country, as well as Provence and
Toulouse, had been put under the protection of the pope,
yet Simon had impudently ravaged them all. His castle
was impregnable, yet he had surrendered it on the mandate
of the pope. All this the Bishop of Toulouse denied,
maintaining that there was no place more reeking with
heresy than the County of Foix.   The count's sister on the
death of her husband had embraced heresy and perverted
many. Mont-segur was specially fortified to protect heretics.
The count had killed many pilgrims (crusaders ?) and had
made many martyrs. Foix retorted hotly: he was not
responsible for his sister: he had no authority over Mont-
segur. He had never molested a single *peaceful* pilgrim ;
but he did not regard crusaders as pilgrims ; they were
robbers and traitors who bore a cross that crushed the
people : there was not one of the people who had been

---

[1] Peter de V. S., ch. 83.
[2] *Chanson*, p. 160, unless, with Fauriel (*introd.* p. lxxxix) we rule
out the garden scene on the ground that it is contrary to conciliar
procedure and etiquette.

captured by the bishop (of Toulouse) whom he had not mutilated : their destruction filled him with joy, their escape with regret. This ex-jongleur bishop was such a high and mighty person that no one dared to contradict him. From jongleur he had become monk, and from monk abbot, but this abbey was so gloomy that he was not content until he came into the sunlight again and was made a bishop ; from that time he had kindled a fire that no water could put out. His words and deeds made him more an anti-Christ than Christ's ambassador. His lying songs had corrupted every one who sang them.

The defence of Foix was not without effect. The pope promised him that his territories should be restored to him, if found innocent.[1] The interests of young Trenceval, the son of the dead Count of Béziers, were pleaded by Raymond de Roquefeuille, He accused Simon of the murder of the count, and if the pope refused to do justice to the orphan of the martyr and reinstate him in his heritage, he would charge the pope with it at the Judgment Day. The Abbot of Beaulieu, ambassador of King John, also supported Raymond and Foix, the more so because his master had a like experience. But the count's enemies were many, powerful and pitiless. The harassed pope retired to his garden, but three hundred(?) prelates followed him and insisted that the restitution of the count meant the destruction of the catholics. ' You will make us all liars, we have preached everywhere that Raymond is guilty of heresy : how can you condone heresy ? ' The Archdeacon of Lyons riposted : ' Raymond was the first to take the cross ; how can the Church persecute the Church's defenders ? It is your preaching, your harsh words and still harsher actions which have brought half a million Christians

---

[1] He received absolution from the legate on payment of 15,000 solidi (melgor), and Honorius III promised him the restoration of his castle, December 8, 1216 (*Epp. Lib.* i. 100) ; Vaissete, viii. 681.

to misery.' But 'their voices prevailed.' The '*servus servorum*' was :—

> A slave who would not be
> In the right with two or three.

But what was the actual sentence ? No historian, so far as I am aware, has noticed that the sentence of Raymond is not included in the decrees of the Council. This is the more remarkable because the Albigensian Heresy was perhaps the most important item upon the Council's agenda, seeing that its affairs involved the three greatest kingdoms in Europe, England, France and Spain, as well as the very status and principle of the Church itself. Mansi[1] knows nothing of the sentence and only quotes from Peter de Vaux-Sarnai, who does not profess to give more than a summary, and from D'Achery's *Spicelegium*. Now D'Achery's authority for the sentence, as for the 'Brief Narrative' (*Narratiuncula*) of the Council itself, is a MS. in the Benedictine Abbey of Lyra, and this, it would seem, is the only existing document purporting to give the sentence in full. This abbey was founded by three men, Robert, Anselm and Daniel, who had abandoned the military for the monastic profession, in 647. In 1176 it became intimately associated with the House of Toulouse through Gilbert, its twenty-second abbot, who negotiated an agreement between the King of England and the Count of Toulouse.[2] If Gilbert's successor forty years later still maintained the same interest in and enjoyed the same favour of the Counts of Toulouse, one can well understand why a decree which deprived the abbey of its patrons should be carefully preserved in the abbey's archives. The *Narratiuncula* expressly separates the sentence from the canons of the Council : ' In that Synod these things had been settled which follow, viz., the canons of the same

---

[1] *Concil.* xxii, p. 1069. [2] v. *supra*, p. 75 note.

Council; and at the end, after the speech of Pope Innocent, the sentence of the land of Albi.' Mansi gives first of all only Peter de Vaux-Sarnai's summary : ' He determined and provided that the city (*civitas*) of Toulouse and other lands acquired (*obtentæ*) by the crusaders should be conceded to the Count de Montfort who in the aforesaid business excelled all men in courageous and ʿaithful labours ; the land, however, which the Count of Toulouse had in Provence, the pope willed should be reserved so that provision should be made in whole or in part for the son of the said Count of Toulouse, provided that he showed himself worthy of compassion by sure evidence of fidelity and good conduct.' Mansi then adds : ' But it is better to give the Decree itself from D'Acheɪy's *Spicelegium*.'

Sententia de terra Albigensi :

Quantum ecclesia laboravit per praedicatores et crucesignatos ad exterminandum haereticos et ruptuarios de provincia Narbonensi et partibus subvicinis, totus pene orbis agnoscit. Et quidem per Dei gratiam et sollicitudinem nostram valde profecit, cum, exterminatis utrisque, terra ipsa in fide catholica et pace fraterna salubriter gubernetur. Quia vero novella plantatio ad huc indiget irrigari, sacro consulto concilio ita duximus providendum : ut Raymundus Tolosanus comes qui culpabilis repertus est, in utroque, nec unquam sub ejus regimine terra possit in fidei statu servari, sicut a longo tempore certis indiciis est compertum ab ejus dominio, quod utique grave gessit, perpetuo sit exclusus, extra terram in loco idoneo moraturus, ut dignam agat poenitentiam de peccatis, verumtamen de proventibus terrae pro substentatione sua quadringentas marcas percipiat annuatim, quamdiu curaverit humiliter obedire. Uxor vero, ipsius comitis, soror quondam regis Arragonorum, cui ab omnibus laudabile testimonium perhibetur, quod sit mulier honesta et catholica, ad suum dotalitium pertinentes integre habeat et quiete. Ita tamen ut eas sic ad mandatum ecclesiae faciat custodiri, quod per ipsas negotium pacis et fidei non valeat perturbari ; vel pro illis secundum apostolicae sedis arbitrium compensationem accipiet competentem. Tota vero terra quam obtinuerunt crucesignati adversus haereticos, credentes et fautores ac receptores eorum, cum Monte Albano, atque Tolosa, quae magis haeretica labe corrupta est, dimittatur et concedatur (salvo per omnia catholicorum jure virorum, mulierum et ecclesiarum), comiti Montisfortis, viro strenuo et catholico, qui plus ceteris in hoc negotio laboravit, ut eam teneat ab ipsis a quibus de jure tenenda est. Residua autem terra, quae non fuit a crucesignatis obtenta, custodiatur ad mandatum ecclesiae per viros idoneos, qui negotium pacis et fidei manuteneant et defendant : ut provideri possit unico adolescenti filio praefati comitis Tolosae, postquam ad legitimam aetatem pervenerit, si talem se studuerit exhibere, quod in toto vel in parte ipsi merito debeat provideri, prout magis videbitur expedire.'

The authenticity of this sentence need not be disputed, although we are dependent for its preservation upon one writer. It is substantially confirmed by the author of *La Chanson* who was present at the Council, and was himself a Tolosan. The verbal similarity, though slight, of Peter de Vaux-Sarnai's summary may indicate that he was writing with a copy before him. We are thankful, however, to have the full text, because it presents the prospects of Raymond, his wife and his son as far more favourable than Peter de Vaux-Sarnai's account would lead us to think. On the one hand de Montfort's power was circumscribed by the existing rights of all catholics and churches within the countries and cities concerned. He held his possessions not as a ' monarcha ' but as a vassal, although the suzerain is not specified. The dignity was personal, given for services rendered, and carried with it no right of transmission to his heirs. Although the word ' heritage ' was pressed upon the pope by Simon's advocates, it is significantly ignored in the sentence. On the other hand, Raymond was not pronounced excommunicate or heretic. His alleged offence was only that he had not destroyed heretics and routiers. On the contrary, the pope, according to the Chanson more than once, and that emphatically, declared him a good and loyal catholic. He was deprived of his land because he could not keep order in it. His son, when he grew to man's estate, provided he showed himself a fit and proper person, should succeed to all the land not actually conquered by the crusaders, for the son ought not to be punished for the father, particularly as the son was but an innocent child when the Crusade first entered his country.　Moreover, Raymond's wife was not to be deprived of her dowry, and was given Venaissin for a residence. Out of the revenues Simon was to pay Raymond 400 marks annually.　Raymond was not ordered off to the Holy Land, but was to abide in a fit place, outside, however, his own country, to fulfil there his penance.　That Simon might be prevented from encroaching on the rest of the land, reserved conditionally for Raymond's son, it was placed in charge of fit persons under the mandate of the Church ; the son himself was placed under the protection of the pope, because, as the Chanson shrewdly observes, Simon would not regard him as a son, and the son would not regard Simon as a father.[1]

The canons of the Council dealt with every heresy ' exalting itself against the Holy Orthodox Catholic Faith ' (as defined in Canon 1) ' under whatever name but having different faces,' but of course they were aimed chiefly at the Albigensian Heresy ; (*a*) after condemnation, heretics were to be left to the secular arm for due punishment (*animadversione debita*), clergy being first unfrocked.　The goods of laymen were to be confiscated, and those of the clergy were to be given to the churches from which they received their stipends ; (*b*) all secular powers were to take an oath to exterminate all heretics in their respective territories ; any power refusing shall after admonition be excommunicated by his metropolitan with his co-provincial bishops.　If still contumacious after a year, to be reported to the pope who shall absolve his vassals from their feudal obedience and permit his land to be occupied by catholics who shall carry out the work of the extermination of and

---

[1] p. 175 (Lafon).

keep it free from heresy ; (*c*) no judge, advocate or notary, if a heretic, to practise ; all decisions, deeds and documents of all such to be null and void. They were to be deprived of all sacraments and refused Christian sepulture. The Church was to refuse their alms and oblations. They were not to be restored to office except by consent of the Apostolic See ; (*d*) no one was to preach publicly or privately without authority ; (*e*) inquiries into cases of suspected heresy based on general and genuine opinion, not on malice, were to be held by the bishop in the presence of the elders (*senioribus*) of the Church ; (*f*) ' Concerning instituting Preachers.' In cathedral and conventual churches fit persons were to be ordained by the bishops as their coadjutors, not only for the office of preaching, but for hearing confessions and enjoining penance and other things which appertain to the salvation of souls.[1]

The Fourth Lateran Council immensely enhanced the power of the papacy. Its claims to supremacy, from Hildebrand onwards, over all matters spiritual and temporal, hitherto based, however contrary to reason and history, upon Scripture, tradition and custom, were now confirmed and authorized by the deliberate decisions of an Oecumenical Council, the largest and most representative ever held. The sun travelled from the West to the East, for the patriarchs of the East acknowledged Rome as the final Court of appeal. A claim which, though thus based, nevertheless owed its execution largely to the vigour and energy of the individual pontiff, was now proclaimed by the Universal Church assembled in Council as inherent in the office itself, and obedience is no longer a question of procedure but an article of faith. All this concentrated power of the ' Catholic Church ' was now brought to bear upon heretics everywhere and upon the Albigensians in

---

[1] Canon x.

particular. Local Councils were no longer necessary ; decrees from Rome took their place. Preachers are no longer a temporary expedient ; they are a permanent part of the Church's constructive machinery ; but as the constructive often necessitates the destructive, so the appointment of the preachers adumbrated the rise of the Inquisition.

IT was a settlement that gave little hope of an abiding peace. The Church would be grateful to Simon for the vindication of her spiritual things, but would jealously resent any encroachment upon her carnal things. The King of France would look askance at this new lease of life which the Church had given to the coveted Marquisate of Toulouse by conceding it to an outsider, in that it dealt a serious blow to his schemes of monarchical expansion. Raymond the elder, cousin-germane to the King of France, brother-in-law to the Emperor Frederick and to the King of England, father-in-law to Sancho, King of Navarre, uncle to the Kings of Castile and Aragon, might invoke pressure from several powerful sources, the convergence of which might cause Simon serious embarrassment. Raymond the younger, more courageous than his father, was not likely to be content with the paternal protection of Rome as an equivalent for the paternal inheritance of Toulouse. Moreover, if so powerful a count as Raymond could be dispossessed on such equivocal grounds, what might not be the fate of other nobles ? If they did these things in the green tree, what would be done in the dry ?

At first, however, things went smoothly. Raymond retired to Spain as the *locus idoneus*. Simon received the oath of allegiance [1] from the burgesses of Toulouse, and his name was entered by the notaries upon the public instruments as ' Count of Toulouse '. In his public address in which he swore to be a true and faithful ruler, he styled himself *also* ' Count of Leicester, Viscount of Béziers and

---

[1] This might also be a test of orthodoxy, v. vol. i, Index, ' oaths '.

Carcassonne,' but not ' Marquis of Provence,' as that title
had been reserved by the Lateran Council for the younger
Raymond.

From Toulouse he went to the Court of France where he
' received his land from the King,' and did homage for his
fiefs, ' as Duke of Narbonne, Count of Toulouse, Viscount
of Béziers and Carcassonne,' ' saving others' right and the
right of those who are our men.' [1]   As he entered Paris,
Simon was greeted by the people shouting : ' Blessed is he
that cometh in the name of the Lord.' (April 1216).   The
title of ' Duke of Narbonne' with which Simon returned
from Paris rankled in the breast of Arnauld, actual Archbishop, and claimant Duke of Narbonne.   He who had
stood as Simon's *amicus curiæ* with the pope and was
largely instrumental in his advancement to power, now saw
this man standing as his *inimicus curiæ* with the king, and
with base ingratitude snatching that rank to which, as
archbishop, he regarded himself as *ex officio* entitled.   If
the priest was to be baulked of his secular power, he would
exercise his spiritual power with compensating severity.
Accusing Simon of robbing the Church, he excommunicated him, and sought confirmation of the ban from the new
Pope, Honorius III.   But Simon not only ignored the
thunder but thrust his way into Narbonne and compelled
the once all-powerful legate to shut himself up in his
palace.

In short the Lateran settlement miscarried.   The old
struggle broke out again but in a new aspect.   It was now
clear that the object of the crusaders was conquest, not
conversion ; and just as the barons of England rose against
the French invaders, so the barons of the Midi likewise,
although in each case the invaders were under the aegis of

---

[1] Vaissete, vol. viii, p. 684.   For Arnauld's arguments and Simon's
violence see the former's long letter to Innocent, September 16, 1216,
in Bouquet, xix, p. 620 ff.   Also Hon. *Epp. Lib.* i., 304, 305.

the Church. The Raymonds, father and son, Foix and others
met at Avignon, and the son canvassed the domains of his
mother, ' of whose sincere catholicity all testified,' [1] and
was received everywhere with enthusiasm ; castles opened
their gates to him and were put into a state of defence.
Raymond entered into a treaty with the Prince of Orange,
and forces came from England and Aragon. Marseilles
revolted against its bishop and trampled crucifix and host
under foot. The younger Raymond captured Beaucaire,[2]
and, when de Montfort came to its relief, drove him back
to Toulouse. For several months the capital was a city
divided against itself. The walls had been partly demolished, but the French in possession of the Castle of
Narbonne and of the country overawed the town, and Fulk,
its bishop, was at hand with his spiritual pains and
penalties for heretics, i.e. rebels, although between Simon
and the citizens he ostensibly acted as mediator. He
assured the latter that Simon would grant a free pardon
if they surrendered ; but upon Simon himself he urged
the city's utter destruction. Trusting their bishop, many
citizens of high rank went out to meet the count, but he
immediately loaded them with chains and put them in the
castle of Narbonne. One escaped and told it in the city,
which at once sprang to arms. Three times was Simon
driven back, and in his chagrin threatened to kill the eighty
citizens in his power. Once more Fulk intervened ; if the
city would only surrender, the eighty would be released,
and their own goods, persons and privileges spared. On
this undertaking, the city opened its gates, but as soon as
he was in possession, Simon broke his oath, made more

---

[1] V. *supra*, p. 90.
[2] By using Greek fire, *Chanson*, pp. 212, 221. James, King of
Aragon was smitten with an interdict by the pope through Bertrand
the legate for harassing the land of Simon de Montfort. Hon. *Epp.
Lib.* iii, 692 (October 23, 1217), see also *Ibid.*, 827.

influential persons prisoners and sent them all to distant prisons.[1]

But the city yearned for its count. Submission to the upstart foreigner was sullen and sluggish, and the smouldering fires of patriotism constantly burst into flame. Simon inflicted a heavy fine upon the city for having aided Beaucaire, and, to enforce payment, ordered the eighty so-called hostages to be dragged through the city, leaving dead and living chained together. With the money raised by the fine he organized an expedition against Montgrenier in the county of Foix ; but in his absence the citizens invited Raymond to return, saying that they loved him more than the hostages. He was received with shouts of ' Toulouse for father and son,' and his restoration was hailed as a resurrection from the dead. Raymond the younger had joined his father with the victorious troops from Beaucaire, and these were supplemented by others from Spain, Foix and Comminges. The force which Simon left behind to keep order attempted in vain to quell the revolt, and was glad to find safety behind the walls of the castle. So black did things look that the Countess de Montfort sent an urgent message to her husband to return at once, otherwise he would lose his wife and son and city. Raymond resumed the government with the active goodwill of the citizens. [2] Barricades were erected in the streets, even little boys and girls helping. Guy de Montfort at the head of a body of knights on foot, endeavoured to cut his way through to the castle, but, although he managed to set part of the city on fire, he was driven back, ' the unarmed beating the armed '. A worse failure befell Simon who hastened to the relief of the garrison by forced marches. His brother was wounded, and he himself almost drowned in the river over which he and his forces were

---

[1] *Chanson*, p. 230. [2] *Ibid.*, p. 254.

driven. Fearing a counter-attack he took refuge in Muret and fortified it. Winter was nigh and the situation desperate. Benevento, the legate, assured Simon that with the spring irresistible reinforcements would rally to his side ; and, that the promise might not be in vain, sent out his preachers everywhere, urging the Crusade. Honorius did his utmost to restrain the foes and stimulate the friends of the Church. He ordered the Tolosans to keep the peace with Simon, and James, King of Aragon to withdraw his forces from Toulouse. He reminded the younger Raymond of the misfortunes of his father and threatened him with the like punishment. The Count of Foix, the citizens of Avignon, Marseilles, Beaucaire and other places received similar admonitions. The Archbishops of Auch, Narbonne and Rheims with their respective suffragans were urged to do their utmost to raise forces to help Simon. And last and most important of all was his letter to the King of France pleading for reinforcements for the home Crusade.[1] But Simon did not wait for them. One bitter night he silently led his knights across the frozen river and attacked Toulouse. But the guards were alert ; and once more ' the unarmed beat the armed '. The ice of the river which had been their bridge became their grave, and hundreds were drowned. Thus winter passed, and neither side dared to molest the other. [2]

In the spring, the Tolosans attacked Muret, but were no more successful than Simon at Toulouse, and only escaped destruction by succours from the city. Yet Simon dare not follow up his success. Indeed in the fray he was unhorsed, but managed to remount and escape. Simon's failure, a growing sense of the real object of the Crusade, all contributed to the late arrival of the auxiliaries this year ; and even when they came there was little zeal and much

[1] Hon. *Epp. Lib.*, ii, 824–30.   [2] *Chanson*, p. 290.

discord. Some feared they were forging a weapon which might be turned by pope or king against themselves. The cardinal legate was challenged by Amauri de Crillon to quote any Scripture authorizing him to deprive an heir of his lands, and declared, ' If I had known in my own land the real secret of this affair, neither I nor my son would have been here.' The Count of Soissons advised Simon to be content with ' the fief of Béziers and leave Toulouse to Raymond's son, if the Apostle of Rome would consent.' [1]

Of these delays and discords Raymond strove to take advantage by repairing the old fortifications and building new ones, while to the crusaders it became clear that delays and discords spelt dangers and difficulties. If Toulouse was to be captured at all, it must be captured at once. Accordingly soon after Whitsun the crusaders marched out of Muret. It had rained in torrents for three days and nights, and the floods had done great damage to the defences of Toulouse. Simon ordered his forces to attack wherever there was an opening, but behind the weakened defences and in the very floods were hearts staunch and true, that met the vigorous assault with a resistance equally vigorous. Day after day the attack was carried on, but everywhere the crusaders were driven back, the mangonels dealing out terrible slaughter. It was one of these, as shown on his tomb, that killed Simon himself. He had rallied his men for a second attack when a stone hurled by a mangonel worked by a woman killed him while bending over his brother Guy who had been dangerously wounded. [2] The assault was called off, and the count's

---

[1] *Chanson*, p. 306.
[2] *Peter de V. S.* ch. 86. The *Chanson* (p. 332) says his head was crushed ; the Chronicle in prose (MSS. Library of Toulouse) says he was decapitated. The tomb was in the Church of St. Nazaire, Carcassonne. His body was later transported to the Abbey of Hautes. Bruyeres, *Hist. Gen. de Lang.* xxiii. 30. Mahul, *Cart. de. Carc.* p. 294.

body was taken to Carcassone where he was buried with all
the honours[1] due to a saint and a martyr (June 25,1218).

For an age which regarded violence as strength, treachery
as cleverness, and mercy as weakness, Simon was above
the average knighthood of his times, a dauntless champion
for the Faith in a war exacerbated by fanaticism and
patriotism. He did not seek the post of leader of the
Church's forces ; he yielded with reluctance. But once in
the saddle he fought with courage, tenacity and skill to
secure victory for the cause. He justified his choice and
was probably the best man for the work. But ' the labourer
is worthy of his hire,' and Simon expected and obtained his
hire in the territory of the vanquished. As general of the
Church, he gained his awards ; as general of the Church he
held them. He was an excellent husband and father ; his
domestic life was irreproachable in a loose age and a
romantic country, in contrast to the life of his chief enemy,
Raymond. His inauguration of a representative government was an instance of an enlightened policy which his still
more famous son copied and developed in England. The
mantle of the crusader fell upon the patriot. Although the
son was only ten years old when his father died, the boy
was old enough to realize the high esteem in which the
services of his parent were held by the Church, an esteem
which increased as the preachers increased. For Dominic
and Simon de Montfort were the closest friends, bound
together by public and private interests; and Dominic, as
we have seen, was the founder of the Preaching Order.
Although the canonization of Simon, proposed by Fulk,
Bishop of Toulouse, was not accepted, yet the General

---

[1] Honours at which the third part of the *Chanson*, entitled ' The
National Revival,' scoffs (p. 340), ' If by murders and treacheries,
burnings, pillage and violence, the fanning of evil and extinguishing
of good, and butcheries of women and children a man can gain the
Kingdom of Jesus Christ, then the count ought to **wear a heavenly
crown.**'

Chapter of the Order in 1256 ordered : ' in every convent '—
and there were many in England then—'in the margin of
the martyrology, the day after the Feast of St. John the
Baptist, let there be added : " This day, in the County of
Toulouse, died the noble Earl, Simon de Montfort, zealous
lover of the Faith, and friend of the Blessed Dominic." '[1]
The parallel between the character and career of the two
Simon de Montforts, father and son, in France and England,
is one of peculiar interest.

[1] Reichert, *Acta Cap. Gen.* vol. i, p. 81.

CHAPTER XV

TO Simon succeeded his son Amauri, and on the surface there seemed every hope of a successful pursuit of the Crusade. In early manhood, with military experience, he inherited the gratitude felt for his father as a champion of catholicity and the reverence as a martyr. He had the whole-hearted support of Honorius. The pope ordered all who had gone to the defence of Toulouse to return at once to their several countries. He once more forbade James King of Aragon, who, like his father, had helped Raymond, to invade the lands of de Montfort ; all matters in dispute were to be settled by the Holy See, not by arms. The younger Raymond he warned by the perils and sufferings of his father not to oppose God. To Philip the King and the Bishops of France he wrote urging them to aid Amauri to the utmost of their power. He confirmed Amauri in all the possessions of his father, i.e., ' all the land which the crusaders had won from the heretics, together with Montauban and Toulouse, saving in all respects the rights of catholics.' [1] But for all practical purposes these letters were not worth their ink. The weight of Simon's personality in the War of Suppression of the Albigensian Heresy may be judged by the confusion into which the Crusade was thrown by his death. Amauri retired from before Toulouse and acted on the defensive for about nine months, i.e., until the following spring.

Things had reached an *impasse* which none could accept. The pope saw heresy exalted, orthodoxy abased. The widow of the Church's soldier-martyr—the mother of her

[1] *Epp. Lib.*, iii. 20, 21, 49, 51 (Bouquet, xix, p. 666)

present champion—was shut up in the Castle of Narbonne.
The older Raymond had torn the sentence of a Great
General Council to pieces ; the younger had laughed the
benevolent ' protection' of the papacy to scorn.   The King
of France, on the other hand, saw ' his man ' defeated and
slain.   The chivalry of the north had been repulsed by the
burgesses of the south.   A dismantled town had proved
more than a match for an organized army.   Thus the *Kingdom*
was gravely challenged.   A situation so serious called for
his prompt and practical interference.   Nevertheless he
did not hesitate to make the embarrassments of the Church
subserve his own political ambitions.   When the cardinal
appealed to him he lent a ready ear, but at the same time
stipulated that he should receive one-twentieth of the
revenues of the Church of France for his expenses.
Honorius, too, proclaimed a new Crusade as comprehensive
as that for the Holy Land.   *All* Christians must unite in
crushing the heretics ; to *all* who responded he promised
plenary absolution.[1]   The cardinal calculated that by
Whitsun an immense army would be in the field, and so
severe would be the punishment of Toulouse that no one
would henceforth dare to lift a hand or move a tongue
against the Church.   Meanwhile neither Amauri nor
Raymond the younger was inactive.   The former moved
northward to join up with the fresh crusaders, and while
they were mobilizing he attacked Marmande.   Raymond,
making a diversion, also moved out of Toulouse, and falling
upon some of these new forces slew hundreds of them and
captured Foucault.   But Marmande's fate was sealed when
Amauri was joined by the young Prince Louis with a force
of 25,000 infantry and 10,000 cavalry.   The town surrendered unconditionally.   The Bishops of Béziers and Saintes
counselled that its commander, Centul d'Astaac, should be

---

[1] *Epp. Lib.*, iii. 246.

burnt or hanged, and that all the inhabitants should be put to the sword. This was opposed by the Archbishop of Auch, not in mercy but from fear of reprisals, pointing out that if Centul were hanged Foucault would be hanged too. William de Roches suggested the exchange of these two prisoners. The decision lay with the young prince, who, while the lives of hundreds hung in the balance, lolled on a cushion in a beautiful pavilion, toying with his glove. Possibly because Marmande was near the royal provinces, and would, he hoped, shortly be included in them, he decided to spare it and its commander, retaining only a few hostages. But this clemency did not commend itself to the new zealot, Amauri, for he secretly sent his soldiers into the disarmed city, massacred about 5,000 without distinction of age or sex, and burnt the city,[1] a second Béziers, in the presence and at the suggestion of its bishop.

The main purpose of the Crusade was now resumed, and the largest force hitherto raised, estimated at 300,000, converged toward Toulouse. The courage of the younger Raymond rose with the danger. It was proposed to him that he should send to Louis acknowledging the King of France as his liege lord and his lands as a royal fief. But he resolutely refused, saying that if Louis had come to him as a friend he would have done so ; but, as he came as an enemy, he would fight him. Elaborate preparations were made for the defence of the city, and, as before, it was solemnly placed under the protection of the Virgin—and no mention is made of heretical rites.[2] Bertrand, the legate, confident of victory, had sworn that Toulouse should be sacked and burnt, and all therein killed. But nothing could intimidate the defenders. From behind their hasty fortifications, they beheld the approach of a foe

---

[1] *Chanson*, p. 351 ff.

[2] *La Chanson*, pp. 307, 358 (Lafon). Here we lose its help, for it ends abruptly.

unequalled in the history of their city for numbers and equipment. 'The kings of the earth stood up and the rulers (of the Church) took counsel together.' The defenders flung them back time after time, until at last with great losses and no gain they abandoned the siege (August 1219). But more than the siege was abandoned : the expedition was abandoned, and Louis returned to his father, who would or could do nothing more, being fully occupied with the English. On the other hand, as nothing succeeds like success, many who had been halting between two opinions, or, having one, had feared to express it, now openly proclaimed themselves on the side of Raymond. Heresy increased : Catholicism decreased.[1]

At a Council held at Toulouse, 1220, by Romano, Cardinal Legate, statutes embodying the decrees of the fourth Lateran Council as to the duty of ecclesiastical and secular powers touching heresy were passed. Also 'all parishioners, masters and mistresses were, on Sundays and Festivals to stop all work and come to Church to hear sermons and the divine offices, and not to leave until they were finished.' But nobody gave heed. The 'preachers' set up a monastery in Narbonne in this year, but the people at once drove them out.[2]

The younger Raymond by his actions had forfeited even those slender promises which Innocent had made him after the Lateran Council, and accordingly Honorius disinherited him ; which made little difference, seeing that he had wrested that very inheritance from the Church's champion with his own right arm.

A new legate, Conrad, Bishop of Portuis, was appointed

---

[1] It was suspected that Philip might use the Crusade to seize land in Poitiers and Gascony from the King of England, and dissension between the prince and the legate brought about the collapse of the expedition. See Bouquet, note, vol. xix, p. 687.

[2] Mamachi, *Annals*, i., 622.

(1221) who with the Pope's permission founded a new society of religious knights,[1] who 'after the example of the Templars fighting in the East against the Saracens should take up arms for the confirmation of the Catholic Faith and the extirpation of heresy.' Its title was 'the Military Order of the Faith of Jesus Christ.' The promise of its first Master to the Count de Montfort was : ' Brother Publius Savaric, the humble and poor Master of the Military Order of the Faith of Jesus Christ, greeting. May your world (*universitas*) know that with the advice and consent of our Brothers we render to Amauri, by the providence of God Duke of Narbonne, Count of Toulouse and Leicester, and his heirs, our help for the defence and protection of his body and his land to the utmost of our power in good faith, and for searching out (*adquirendum*) and destroying the wicked heretics and their land.' In return the Order was to receive only such reasonable alms as Holy Church could give. But we hear nothing further of it, and in any case it was ineffective. The pope's appeal, too, to Philip fell upon deaf ears. ' The heretics,' he confessed, ' hold their schools and preach their errors openly. The secular powers must repress wickedness when the spiritual cannot. . . Almost everything has reverted to its old confusion.' That even the higher ranks of the clergy were not untainted with heresy is illustrated by the case of the Abbot of Electe, in the Diocese of Narbonne, where the abbot and monks were condemned. Describing them as ' *non monachos sed demoniacos* ' and in other terms scarcely decent, Arnauld handed them over to Satan (secular arm) as the equals of Judas, expelled them from the abbey, confiscated all their goods, and gave them with the abbey to his beloved chapter of the Greater Church of Narbonne. He reserved to himself the appointment of other monks in their stead,

---

[1] Vaissete, *Hist. de Lang*. viii. pp. 740, 743.

and the allotment of the rents and revenues. This sentence was confirmed by Honorius. Eventually the legate installed twelve canons, of whom six were presbyters, and of deacons, sub-deacons and acolytes, two each. The previous monks were reinstated by Gregory IX.[1]

The following year the old Count of Toulouse died. Just before his death he lost his speech but retained consciousness. Jordan, the Abbot of St. Saturnin, who happened to be present when the count was seized with paralysis, ran to his aid, and to him the count made the motion of prayer. The alarm soon spread, and the Brothers of the Hospital of St. John of Jerusalem were summoned. They brought with them a cross which the count devoutly kissed, and immediately expired. Thus with his last breath he did his best to prove his orthodoxy, but it availed nothing to save his remains from the penalty of heresy. Being excommunicate, he was buried in a dark unconsecrated corner in the grounds of the Hospital of St. John, situated in the middle of one of the streets of Toulouse. Nor could his son, who had long since made his peace with the Church, twenty-five years afterwards get the ban removed so that his father's body might be exhumed and placed in consecrated ground.

Was the Count truly repentant ? Nearly 300 years after his death, Bertrandi, a lawyer of Toulouse, published a history of the city—of which he was a native—in which he says he had seen the tomb of Raymond with the following inscription :—

> Non y a home sus terra per gran senhor que fos,
> Quem gites de ma terra, si la glieza non fos.

(Translation : There would have been no one in the world strong enough to rob me of my country if the Church had not existed.)

---

[1] Mansi *Concil*. xxii ; Bouquet, vol. xix. p. 718.

This corresponds to lines 380. 6–7 in La Chanson :

> Non es en est mon nuls om tan poderos,
> Que mi pogues destruire si la glieza non fos.

The genuineness of the inscription has been denied, but Fauriel accepts it.[1] The lines are well known and are often quoted by historians, e.g. Cæsar Nostradamus, who believed them to have been composed expressly for this epitaph.[2]

---

[1] Introduction to *Chanson*.

[2] ' The most remarkable seal and the most ancient (in Languedoc) is that of Raymond VI, seated between the sun and the moon, indicative of the great extent of his dominions and holding in his left hand a building of three towers which is the Castle of Narbonne in Toulouse, the old residence of the Gothic and Carlovingian Kings.' (E. Roschach, *Hist. de Languedoc*, vol. xvi). The seal of Raymond VII is the same. Raymond's character, according to Innocent III, was ' subtle and sly, slippery and fickle, pretending penitence to secure absolution but harbouring hatred.' (*Regesta*, xi. 26).

THE death of Raymond reopened the question of succession, and his son appealed to Philip for his co-operation in recovering his ancestral lands. On the other hand the legate and certain bishops approached the same monarch with the utmost servility, imploring 'the most revered King, on bended knee, with floods of tears, and rent with sobs, to hasten to the aid of the Church, otherwise it will be overthrown, so strong and numerous are the heretics.'[1] But the death of the king rendered void both appeals. Louis, his successor, quietly dropped Amauri, who with no money and no reinforcements was glad to come to terms with his adversaries. Amauri lacked the military skill and the indomitable will of his father, qualities which, conversely, were lacking in the older Raymond but strikingly exhibited in the younger. Accordingly the two met at Carcassonne (January 14, 1224) and patched up a sort of peace. The 'conventions' were announced as being 'made between us the Counts of Toulouse and Foix, for the one part, and Count Amauri and his (supporters) for the other part.' This preamble is remarkable in that it describes Raymond as Count of Toulouse and Amauri as Count of nowhere, and the more so because a deed was issued the same day to a monastery in the name of Amauri 'Duke of Narbonne and Count of Toulouse.' Amauri agreed to abide by the decision of the King of France on the relation of the two counts, (Toulouse and Foix) to the Church and to himself in matters territorial. His men were to be allowed to disperse un-molested, and those of his local partisans who had been

---

[1] Vaissete, viii, 765.

deprived of their properties in the war were to have them restored. Toulouse and Foix were to have the right to enter Narbonne and Agde after two months.[1] But what of the chief matter—the suppression of heresy ? Of this not a word. Amauri was treated as an invader, not as a defender of the Faith. The restoration of Narbonne to Raymond was a surrender to the heretics. A compact in which Rome was not consulted constituted a challenge to the papacy. Everywhere the Albigenses became more defiant and aggressive. The archbishop and bishops of the Province of Narbonne complained to Louis that owing to the transfer of Narbonne from Amauri to Raymond ' Pharoah's serpents had devoured Moses' serpent.' Honorius described the land as ' worthless metal ' (Jer. vi. 29, 30). He was tortured with anxiety, for the heresy had spread to the Tarn, Provence, Embrun, Arles, and Vienne. He too appealed to the king ; but the king replied that it was not *his* duty to examine articles of faith ; *that* appertained to the Church. It was his strong desire, however, that the Church should come to terms with Raymond, saving the rights of himself and his feudatories. His price for military aid was £60,000 (Paris) per annum for ten years.

The optimism on the other hand of the Albigenses was shown by their election of a ' Pope ' Bartholomew Cortés, a native of Carcassonne, under whom their scattered communities would become united and their organization consolidated. This ' perambulating heresiarch ' had been sent by the Catharists of Bulgaria, Croatia, and Dalmatia who offered a home there to any refugee co-religionists.[2] ' Pope ' Bartholomew adopted papal titles and claimed papal powers. He signed himself ' servus servorum Sanctæ Fidei.' He created bishops and consecrated churches, and paid official visits throughout Toulouse. At a meeting at Pieussan in the Diocese of Narbonne arrangements were made to form a new ' Diocese,' the bishop of which was to be elected by the Perfects of Carcassonne and consecrated by the ' Bishop ' of Toulouse, under the title of the ' Bishop ' of Rodez. Agen too, which had almost been destroyed, put forth fresh growth by the ' Bishop ' of Toulouse consecrating for it a ' Bishop ' with major and minor sons.[1] Heretics from all parts came to consult Bartholomew. But his sudden death, although it brought to an end the Council which had been summoned at Sens—and adjourned to Paris that the king might personally attend—did not bring to an end the alarm of the Church.

This alarm reacted upon the pair who had caused it. Raymond had no mind to champion heresy at the cost of another war, and, probably, further loss of land. Amauri's confederates had no mind to be robbed of the fruits of their labours. Raymond saw that he must make his position in relation to the Church clearer. So at a Council held at Montpellier the same year he promised : (*a*) to keep the Catholic Faith, as preached by the Roman Church, (*b*) to purge his land of heretics, (*c*) to expel all routiers, (*d*) to restore all rights to the Churches, (*e*) to pay 20,000 silver marks, on condition that Amauri renounced all claim upon his lands and those of his allies. Amauri countered with a letter to the Council urging that peace should not be concluded, ' as they were just about to reap the harvest.' Ambassadors from both went to Rome, and Honorius who was really anxious to stop the Crusade in the West, in order to strengthen the Crusade in the East, wrote to the legate, Romano, Cardinal of St. Angelo, who summoned what he intended to be a Council at Béziers on November 30, 1225, but those who attended disputed so hotly as to priority of rank that they sat ' in

---

[1] Doat, *Inq. of Carcassonne*, xxiii. 260. v. also vol. i, p. 77.

consilio non in concilio.'[1]   At this conference were present the King of France, several archbishops and over a hundred bishops.   Amauri reviewed his claims and Raymond his promises made at Montpellier.   Amauri challenged Raymond to submit his case to the ' Judgment of the Twelve Parts of Gaul.'   This Raymond declined, but offered to do homage to the king for his land.   After much altercation, the legate proposed that each archbishop should sit separately with his suffragans, and send to him their several opinions in writing.   These he would treat as confidential, only laying them before the pope and the king for their decision.[2]

The pope's decision was made known at a council held early in the following year at Paris, at which the legate excommunicated Raymond and his allies, and gave their lands to Louis and his heirs for ever.   Amauri and his uncle Guy surrendered (*quitaverunt*) to Louis and his heirs whatever they had of right in the south of France.[3] Romano also went through the Kingdom, seeking men to take up the cross against the Count of Toulouse, promising full remission of sins and absolution of all vows, the vow of the pilgrimage to Jerusalem only except.   Also, with the consent of several bishops, he promised the king for five years, if the war lasted so long, a tenth of all the revenues of the clergy ; and if this proved insufficient for the war's expenses, more from the treasury of the Church. This tenth was not to be paid by those prelates and clergy who took part personally in the Crusade.   The tenth was to be paid twice a year, at Easter and All Saints' Day.   The king in response to all this called a council likewise at Paris on April 4, and ordered all who owed him military service to meet him on the fourth Sunday of that month at

[1] Matthew Paris, p. 277.   [2] *Ibid.*, Mansi *Concil*, xxii, 1113.
[3] Mansi *Concil*, xxiii, 10.

Bourges with their horses, duly equipped, 'in order that
from the vineyard of the Lord God of Hosts, which that
wild boar of Toulouse had ravaged, they might root up all
the weeds (*inutilia*) and plant therein all that was fruitful
(*utilia*).'

But no weeds were rooted up, and these elaborate preparations planted nothing in. For the French nobles, whatever
might be the feeling of the bishops, had little heart for the
campaign, for ' it seemed to them a gross abuse of power
to deprive a Christian man and a Catholic of his inheritance ;
for such the Count of Toulouse by his avowals at the
Council of Béziers had proved himself to be.'[1] So far from
the war lasting five years it lasted barely five months. Louis
marched south with a force of 50,000, and his passage
across the Rhone was facilitated by the Avignonese; but they
refused the entrance to so large a force into their city. The
siege of it lasted three months, during which the king's army
suffered so much from disease and attacks from the enemy
that while he captured the city he abandoned the Crusade
and retired to Montpensier where he died (November 1226.)
Matthew Paris in his vivid description of the siege gives us
what is probably the longest list in contemporary writings
of mediæval weapons offensive and defensive ; the *petraria*,
*balista, scrofa, catus, funda, ensis, lancea, scutum, clava, lorica,
sagitta*, of the French were met by *cuneis, fassatis, moeniis,
turribus,propugnaculis, lapidibus, comportatibus, spiculis, repa-
gulis et machinis aptatis*, of the Avignonese. ' They also
met argument with argument.' The Count of Toulouse as a
skilled warrior had removed all the old men and the women
and children, and had destroyed the crops in the surround-
ing country. The corpses of men and beasts of the
besiegers bred swarms of fat black flies which poisoned food
and drink, and made sleep impossible. The French were

---

[1] Mathew Paris, p. 279.

incessantly harassed by the enemy ; at one sortie they lost 2,000 men, being surprised when at a meal. A plague broke out to which many succumbed. When the king died, the legate concealed the fact, and in the name of the king promised the citizens their lives, liberty, goods and rights as before, if they would open their gates. They replied that they had suffered too much from France to live under its government. The legate then asked that he and the bishops might be allowed to enter to prove their personal goodwill. With this the citizens complied, but on the gates being opened, the French rushed in and overwhelmed the defenders.[1]

[1] Matthew Paris, p. 281.

CHAPTER XVII

WITH the accession of the young Louis IX, the pattern hero and saint of the Middle Ages, began the decline and fall of the Albigensian Heresy. He, not pope, prelate or preacher, set the ideal of personal sanctity and religious zeal. No more formidable suppressor of heresy could have been raised up than St. Louis, because the real force brought against it was moral and not military. Different from his predecessors who served the Church little that they might serve themselves much, he believed conscientiously, that in killing Jews, Turks, Infidels and Heretics he ' was doing God service.' He was no docile instrument of Rome,[1] but the God-appointed champion of the Catholic Church. Not to extend the Kingdom of France but the Kingdom of God did he 'endure hardness.' The royal domains were even reduced; where it was found that in the last two reigns lands had been unjustly annexed, they were restored to their rightful owners ; or, where this was impossible, money of equal value was given to the poor. ' St. Louis was above all a conscientious man, a man who before acting weighed the question to himself of the moral good or evil—independently of all utility, of all consequences.'[2] Now a man of such transcendent piety, as then understood, impregnable integrity and utter devotion to duty was just the one who would *not* extend his policy of restitution to a man who ruled over a country infested with heresy and was himself excommunicated for protecting it.

Although Louis was only eleven years old when he began to reign and a Regency was set up under his mother, his

---

[1] Joinville, p. 140.
[2] Guizot, *Civilization in France*, Lecture xiv.

sense of religious duty was so precocious that it was quite clear to all from the beginning what would be his policy with regard to heresy. Thus in the Lent following his accession (1227) a Council was held at Narbonne,[1] the very first canon of which dealt with heresy. The king, it stated, had heard that the laity of the province of Narbonne and other parts adjacent ignored their sentences of excommunication. Such were to be admonished three times, and, if recalcitrant, to be fined nine pounds and a penny. If still obstinate for a year, all their goods were to be forfeited. The sixth canon complained of the prevalence of perjury and false evidence ; it ordered that perjurers were to be denounced in church, and, if obdurate, to be excommunicated with candle and bell. The fourteenth renewed the decree of Lucius III as to ' testes synodales '. The fifteenth required all counts, barons and castellans to renounce heretics and their abetters. The sixteenth ordered all ' vested ' heretics, or who were known or justly suspected to be heretics, to be removed from all public offices. The seventeenth stated : ' Raymond, son of Raymond, once Count of Toulouse, the Count of Foix and Trenceval who is said to be Viscount of Béziers, the heretics of Toulouse, credents, abetters, defenders, receivers, and especially those of Limoges and others who had sworn to the Lord Louis, King of France, of happy memory, and afterwards forsook the Church, also all who aid them with arms, horses, or victuals, or sell, give, send, or knowingly help them in any way, shall be denounced and excommunicated with candle and bell.'

This Council, to which too little attention has been given and whose importance has been underestimated, paved the way to the decisive Treaty of Paris, for it was a restatement in vigorous terms of the policy of the State rather

---

[1] Mansi, *Concil.* xxiii, p. 21.

than of the Church. Raymond saw in it no hope of relief
from the new king. On the contrary, he was faced with all
the forces of a monarch who required no encouragement
however servile, or threats however severe, from the
Church, inasmuch as he was himself fervent in the Faith.
In May 1228 he sent ' a no inconsiderable expedition '
against Raymond, but it was destroyed in an ambush near
Castle Sarcin, 500 being captured. These, after being
horribly mutilated, were sent back to the north as a
warning not to interfere with the south. Three other
expeditions that summer were equally disastrous.[1] Yet
Raymond had no desire to be a martyr for heresy ; the
salving of his inheritance appealed to him more. Not the
less was the pope anxious that the Albigensian Crusade
should cease so that the full weight of France should be
thrown into the Palestinian Crusade. Another force too,
more under the control of the pope, less costly and more
potent than carnal weapons of warfare, was being
developed—the Inquisition. To all parties therefore,
except the most ardent heretics, peace was desirable.

Accordingly feelers were put out. Romano, the Legate,
instructed the Abbot of Grande-Selve, Helios Garini, to
sound Raymond ; and, he being favourably inclined, a
preliminary meeting was held at Meaux at which were
present the Legate, the Archbishop of Narbonne, and other
prelates, the Count of Toulouse and men of position in the
city. The exchange of views being satisfactory, these set
out for Paris that the matter might be completed
(*consummari*) before the king. Here was drawn up in
Lent, 1229 the important Treaty of Paris,[2] between the
King of France and the Church for one part, and Raymond
for the other part. Raymond promised to be true to the
Roman Church and the king and his heirs unto death : to

---

[1] Matthew Paris, p. 294.   [2] Vaissete, viii. 883 ff.

attack to his utmost all heretics, their aiders, abetters and receivers, sparing neither neighbour, vassal, relation nor friend : to purge his lands of all heretics and help to purge and defend the lands of the king and the Church : to make diligent search for heretics, and to pay for two years two silver marks, and after that one mark for ever to any one who captured a heretic : to expel all routiers and their receivers from his lands and punish them with due punishment : to defend all churches, ecclesiastics and their liberties : if any person remained obdurate after excommunication, to deprive such of all his property real and personal, and to hold such until he recanted : to cause all bailiffs on appointment to carry out their regulations : no Jew or one suspected of heresy to be appointed bailiff, but only catholics : all real estate held by churches and ecclesiastics before the first crusade to be restored to them : to pay as reparation for the destruction of castles and houses 10,000 silver marks, to be distributed by a commission appointed by the legate and the church ; to pay to the Abbot of Citeaux 2,000 silver marks, to the Abbot of Clairvaux 500, to the Abbot of Grand-Selve 1,000, etc. ; to pay 6,000 marks for rebuilding the Castle of Narbonne and other castles, to be held by the king and the Church as security for ten years : to pay 4,000 marks for two masters of theology, two decretists, six masters of the liberal arts and two masters of grammar at Toulouse. after his absolution to take the cross against the Saracens within two years and remain in Palestine for five years : to take no revenge against or in any way injure the Church and its adherents, or the Counts de Montfort and their adherents, except those who did not come with him (Raymond) into the Peace : his daughter, Jeanne, to marry one of the king's brothers : if he (Raymond) died without legitimate sons, his land to descend to his daughter, Jeanne, and her heirs. In return the king granted to Raymond the whole country and Diocese of

Toulouse, except the land of the Marshal which he, the Marshal, held of the King.   After the death of Raymond the See of Toulouse was to come to the king's brother, who married Jeanne, and their sons.   If he died without sons of her, Toulouse and the See of Toulouse, to come to the king and his heirs.   The king also granted (*dimittimus*) to Raymond the Sees of Agen and Cahors,[1] also of the See of Albi all on the south side of the Tarn to the middle of the river.   All native feudatories who had fled from their country because of their adhesion to the Church, the king's father or the counts de Montfort, to be restored to all their former inheritances and possessions which they held of the king's father, himself or the counts de Montfort, unless they were convicted heretics.   If, however, any who remained in the country were unwilling to return to the government of the Church or king, especially the count de Foix, Raymond was to make vigorous (*vivum*) war against them and make no truce without the consent of the Church and the king.   If Raymond gained the victory, the land conquered to be his, but he must destroy all forts and defensive walls, unless for the Church's and the king's security they wished to retain them for ten years ; after which they were to fall to the king with all their revenues. Thirty towns (*named*)[2] were to be dismantled of their fortifications and not rebuilt without the permission of the Church and king.   As security Raymond was to hand over seven castles, including the castle of Narbonne, for ten years, which the king might fortify if he chose.

Stripped to his shirt and breeches, and barefoot, Raymond took the oath before the doors of Notre Dame on Good Friday (April 12, 1229).[3]   He was then admitted to

---

[1] Except certain fiefs in Cahors which Philip held at his death.

[2] e.g. Castelnaudary, Fanjeaux, Avignonet, Gaillac, Verdun, Agen, Montauban.

[3] Vaissete, viii, p. 893.

the Church, but, unlike his father, the scourging was omitted. Before the altar he did homage to the king for whatever land of his vast and beautiful inheritance the Treaty spared him ; but the precaution was taken of detaining him in Paris until the terms were ratified in Toulouse, and his castles and his daughter (aged nine) handed over.

As was suspected, the Count of Foix proved less tractable than his *ci-devant* comrade-in-arms. He protested the indefeasible right of every man to religious liberty. ' This liberty my father had always impressed upon me, assuring me that, with it and will resolved to maintain it, I might look on calmly, though the very vault of heaven gave way and broke over my head, for I had nothing to fear.'[1] He yielded only when he saw that resistance was hopeless and would cause useless bloodshed. The Count of Comminges readily accepted the arguments of Raymond, his over-lord, although Raymond was now no longer Duke of Narbonne, and so of the first rank, but reduced to the fourth among the six peers of the realm.

[1] Percin, *Hist. des Albig*. p. 141 from a MS. account of his life. Vaissete, viii. 903.

CHAPTER XVIII

A S soon as the Treaty of Paris was signed, Romano hastened to Toulouse where he assembled a great Council at which, *inter alia*, the following decrees were passed : (1) The archbishops and bishops shall in each parish in town or country bind one priest and two or three respectable laymen (or more if necessary) by an oath that they will make diligent, faithful, and frequent search (*inquirant*) for heretics in their respective parishes, searching every suspected house, cellar, shed or other hiding place, and destroy all such places ; and, if they find any heretics, credents, abetters, receivers or defenders, they shall take precautions to prevent their escape. The archbishops and bishops shall strictly enjoin the lords of such places or their bailiffs to inflict upon such the proper punishment (*animadversio debita*). (4) If any landowner allows heretics to be on his lands, he shall lose his land for ever, and his body be handed over to his lord for his disposal (*quod debebit*). (6) Houses where heretics are found shall be destroyed.[1] (7) If bailiffs protect heretics they shall lose their goods and their office, and be deprived of the right to exercise it for ever. (8) No heretic shall be punished except by the bishop or other authorized ecclesiastic. (9) Anyone may search for and arrest heretics in the land of another, and the bailiffs of the place shall be bound to render such all possible assistance ; that is to say, king's bailiffs can search in the territory of the Count of Toulouse and others, and

---

[1] One such hiding place is described : ' In their house is a cupboard (*archa*) for storing corn, and in the cupboard a recess or hiding place in which the heretics were wont to be concealed' (Nat. Lib. Mss. lat. 4269, f. 17). Some houses had secret doors. Limborch *Inq.* (*Sentences of Toulouse*, pp. 63, 107, 193).

the Count of Toulouse and others can do the same in the territory of the king. (10) If any heretics of their own freewill renounce their heresy and return to the Catholic Faith, they shall not remain in the place where they have been wont to live, if that place be suspected of heresy ; but they shall be put into a Catholic town. As a mark also of detestation of their previous error they shall wear two crosses of a colour different from that of their clothing, one on the right and the other on the left. And no one shall be excused the crosses unless he has a letter from the bishop to certify that he has been reconciled. Such heretics shall not hold any public office and shall not take part in any lawsuit, unless they have been fully restored by the pope or his legate after proper penance. (11) If, however, heretics return to the Catholic unity, not voluntarily but by fear of death or for some other cause, for their penance they shall be immured in some place by the bishop with proper safeguards, so that they may have no opportunity of corrupting others. They shall be maintained by those who received their forfeited goods; and if they have none, then by the bishop. (12) All males from fourteen years of age, and all females from twelve years of age upwards shall swear to keep the orthodox faith. A list of their names shall be kept in each parish, and all shall take the oath before the bishop or other men of position (*bonos viros*).[1] If anyone shall be absent on the days appointed for taking the oath (which shall be twice a year), and does not report himself within fifteen days, he shall be suspect. (13) All males and females who have reached years of discretion shall confess and communicate at least three times a year, viz., Easter, Whitsun and Christmas. (14) The laity shall be prohibited[2] from

---

[1] Heretics were called ' boni homines ', never ' boni viri '.
[2] Cf. The Council of Béziers (1246), canon 36 ; ' De libris theologicis non tenendis etiam a laicis in latino, et neque ab ipsis neque a clericis in vulgari teneri faciatis ad plenum.'

having the Old and New Testaments.   Anyone who wishes, however, may have the Psalter or the Breviary or the Hours of the Blessed Mary for the purposes of devotion, but everyone is strictly forbidden to have the aforesaid books translated into the vulgar tongue. (15) No one shall employ a doctor accused of heresy. When the sick man has received the Holy Communion from the hand of his priest (*presbyteri*), great care shall be taken until the day of his death or recovery that no heretic or one suspected of heresy approach him, ' since we understand enormous abominations have happened thereby.' (28) All persons from fourteen years of age shall swear to keep the peace. (42) Widows and heiresses who own forts and castles shall not marry the enemies of the Faith. If they do, their property shall be confiscated, but shall be restored to their heirs. By the Treaty of Paris there were annexed to the Kingdom of France ' the Duchy of Narbonne, the Counties of Béziers, Agde, Maguelone, Nîmes, Uzes and Viviers, a part of the County of Toulouse, half of the County of Albi, the Viscounty of Gevaudan, and the claims of the Count of Toulouse over the ancient Counties of Velaz, Gevaudan and Lodève.' [1]

Possibly they were the best terms Raymond could secure short of absolute deprivation such as his father suffered ; but the surrender carried with it the surrender of municipal rights which the capitouls and citizens regarded as inalienable. The towns in the south were larger, wealthier and stronger than those in the north, and municipal patriotism refused to accept such an agreement which bartered away municipal freedom. Hence the struggle took on for some years a new aspect which lasted until the towns realized, like Raymond, that their resistance was hopeless. The measures for the suppression of heresy taken by the Church

---

[1] Guizot, *Civ. in France*, Lecture xiv.

in conjunction with the secular arm were resisted even by consuls, capitouls, castellans and other secular persons. The co-operation of those who were citizens before catholics accounts largely for the length and strength of the resistance which the heretics offered to the increased dangers which threatened them. Those dangers lay not in the severity of the penalties which the Council of Toulouse imposed, but in the rigour with which this formidable and cordial union of Rome and France determined to enforce obedience.

The legate ' a wary and prudent man ', leaving nothing to chance, ' ordered *an* inquisition to be made against those suspected of heresy.'[1] All the bishops present at the inquiry had to examine the witnesses[2] whom the Bishop of Toulouse brought forward ; their evidence was reduced to writing, and the records were entrusted for safety to the bishop. Some submitted at once and were pardoned. Others yielded under pressure and were severely punished. But bolder spirits demanded the names of their accusers, on the ground that such were guilty of treason. Riots broke out everywhere, and so general and terrible was the storm that the legates and those inquisitors who survived fled to Rome. Witnesses came forward at the risk of their lives, and several were killed.[3]

The contemporary, William de Puy-Laurent, chaplain and almoner of Raymond, affirmed that these disturbances were fomented by the bishop who wished to embroil the Count of Toulouse anew with the pope and the king ; and this view is supported by Raymond's letter to Gregory IX, as well as by the latter's letter to several bishops bidding them treat Raymond with kindness. But there can be no doubt that

---

[1] William de Puy-Laurent, 40.
[2] One such was William de Solier, once a ' perfect ', and therefore particularly dangerous. Theodoric, however, once Dean of Nevers, stood firm and was burnt (Greg. ix, *epp*. xxii). See *supra*, p. 22.
[3] William de Puy-Laurent, 40.

the trouble was due chiefly to the natural irritation at this systematic inquiry into a man's religious opinions, and to anger at the loss of municipal liberties. At Conchis the abbot of the convent was seized at Mass by Bernard, Count de Comminges, and other vassals of Raymond, beaten unconscious, dragged out of church and hanged on a gibbet. A monk took him down whilst still alive, but they put him up again. The convent of preaching friars was re-started at Toulouse (1228), two monks taking possession of a house and grounds in the name of the Master-General of the Dominican Order and of the Provincial Prior of Provence. At Narbonne the archbishop gave the convent of Preaching Friars a Church and a nucleus of a library, and conferred upon them the right of burial. All decrees, including those of the Council of Toulouse, against heretics, were adopted as by-laws of the city. But between the city—or old part of Narbonne—and the borough—or new part, there was always considerable jealousy ; and the ' peaceful penetration ' of preachers, who did as much prying as preaching, produced further friction. The vapour was highly inflammable, and only a spark was wanting to cause an explosion. That spark was the definite investiture of the Preaching Order with inquisitorial powers from Bourdeaux to Narbonne by the two bulls of Gregory IX (1233).[1] Ferrier was appointed inquisitor for Narbonne, William Arnauld and Peter deCella for Toulouse and Carcassonne, Arnauld Cathala and William Pelisse for Albi.[2]

[1] Potthast, 9153, 9155. Bernard Gui, *Life of Greg. IX ;* Muratori iii, 1,573.

[2] Douais, *Albigensianism and the Preaching Friars at Narbonne*, p. 19. Bernard Gui, punning on Ferrier's name, describes him as ' in virga ferrea malleans . . . adeo quod nomen ejus quasi gladiosum in auribus hereticorum resonat ; *MSS.* 609 (*Lib. of Toulouse*) which by giving the depositions of 5,638 witnesses before the Inquisition (1245) testifies to Ferrier's activity. In 1252 he was made Prior of the Preaching Order at Carcassonne, and a few months later he became a Prior at Béziers where he lived two years. This Convent was of royal found-

The Narbonnese had been quite happy under the easy rule of their late archbishop and were not prepared to be driven into orthodoxy by the truculent methods which his successor, Arnauld, had pursued as legate and leader of the crusades. Arnauld found both from within and from without that his new appointment was no *otium cum dignitate*. His flock, at any rate in the borough, received him sullenly, and he quarrelled with his late colleague, Simon de Montfort, over the Dukedom. Conrad, Bishop of Portuis, dare not enter Narbonne by land as legate, and had to slip in by sea (1219) ; and when three years later he excommunicated the borough and villages around, they retaliated by attacking the city and driving out the Preaching Friars,[1] and they did not dare to return until 1228, and found no rest for the sole of their feet until 1231 in a property given to them by Peter Améli.[2] Owing to the central position of Narbonne for traffic, heresy made a determined effort to win it. Even under the eyes of the archbishop-legate heretics came and went unmolested.[3]

The municipal situation was peculiar ; the city was zealously orthodox, the borough, which had grown up round the city, tolerant of, if not actually favourably disposed towards, heresy. Ferrier charged the burgesses with being directly guilty of heresy. In real or pretended indignation they rose up, ransacked the convent of the Preaching Friars, and ravaged its grounds, its library, cellars, refectory, kitchen ; nothing was spared. The archbishop was wounded, his live stock driven away, his vestments and saddlery stolen. This open rupture brought the difference between city and borough to a point, and

ation, owing its origin to a donation of Louis IX (1247), and enjoying his patronage. (Granier, *The Preaching Friars of Béziers* in *Mélanges de littérature et d'histoire religieuse*, vol. i, an. 1899).

[1] Vaissete, iv, 545, 546.
[2] *Gallia Christiana*, vi, 61.
[3] *Mss.* 609 (*Lib. of Toulouse*).

the point was,, ' Art thou for us or for our adversaries ? '
Are you for the Church or for Heresy ? So the city drew
up nine Articles and issued them by the archbishop with
the approval of the legate, the Archbishop of Vienne,
and the Bishops of Nîmes, Béziers and Toulouse. They
were—

(1) The borough must swear to hold the Catholic Faith
and aid in every way the archbishop's court in discovering,
arresting and punishing heretics and those suspected of
heresy.

(2) All above the age of fourteen both in the borough
and city must renew their oath as prescribed by the Council
of Toulouse.

(3) No alliance must be made with the enemies of the
Faith or of peace.

(4) All leagues already made must be dissolved, and
no fresh leagues entered into without the permission of the
archbishop and his successors.

(5) The domain and jurisdiction of the archbishop
must be acknowledged.

(6) Houses in which heretics are found must be pulled
down.

(7) All forfeits or monies which had been taken from
persons in the borough who had refused to take the oath
to the consuls must be restored to them.

(8) Arnauld le Long and his brother were to be restored
to the city, and the two men who had arrested them must
go to Rome before Easter to obtain absolution from the
pope.

(9) Reparation must be made for all damages.[1]

The consuls of the borough accepted all these Articles
but the fourth. To gain outside support they wrote to
other consuls, e.g., those of Nîmes, pointing out the effect

[1] Vaissete, viii, 981.

of these Articles upon their authority, and complaining of the mischievous influence which the Preaching Friars were having upon the archbishop. Under their pressure he had excommunicated them (the consuls), laid an interdict upon them, forbade lawyers or doctors to practise, or priests to hear confessions, except of persons ' *in articulo mortis.*' The Preachers arrested innocent persons, despoiled them of their goods and thrust them into prison. They entrapped the simple and illiterate with tricky questions.[1] The consuls said they had given their word to support the inquisitors, but only if they followed the Council of Toulouse. They had proved their *bona fides* by punishing heretics, and had promised to repair the damages sustained by the archbishop and convent, but they refused to pay the sum demanded by the archbishop to remove the excommunication, because they were not guilty. Also they resented the discourtesy of the archbishop in that he no longer addressed the burgesses as ' sons ' or ' brothers ', much less as ' fathers of the work of Jesus Christ '. He forgot what they had done in the days of Simon de Montfort.[2] The archbishop and the consuls of the city countered this move with a letter to Louis, in which, after exaggerating the violence of the burgesses, they sought to incriminate Raymond as well, alleging that he had come to Narbonne, ostensibly as a peacemaker, but really as a mischief-maker, and acted as if *he* were king. They urged Louis to assert his authority in the interests of peace.[3] The dreary struggle dragged on until 1236, when a truce was made between city and borough which matured into a peace the following year.[4] By 1242 the authority of the Inquisition was so firmly established both in borough and

[1] e.g. ' Who makes a woman a mother—God or man ? '
[2] *Hist. de la Ville de Nîmes, Preuves,* 73–75.
[3] Teulet, *Layettes* pp. 321–323.
[4] Vaissete, viii, 1000–1008, Doat, L., 109.

city that any stranger before entering, had to take an oath that he had had nothing to do with the death of the prior of Carcassonne, or the Friar Preachers at Avignonet or with burning the books of the Inquisition.[1]

Reverting to Toulouse, special provision was made by the Council of 1229 for the education of the young, but it was four years before anything was done. Then a college was opened at Toulouse, the masters and scholars of which were to have the same privileges as those of Paris. The expenses were to be paid by the Count of Toulouse, and a Housing Board was set up consisting of two clergy and two laity, publicly elected and tactful, but duly sworn catholics, with power to compel any citizen who had an empty house to let it to the scholars at a fair rent to be fixed by the Board. The count was to afford the masters, scholars and their servants every protection, but was to have no control over their opinions or conduct.[2]

The delay in setting up this college was probably due to Raymond. The long struggle had left him with an empty treasury, and he found that in signing the Decrees of the Treaty of Paris and the Council of Toulouse he had promised more than he could fulfil. He took the earliest opportunity that prudence suggested of pleading with the pope for a postponement of the payment of the huge sums demanded. He intimated that help in paying the fine should be forthcoming from the ecclesiastics of his country, and the pope, Gregory IX, ordered his master-chaplain to inquire whether this was feasible.[3] He claimed the restoration of Venaissin under the terms of the Treaty.[4] He postponed his journey to Palestine under various pretexts for nearly twenty years. Yet to prove his *bona fides* in suppressing the Albigensian Heresy he issued

---

[1] *Archives of Narbonne*, Annexe, xvii. 196 ; also *infra* p. 199.
[2] Percin, *Monumenta*, xxiii, 923.
[3] Vaissete viii. 931.   [4] *Ibid.*, 979.

(April 1233) the Statutes of Toulouse which tightened the screw of the Treaty Decrees. Inquiry was to be made for all who killed the prosecutors (*persecutores*) of heretics, or who consented to their murder. An informer was to be rewarded with one mark. Seneschals and bailiffs merely suspected of heresy were to be removed from their office. All houses in which from the time of the Peace of Paris a heretic had been found alive or buried were to be pulled down, and all goods were to be confiscated, unless the owners could prove their innocence. All huts at a distance from the castle, all fortified caves and inclosures suspected or reputed to be occupied by heretics were to be destroyed or stopped up, and all goods there to be confiscated. The lord of the castle in whose domains such places were discovered was to be fined £25 (Tolosan) in each case. All inheritances of heretics were to be forfeited unless their children could prove their own orthodoxy, but such children could not succeed to the property if, in the meanwhile, between such forfeiture and proof, the inheritance had been sold or given away. Nor did such succession apply to the houses where the said heretics had lived since the Peace of Paris; these were to be destroyed without any mercy whatever. All who prevented inquisitors from entering a village, house, inclosure or wood, or defended heretics found in such places, or refused to help or abstained from helping inquisitors, were liable to confiscation of their goods and other lawful penalties. If anybody were discovered after death to be a heretic since the Treaty of Paris, his goods were to be confiscated and his house destroyed. 'Vested' heretics who had been reconciled to the Church were to have certificates from well-known catholics, and must wear the crosses in a conspicuous position on pain of confiscation of goods. Those heretics who had no goods to be confiscated were to wear the crosses. If a person intending to go over to heresy sold or mortgaged his property or parted with it in

other ways, all such contracts were to be null and void.   If
a person under pretence of business or pilgrimage should
visit a heretic, and during such absence from home thus
elude his taxes and remove his goods, he must obtain
permission for such absence from his bishop on the security
of his relations and trustees of his goods ; such absence
must not exceed a year.   Otherwise he would be adjudged
a heretic, with the consequent penalties.   That the keys of
the Church might not be despised, contumacy after one
year was to be punished with confiscation.   All who
violated the Peace of Paris were to be punished.   No one
was to injure or oppress convents, especially those of the
Cistercian Order.[1]

Decrees and Statutes served one great purpose.   They
showed those heretics who were sincere that they must no
longer ' put their trust in princes or in any child of man.'
Never had the issue been so sharply defined.   It was a long,
dreary and bitter struggle, lasting for another hundred
years, for what each side believed to be the truth.   War in
the ordinary sense ceased, and there were no more great
battles, except at Mont-segur, the last stronghold,[2]
Heretics no longer perished in thousands, but singly or in
small groups at the stake, or by torture and disease in
prisons, or by starvation in exile.   Reprisals and revivals
were to be expected ; but surely, if slowly, the Church
removed from her path a heresy or combination of heresies
which had in various guises troubled her from early ages,
by a weapon which this age forged out of old materials
and subsequent ages perfected—the Inquisition.

---

[1] Vaissete, viii. 963.   Teulet, *Layettes*, ii, p. 248.   [2] See p. 152.

Part II.—THE INQUISITION

CHAPTER I

THE Inquisition was not, as is often assumed, a new office specially invented by the popes for the extirpation of heresy. The principle of the Inquisition may be traced back to the early days of the Roman Republic, and, indeed, is indispensable to the stability of any form of government, viz., an inquiry into rumoured movements for its overthrow, and the restraint and punishment of the guilty. The methods taken to attain these objects will differ in nature and number, but the underlying principle will be the same. The Roman Republic had its Inquisitio, and this naturally passed over into the Roman Empire, which, according to the first Augustus, was but the Republic under a new name. And when the Roman Empire became the *Holy* Roman Empire, the Inquisitio still remained as a legal process for the preservation of authority. This would apply alike to matters religious and secular.[1] Manichee, Arian, semi-Arian, Athanasian, Donatist, all were exposed to persecution by the secular arm.[2] *The* Inquisition therefore, which was successful in the suppression of the Albigensian Heresy, was no new

---

[1] Theod. ii, *Nov. tit.*, iii, 438. ' Praecipuam imperatoriae majestatis curam esse perspicimus verae religionis indaginem. Cujus si cultum tenere potuerimus, iter prosperitatis humanis aperimus inceptis . . ' ' Ubicumque Manichaei inveniantur, capite damnandi sunt.' Code II, v. also 12 (Tanon, pp. 127 foll.).

[2] But even then only for overt acts. ' How laxly the laws (against heresy) were applied may be seen in Austin's case. Manichees were certainly not hunted and punished, however fierce the laws which had been registered ' (Bussell's *Religious Thought and Heresy in the Middle Ages*, p. 739).

invention, but something which the Church, at first condemning, took from the armouries of the State and shaped
and sharpened for her own ends.[1]

The theory of the Holy Roman Empire—of the co-operation of the Church and State for a common religious end—
though possibly a splendid ideal, was never fully realized;
and the attempts at a working co-ordination of their
respective powers and prerogatives caused long and bloody
struggles, and furnishes the frame-work of European
history for some ten centuries—from Charlemagne to
Napoleon. The amalgamation of temporal and spiritual
interests called for the most delicate manipulation and
tactful adjustment; and as at first the Church was 'the
weaker vessel' in this union, she had to walk warily,
dependent as she was on the temporal power for the
temporal punishment of evil doers, as well as the praise
of them that did well. Hence not only was there no
necessity for calling into being an entirely new organization, but such a policy would have been highly im-
prudent; for those against whom it would have been
directed were subjects of a State as well as members of a
Church. Not only, therefore, would the State have vigorously questioned the right of its partner to set up a
tribunal over whose decisions it could exercise no control,
but it would have flatly refused to carry out those decisions,
when called upon to do so, in all cases where allegiance to
the Church conflicted with allegiance to the State. Justinian had laid it down that 'if anyone of the impious
superstition of the Manichees, after many cautions and
plenty of time for repentance, persisted in his errors, he

---

[1] Bernard of Clairvaux (*Serm*. LXIV, Migne, *P.L.*t. 183, p. 1086);
'Haeretici . . capiantur non armis sed argumentis,' quoting 1
Tim. ii. 4; but in Serm. LXVI (p. 1101) advocates penal measures:
'Melius procul dubio gladio coercentur, illius videlicet qui non sine
causa gladium portat, quam in suum errorem multos trajicere
permittantur.'

became liable to the extreme punishment.' This virtually conceded all that the Inquisition claimed ; but even
Charlemagne, who based his legislative policy upon that of
Justinian and empowered the secular and ecclesiastical
courts to inquire into all charges of superstition and
paganism, required all their judgments to be endorsed by
himself.   At his decease the break-up of his vast kingdom
gave greater independence to the bishops and to the
bishop's court.   Hence arose the need for the systematization and codification of the Church's law, known as Canon
Law.   It was claimed that this was nothing else than the
application of Roman law to Church affairs, and not an
innovation of the Church.   And as none studied law either
of Church or State except ecclesiastics, there was none to
contradict their conclusions.   These were set forth in the
famous Decretum of Gratian (c. 1150), of which a modern
Roman Catholic writer observes ; ' no work has ever come
near it in its influence in the Church, although there is
scarcely another so chokeful of gross errors both intentional and unintentional.'[1]   What the great canonist,
Gratian, dogmatized in the middle of the twelfth century
the great Summist, Aquinas, justified a century later. [2]

' Inquisitio ' was the technical term in Roman Law for
the process of obtaining evidence, and the person who
sought for it was called an ' Inquisitor.'   Such evidence
might be obtained by (*a*) *Denuntiatio*, (*b*) *Accusatio* or
(*c*) *Diffamatio*.   ' *Denuntiatio* ' was the charge made by one
in authority : ' *Accusatio*,' by a private person : ' *Diffamatio*,'
by common report.   This process applied to all kinds of
offences, religious, political, civil.   The early Christians
would be punished as heretics against the State religion ;
and when Christianity became the State religion, it was

[1] Janus, *The Pope and the Council*, p. 143.
[2] *Summa*, ii. 9. 11.

natural and rational that *Inquisitio* should be made in all cases of suspected dissidents, as against rebels and other criminals. There were, however, under the Roman system, safeguards against injustice which were absent from the Church system. In the former there was no secrecy, witnesses were known to the accused and confronted with him. The accused was allowed the aid of counsel. No women, children or biassed persons were permitted to give evidence. If the charge failed, the accuser was liable to the penalty instead. Under the Roman system, the accused was innocent until proved guilty; under the Church system the accused was guilty until proved innocent. As the Inquisition developed and grew more searching, more scientific, its zeal for the whole blinded it to the most elementary justice for the individual.

It spread into every European country, with one exception, and that exception was England. In the publicity, fairness and freedom of English justice, the secrecy, prejudice and craft of the Inquisition found no place.

CHAPTER II

A S the Inquisition now came to be set up in all the chief
cities of Southern France it may be convenient at
this point to attempt to gain a comprehensive view of its
operations. The Albigensian Heresy called the Inquisition,
as a distinct office, into being, but the principle of an
Inquisition was, as we have seen, no new thing. ' The
Church was armed about A.D. 1230 like the armoured
knights of the time. . . . but the armour was not made in
a day ; centuries put it together piece by piece.'[1] The
decrees of Verona,[2] and of Narbonne[3] which appointed
periodical visitations of bishops, assisted by synodsmen,
were either never acted upon or proved ineffective. Those
in authority might be indifferent to or themselves infected
with heresy. Where a whole town favoured heresy, it
would be impossible to obtain a *diffamatio ;* and hence
suppression was least possible where most needed. Moreover, a heretic finding one diocese too hot for him might
seek an asylum in another where the bishop was less
zealous. In short, there were many gaps in the fence
through which a heretic could slip. To be successful the
inquisitor must be an officer of a *system* established to deal
exclusively with heresy, and behind that system must stand
the whole power of the Church centralized in the pope.
From the pope alone he must receive his authority, to the
pope alone he must be responsible. To save Church order
he was nominally the assistant of the bishop in his supreme
duty of the suppression of heresy, but in reality he was
independent of him.

[1] De Cauzons, *Hist. de l'Inq.*, vol. 1, p. 492. See also Tanon,
p. 255 ff.
[2] v., p. 8.   [3] v., p. 115.

To that one work he must devote all his energies untrammelled by legatine, episcopal or political duties. For that one work he must sever himself from all earthly ties ; for that sacrifice all private interests. On the other hand, a mere recluse, with no knowledge of human nature or worldly affairs, would be worthless. An inquisitor must be in the world, but not of it ; innocent as a dove, but wise as a serpent. He must be thoroughly intimate with all the tenets and all the wiles of heresy, with all the arguments and all the ways by which it was propagated. He must not be as one that beateth the air. He must not draw a bow at a venture, or shoot the arrow of the Lord's deliverance thrice only, but his whole quiverful against the heretics until he had consumed them.

Where could the pope find machinery capable of dealing effectually with the evil ? It must work swiftly, smoothly, decisively. The ordinary organization of the Church was too clumsy, too general. It was in the Preaching Friars that the requisite machinery was found.

Strictly speaking, a preacher functions in the pulpit or in ' the streets and lanes of the city '—*not* in a court of law. A Preaching Order should have no tribunal. It aims at breaking down all resistance to its message by proclaiming the truth and awakening a sense of sin, and the realization that ' it is appointed unto man once to die and after that the judgment.' And *this* theory of persuasion was maintained in the *official* repudiation of the prying and coercive powers implied in the title ' Inquisitores.'[1] The minutes of their provincial Chapters consist for the most part of lists of lectures and the subjects upon which and the places in which they are to lecture, Logic, Philosophy, Theology, and the Holy Scriptures being most frequently mentioned ; also

---

[1] General Chapter of Paris, 1256 : ' Item, quod fratres nostri vocantur Fratres Praedicatores, *et non aliis nominibus.*'

inasmuch as one cannot give out if one does not take in, the subjects to be studied and the places where such studies might be most profitably pursued were carefully allotted. Logic and Natural Philosophy were but ancillary to the study of Theology (the Sentences and Holy Scriptures).[1] Lecturers in Theology as a distinct office were appointed about the last quarter of the thirteenth century, the first mention of such (with sub-lecturers) being at the Chapter of Bordeaux in 1277. To all the lectures young students were admitted, and the regulations for their behaviour show that boys were boys then as now : ' we will (or advise)[2] that youths who are sent to study shall be diligent in their study and strive to conduct themselves religiously and quietly ; but those who are found to be useless in study or insolent to others or disturbers of peace, the priors, with the advice and consent of the lecturers, sub-prior and three other discreet friars, shall (*possint*) send back to their convents, if after the first warning they do not amend.' Preachers carried an official summary of arguments wherewith to refute the heretics, but out of more than 1,000 passages from the Bible only twenty-one are taken from the Old Testament.[3]

It is almost inconceivable that men of this vocation could pass without a qualm from the ' *beata tranquillitas* ' of the library, lecture room or pulpit to the horrors of the Inquisition. But inevitably in the atmosphere of the

[1] *Les Frères Prêcheurs en Gascoigne* by Douais, passim; also *Les Fr. Prêch. en Narbonne*, pp. 58 ff. The earliest written statute of the University of Oxford (under the influence of Dominicans) to which a date can be assigned (1253) is : Quod nullus in eadem Universitate incipiat in theologia nisi prius rexerit in artibus in aliqua Universitate.' Malet, *History of Oxford*.

[2] Volumus (v. l. monemus). Chapter of Bordeaux, i, 287. Also Douais, ' *Studies under the Preaching Friars in 13th and 14th centuries.*'

[3] *Summula contra herrores notatos hereticorum*, MSS. 301, Lib. of Toulouse.

Middle Ages 'Fratres Prædicatores' became 'Fratres Persecutores.' A preacher may surely 'inquire' how far the people are 'doers of the Word and not hearers only.' He must reprove and rebuke as well as exhort; and if all three fail, heresy, being rebellion against the Church, as treason is against the State, and the salvation of the soul being the highest concern of the former, as loyalty that of the latter, means must be found in the interests of the offender to bring him to a proper frame of mind. According to the Bull 'Ad extirpanda' (1252) of Innocent IV, heretics were 'robbers and murderers of souls, thieves of the sacraments of God and the Christian Faith.' But the weapons of the Church's warfare are not carnal but spiritual; therefore it was forbidden her to inflict physical punishment, much more to shed blood. This was the province of the State, the secular arm, her other partner; and it was its bounden duty to carry out the behests of the Church. Thus while the inquisitors never, in theory, imprisoned, tortured or burnt heretics, yet they pronounced such sentences that the secular arm, under fear of a worse punishment (excommunication or interdict), had no option but to execute them. The provincial Chapter of Montpellier (1242) ruled: 'We order (*precipimus*) that the Preachers altogether abstain from the execution of sentences, such as building prisons, arresting, detaining, imprisoning, exhuming the dead, and burning and other punishments, *except so far as it is granted them.*'[1] 'Our pope does not kill but orders (*precipit*) some one to be killed. It is the law that kills those whom the pope allows to be killed.'[2]

We have already seen the advent of the Preaching Order of the Dominicans into Toulouse and other places, and if an exact date be sought for the conversion or evolution of the

---

[1] Douais, *Fr Prêch, en Gascoigne*, p. 64.
[2] Discussion between a Catholic and a Paterine. Martene and Durand, *Thes.*, v. 1741.

Preaching Orders into the Inquisition we might assign April 1233, when Gregory IX issued three Bulls, the first issued April 13, the second April 20, and the third April 22. The first was addressed to all the prelates of France, in which after pointing out that heresy must be suppressed and that God had raised up the Preaching Friars for this purpose, he proceeded : ' We, seeing you are engrossed in a whirlwind of cares and scarce able to breathe by the pressure of over-whelming anxieties, think it well to divide your burdens. . . . We have therefore determined to send Preaching Friars against the heretics of France and the adjoining provinces, and we beg, warn and exhort you, as you reverence the Holy See, to receive them kindly and treat them well. . . . '

The second Bull was addressed to the Prior and Friars of the Order of Preachers in Béziers, directing them in order to capture the little foxes (i.e. heretics) in Béziers, Narbonne etc., to choose and send out prudent friars zealous for the Faith, who, wherever they might preach, should have power to deprive clerks who defended heresy of their benefices ' and to proceed against them and all others, calling in the aid of the secular arm, if necessary, and restraining opposition, if requisite, with the censures of the Church, *without appeal.*'

Two days later this was confirmed and enlarged by a monition to the Provincial of Toulouse, bidding him to choose out of his friars fit and proper persons ' learned in the law of the Lord,' to conduct within the limits of his province a general Preaching, wherever he deemed it expedient, to which the clergy and people alike were to be summoned. For the more effective discharge of their mission they could call to their aid other discreet persons. They were to examine any reputed heretics, and those who refused to render absolute obedience to the Church were to be proceeded against according to the Statutes. The absolution of those who wished to recant must be granted warily. The preachers were to remain in each station twenty days. To those who attacked heretics and their defenders in their castles and other fortified places the preachers were to render every possible help, and if they were performing a penance, to reduce it by three years.[1]

No ampler powers could be conferred upon any body of men. Not only were the bishops at a stroke deprived of all *final* discipline over their clergy and their flocks (for any offence might be interpreted as heresy), but the bishops themselves and the legates as well as the laity and the monastic orders were swept under the despotism of the inquisitors. They were both police and judges, and their judgment was, with the exception of difficult appeals to Rome, final. They were chosen not by bishop or legate, but by their provincial. The pope however, reserved to himself the right of suspending the Inquisition in any place, as he did in Toulouse (1237), and of hearing appeals against its decisions in cases of special difficulty. Only gradually was the relationship between bishop and inquisitor settled.

As we should expect, and as we shall see, there was thus let loose a poison-gas of suspicion and distrust, of hatred and cruelty, that blasted all peace of mind and asphyxiated all social amity, all family affection, all ecclesiastical unity. It did its deadly work effectually for a time, and it was at least three centuries before the counter-blast of the Reformation swept it all away.

---

[1] Percin, *Mon.* vol. iv, p. 92 ; Ripoll, vol. i, p. 47. The Statutes had been put forth on March 7, 1232.

SOME writers in their admiration for Dominic would ascribe to him whatever credit there may be in being the first to suggest the Inquisition and in being the first Inquisitor. Thus Louis à Peramo states that: 'Dominic opened his mind to the Cistercian Abbot (Arnauld), who was legate in the kingdom of France, about introducing the (or an) Inquisition, and that he, while ordering the matter to be referred to the pope, charged Dominic with the office of the Inquisition; but that after the Lateran Council of A.D. 1216, Dominic was created Inquisitor on the authority of papal letters, a copy of which some authors assert they have seen.'[1] Bernard Gui, in his life of St. Dominic says: 'He filled the office of the Inquisition against the disease of heresy by the authority of the Holy See committed to him in the parts about Toulouse.' The amount of historical accuracy in these and similar statements may be tested by the facts given above. Dominic was appointed head of a mobile force of Preachers, without any inquisitorial or punitive powers. Their official title was neither Dominican nor Inquisitor but Preaching Brother.[2] So Gregory IX in proclaiming the canonization of Dominic and fixing his day on August 4, praises him as 'Pastor et Dux inclytus,' and says that he meritoriously started the new Order of Preachers, but calls neither him nor them 'Inquisitors.' The confirmation of Prouille by Innocent and Honorius was not the inauguration of an authorized world-wide order of Preachers but exclusively of Prouille itself as a convent. The

[1] Lib. 2, tit. i, cap. 1, quoted by Limborch, *Hist. of Inq.* (Amsterdam).
[2] v. *supra*, p. 136.

donation of St. Romans at Toulouse was made to ' Brother Dominic, Prior and Master of the Preachers and his companions present and future,' [1] and contemplated an autonomous community at St. Romans without any supervision from outside. Neither bulls nor donation can be construed into the foundation of a separate order. [2] So in the deed of the conveyance of the Church of St. Mary of Prouille, they are described as ' Preachers delegated to preach against heretics and to drive away heresy,' and Humbert [3] declares that the object of the Order is ' study as a preparation for preaching, and preaching as a means of saving souls.'

But in the atmosphere of that age it was almost inevitable that conversion could only grow out of coercion— that powers of preaching would bring in their train powers of pressure. Frederick II, by the Four Constitutions, which he issued from Padua (1222) allowed the Order of Preachers to go anywhere in the Empire under his special protection. Their persons were to be sacred ; they were to deliver heretics, among whom are mentioned Cathari and Waldenses, to the archbishops, dukes, etc., by whom they were to be retained until they had completed their sentences. It is not clear who were to pronounce the sentences, but authority to arrest and to deliver to trial those suspected of heresy could not fail to increase the importance of the Preachers ; and although these Constitutions did not apply to France, yet the fact that some members of the Order were exercising such powers could not fail indirectly to enhance the position of the Order generally.

At first the Inquisition was only local and confined to such places as Toulouse, Albi, Carcassonne and Agen, [4]

[1] Cartulaire, ii, p. 58.   [2] Jarrett, pp. 65 ff. Guiraud, pp. 80 ff.
[3] ii, 28.   [4] Potthast, 9155.

and of these, Toulouse, on account of its connection with Dominic, the establishment of the first Dominican Monastery and as the metropolis of the county, claimed priority of dignity over the others. It was not until 1255 that this priority was supplanted by that of Paris, when, at the request of Louis IX, the pope elevated the prior of the Order in Paris to be the master-general of France and Toulouse.

Toulouse received its new honours coldly, and the prior hesitated to act. Even when he received a command from the pope three months later (July) to ' elect several learned friars to preach the Cross and proceed against the heretics according to the statutes recently promulgated,' no progress was made. Not indeed that there was no zeal. The two Inquisitors, Peter de Cella and William Arnauld, set about their work with ardour, but it was the ardour of official youth and inexperience, so confident were they in their omnipotence that at the mere announcement of their authority heresy would crumble to dust. The first executions under the Inquisition took place at Toulouse, several heretics of high and low estate being sent to the stake. John, the weaver, was delivered from prison by the people, but was recaptured shortly afterwards and burnt, protesting his orthodoxy. ' I am not a heretic, for I have a wife and children, and eat flesh, and lie and swear, and am a faithful Christian.' But persons of high and low estate retaliated by defending and concealing heretics, and by wounding and killing their persecutors.[1] The Bishop, William de Fauga, and the Inquisitors indeed were of one

---

[1] *Chron. of W. Pelhisse*, p. 90. His point of view may be gathered from the following sentence : ' Eorum nomina non sunt scripta in Libro vitae, sed corpora hic combusta et animae cruciantur in inferno.' (*Chron.* p. 51). See C. Molinier, *Etude de l'Inq.*, who first published Pelhisse's *Chron.* from the MS. in the Library of Carcassonne.

mind, for all were Dominicans, but between them and the
capitouls there was the same antipathy as elsewhere.
The climax came on August 5. Returning from the
service of the canonization of St. Dominic, the bishop was
informed that a matron, dying of fever, was about to be
hereticated. The bishop went to the house. The woman supposed she was talking to the Catharist Bishop of Toulouse,
the mistake was artfully encouraged, and she unfolded to
him all her mind. At the close he said : ' Dismiss all that ;
I am your Bishop of Toulouse,' and ordered her to be burnt
in her bed which was immediately done. The bishop and
his company then returned to the palace for the feast.[1]
Pons of St. Gilles, the prior, went further. The same day
in the evening, in the presence of a huge assembly, he based
a violent harangue on Ecclus. xlviii, *v.* 1, Then stood up
Elias the prophet as fire, and his word burnt as a lamp.'
Turning to all parts of the compass, he shouted several
times : ' From this hour I cut off [2] all heretics and their
supporters, in the name of God and His servant, blessed
Dominic ; and I call upon all catholics fearlessly to bear
witness to the truth.' But the burning of the living in the
morning followed by the oration to the living in the
evening had an effect the reverse of that intended. As at
Narbonne, the populace were infuriated ; they broke open
the prison and released the heretics. The capitouls forbade anyone to provide the preachers with food,[3] and
set guards at the convent gates. At last the capitouls
drove the friars out of the city through throngs of people
mocking and jeering. They went to Carcassonne and
there issued citations to the capitouls to appear before

---

[1] Pelhisse, *Chron.*, pp. 97, 98. Venerunt ad refectionem, et quae
parata erant cum laetitia comederunt, gratias agentes Deo et beato
Dominico.' Aug. 5 was fixed by the Bull from Spoleto, July 13, 1234.
[2] ' Diffido,' a mistake for ' diffindo.'
[3] Doat xxi, f. 160 ; xxx, f. 146.

them, but the latter threatened the bearers of them with death if they did not at once quit the city.[1] On the capitouls defaulting, the bishop of Toulouse who had joined the preachers at Carcassonne excommunicated the city. Raymond the Count, whose interests were wholly self-centred, feared lest these disturbances might be made the ground for questioning his *bona fides*, and to remove all suspicion he issued (1233) statutes reiterating those of the Council of Toulouse.

Driven from Toulouse, William Arnauld and Peter de Cella, undismayed, went far afield, but wherever they went, either together or separately, their attempts to set up the Inquisition only provoked riots, at Niort, Moissac, Montauban, Cahors, Avignonet, Albi.

Clearly the crushing machine was not fulfilling expectations. Gregory, therefore, first of all ordered that for the sake of uniformity in all the proceedings of the Inquisition the compilation of the Decretals drawn up by Raymond de Pennaforte should be universally observed by the preaching friars (September 5, 1234). Six months later he complained that Raymond and the capitouls were not co-operating with the preachers and insisted upon amendment. (March 1235). Some of the preachers themselves were getting slack or afraid, and had sought the peace of Cistercian cloisters. Gregory sternly ordered them to resume their preacher's habit and forbade the Cistercians to receive any friar without the licence of the Apostolic See or a prior of the Preaching Order (June). This was followed by the famous Bull ' *Excommunicamus* ' of November 8, 1235, whereby he excommunicated, anathematized and left to the secular arm all heretics, of whatever name and kind, condemned by the Church, to be punished ' *animadversione*

---

[1] Pelhisse, *Chron.*, pp. 11 ff. MSS. 490 f. 118 b. ff. of Toulouse. Cf. Douais, *Les Sources de l'Inq.*, pp. 89, 96.

debita.' Guilty clergy were first to be degraded from their orders. If any such clergy wished [1] to recant, they were to be thrust into perpetual prison for fitting penance. Credents were to be punished in the same way. Their aiders were to be excommunicated, not to be admitted to any public office, and not to appoint or recommend any to such. Their oath was worthless. They could not inherit any property, or make a will or claim payment of debts. If any were under suspicion and refused to purge themselves of it, they were to be smitten with the sword of anathema, and avoided by all until they had made due satisfaction. A year's contumacy rendered them liable to perpetual imprisonment as actual heretics. Clergy must refuse to give such the sacraments of the Church, or to accept their alms and oblations. Whoever buried such incurred excommunication, from which he could not be absolved, unless he exhumed the body with his own hands. The grave itself was defiled, and no one could ever be buried therein. No layman was to dispute about the Catholic Faith, either privately or publicly, under pain of excommunication. All meeting-places of heretics and all persons who differed from the faithful in speech, life or behaviour were to be notified to the authorities. No son or grandson of heretics or of their supporters was to be admitted to any ecclesiastical office or benefice.

This the pope followed up with a letter to Louis IX, complaining that Raymond, Count of Toulouse, had done nothing to extirpate heretics, but rather had allowed his land to become a refuge for them.[2] He urged the king to compel the count and capitouls to mend their ways.

---

[1] 'Voluerunt,' but Decret. v. 7. 15 and Letters read 'noluerunt'. See De Cauzon's *Hist. de l'Inq.*, vol. i, p. 301, note 4.

[2] Arnauld Dominic, e.g., who had betrayed to the Abbot of St. Sernin the hiding place of seven heretics this year, was killed in his bed.

Things would improve if Raymond went to Jerusalem in the following Spring, and Alfonse, the king's brother and Raymond's son-in-law, took charge of the county. The appeal was fruitless, but the bull remained for further reference.

Meanwhile the heretics could not view these attacks without concern. But where should the timid find safety? In the Pyrenees? Here the law was more severe than in France, for King James with his bishops at the Council of Tarragona (1234) had drawn up certain ' Sanctions '[1] whereby (1) No one was to have the Old or New Testament in the Roman language. (2) No one reputed or suspected to be a heretic was to be admitted to any public office. (3) Houses which had been proved to have hiding places for heretics were to be destroyed if freehold, or to revert to their owners if leasehold. (4) No credent or heretic was to be punished unless condemned as such by the bishop of the place or other ecclesiastic. (5) Anyone knowingly or carelessly permitting a heretic to stay on his land was to lose such land for ever ; the land, if feudal, to revert to its owner : if freehold, to be confiscated to the king and the person's body to be delivered to the king for fitting punishment. (6) In places suspected of heresy, where the bishop thought it expedient, one priest or clerk was to be appointed by the bishop, and two or three laymen by the king or his vicar or bailiff, to search for heretics in their parishes without let or hindrance. Anyone obstructing such search was to be punished as the bishop, with the king's authority, should think fit. (7) Spies[2] on discovering heretics were to take precautions against their escape and denounce them to the archbishop, bishop, or the king's vicar or bailiff. Neglect to do so was to be

[1] Mansi, *Concil.* xxiii. pp. 331, 332 ; cf. pp. 103 ff.
[2] ' Inquisitores ' not in the official sense.

punished with loss of benefice, if a clergyman : by fine, if a layman.

Deterred, therefore, by these Sanctions, many heretics migrated to Lombardy, and here in comparative safety they carried on their services with their ' bishops,' ' perfects ', etc. ; for although Frederick II had put forth his Constitutions (February and March 1232),[1] of which the Bull ' *Excommunicamus* ' was but the papal edition, they were less strictly enforced. Across the frontier there was a constant coming and going, and contact was kept up with the main body in France. Thus a William Fournier [2] set out from Toulouse for Lombardy with five companions, two of them being women. There was a complete chain of heretical stations on the road, at which they were hospitably received. At Pavia for instance, Raymond Mercier, a ' deacon ' of Toulouse, entertained them, and gave Fournier ' heretication.' At another place they met a member of the Roaix family of Toulouse, noted for its adherence to Catharism. William Fournier, however, was not a good specimen of a pilgrim. He tried to serve God and Mammon, combining religious professions with commercial interests. He soon returned to France, and lifted up his heel against those whose bread he had eaten. His depositions were made, April 2, 1237, before William de Bonsolas, sub-prior of the Convent of Preaching Friars at Toulouse, Friar John, a Minorite [3] of Gascony, and certain high dignitaries of the Church, delegates for the Inquisitors, William Arnauld and Peter de Cella, in their enforced absence. Another traitor at Toulouse, whose disclosures

---

[1] Pertz, vol. ii, p. 287 ff.   [2] Cf. p. 130.
[3] This introduction of a Minorite to the bench was made at the suggestion of the Archbishop of Vienne, to temper the severity of Dominicans with the mildness of the Franciscans. Franciscans are also associated with the Preaching Friars in the Inquisition at the request of Raymond VII, Count of Toulouse, April 1243. See Vaissete, vol. viii, p. 1121.

caused the greatest consternation to the heretics, was Raymond Gros, who had been a ' perfect,' more than twenty years before. He alleged against the accused many things which they could not refute, because they could not remember whether they had done them or not. The prisons *available* were insufficient for the numbers that were arrested ; but that does not necessarily imply that the number was large. The count being supine or impotent and the capitouls hostile, the municipal prisons would not be placed at the disposal of the Church; and the only place of incarceration would be the bishop's palace and make-shifts. Those for whom no secure place of detention could be found had to swear that they would not attempt to escape while prison accommodation was being provided ; but as the heretics held all oaths to be wicked, this safe-guard in conjunction with popular opinion was worthless. The capitouls refused the members of the Inquisition the use of the public mills, ovens, or wells, and in every way their lives were made intolerable. Legislation in advance of public opinion was generating a heat which might at any time produce a violent explosion. When a priest tried to stop the giving of the Consolamentum[1] to a lady at Toulouse, the people smashed his windows. Raymond, remembering what had occurred ten years before, grew nervous, and on his petition the pope ordered Raymond, the Dominican Bishop of Toulouse, and the inquisitors to suspend the Inquisition and the execution of its sentences for three months (May 13, 1238).[2]

[1] See vol. i, Index s. v.
[2] Potthast, 10598.

THE amnesty of three months was prolonged to nearly twice the number of years ; but an amnesty is not a Peace Treaty, and heretics were still under the sword of Damocles. The Inquisition in its punitive operations was suspended, not removed, and the friars, gathering strength as controversialists, went about in their original capacity as preachers, refuting heretics and accumulating evidence against them. Moreover these exclusively ecclesiastical tribunals were regarded as a serious encroachment upon the juridical authority of the State. Magistrates were called upon to punish persons condemned upon charges of which they, the magistrates, had no cognizance, and about which they had never been consulted. Even Louis IX resented this, for in 1236 he forbade his subjects to appear before such tribunals ; and if anyone punished such for contumacy, his goods were to be seized, and not released until the sentence had been revoked. Only after the pope, in a historical letter in which flattery and menace were cleverly blended, had assured the king that Charlemagne, Theodosius and Valentinus had always admitted the Church's right to judge heresy,—a right that, so far from dimming the splendour of the throne, enhanced it—and, further that, unless the law was withdrawn within two months, those that originated it would entangle themselves in the net of anathema, did Louis yield. The pope, already an old man when elevated to the popedom in 1227, had been worsted in his struggles with the emperor, and, broken in heart and enfeebled by age, sank into his grave, 1241. An interregnum of two years followed, for his successor, Coelestine IV, died before his consecration.

The aggressiveness of the preachers, the zealousness of the secular powers, the dissatisfaction with the Simon de Montfort settlement of estates, tolls and villeinage, the depraved character of the Bishop of Toulouse, the preoccupation of the pope and king with the preparations for the Palestinian Crusade, the diversion of the united strength of the Church and State in the West to the conquest of the East, all constituted in the eyes of the Albigenses a favourable opportunity to rise against their oppressors. In 1242 they attacked the inquisitors at Avignonet and killed William Arnauld and all his assistants. About thirty men were secretly admitted at dead of night into the castle by a confederate. They burst into a room, known as the Sala of the Count of Toulouse, and murdered all the members of the Inquisition in their beds. They broke open all their boxes and took away all their books and records. Their weapons were crude, one boasting that he had killed some of the party with a stick (*clava lignea*). Peter Roger de Mirapoix asked to have the head of William Arnauld, and was afterwards charged with having converted it into a drinking cup. After the massacre they escaped to Mont-segur.[1] An outbreak at Toulouse also caused the death of six members of the Inquisition. The interregnum in the papacy, however, had postponed the Crusade to the East; and when Louis heard of this revival of heresy, the spirit of the Crusader came upon him and drove him south instead of east. Having exacted the promise [2] of one-twentieth of clerical incomes for his expenses, he marched against the enemies of the Faith at home and attacked Mont-segur, heresy's chief stronghold. An assault in 1238 had been beaten off. Its natural advantages had been strengthened by skilful fortifications. Bertrand Roqua, its

---

[1] Vaissete, viii, p. 1151 ff. (details vary).
[2] M. Paris, p. 527.

chief engineer, was, significantly, a bailiff of the Count of Toulouse ; and its defence was entrusted to Raymond de Perelle, whose daughter had been burnt as a heretic. It was kept well supplied with food, munitions and money, and heretics hastened from all parts to its aid, but all in vain against the army and zeal of the King. A few, including four ' perfects,' escaped by sliding down the rocks upon which it stood. Two hundred and five persons, male and female, were burnt at the foot of the mount, and others were condemned to various punishments (1243). For this revival Raymond, Count of Toulouse, was held responsible, and the redoubtable Ferrier and the disreputable William, Bishop of Toulouse, promptly excommunicated him. But on appeal to the new Pope, Innocent IV, the sentence was as promptly quashed.[1]

A Church at unity with itself was indispensable to the success of that Church's most pressing duty—the conquest of the Holy Land, and to secure this the pope was prepared, not indeed to grant concessions to heresy, but to show clemency to heretics, real or suspected. Raymond had not yet fulfilled his oath to go east to fight for the Cross, but if he were now excommunicated he could neither go himself nor send aid. The pope therefore, issued a bull to all inquisitors in Narbonne and France, ordering that all the heretics of whatever name who had not been condemned, and who returned voluntarily to the unity of the Church, should be received without the imposition of any penalty whatever ; the inquisitors were to publish this everywhere ; a reasonable (*competentem*) time should be set, within which this offer was available ; after which they were to proceed against heretics in the usual way, but with the

---

[1] Potthast, 11390, 11392. Vaissete, viii, 1142. Raymond could justly plead that it was at his request to the Bishops of Toulouse, Agen, Cahors and Rodez, the Inquisition had been revived, and that he had promised his support (April, 1243). *Ibid.*, viii, 1121.

permission of the ordinary. On receiving this mandate, the inquisitors presented themselves at Narbonne, where a Council was held, presided over by the archbishop, but its decisions were less favourable to heretics than the bull. Heretics who surrendered voluntarily were not indeed imprisoned, but had to make their confession publicly at the church door each Sunday, semi-nude, wearing crosses and bearing rods in their hands.[1] In fact the canons of this Council formed the basis for future inquisitorial procedure, although some points were referred to the pope for settlement ; for instance, the granting of absolution and the imposition of penance should be left to the confessor alone. Canon IV ordered that prisons should be built and fully equipped for the accommodation of poor persons convicted of heresy, so that the expense should not fall on the bishop.

The resuscitated activity of the Albigenses aroused a corresponding activity of the Church—an activity which never ceased until the heresy was finally suppressed. But the machinery was far from perfect, and reference was being constantly made to Rome for instructions. And in Innocent IV (1243-1254) is found one of the great legislators of the Inquisition. One of his first acts was to publish his approval of the Twelve Statutes of the Emperor Frederick against heretics, which were as follows : (1) Heaven had entrusted him with the material sword, as distinct from the Priesthood, against the enemies of the Faith and those who insulted the Church (*tanquam materni uteri corrosores*). (2) Those condemned by the Church were to be handed over to the secular arm. (3) If they returned through fear of death they were, according to canonical sanction, to be thrust into perpetual imprisonment to fulfil their penance. (4) Magistrates, etc., were to arrest and keep in strict custody

---

[1] Canon I. Mansi dates this Council A.D. 1235, but probably 1243-1245 is correct. See Vaissete, iii, p. 585 ff.

all those pointed out to them by inquisitors and others zealous for the orthodox Faith until they were damned by the Church. (5) Favourers, etc., of heretics were to be treated in the same way. (6) Those who were convicted of heresy in one place, and who removed to another to propagate it, were to receive the same punishment. (7) If a convicted heretic was at the point of death and abjured his heresy and recovered, and it was found that his abjuration was insincere, then the original sentence of death should be carried out. (8) No appeal against a sentence to be allowed. (9) As blasphemy is worse than treason,—the former being against God, the latter against man,—heirs and successors of heretics and of their aiders and abetters were to be deprived of all temporal benefits, public offices and honours. (10) Provided that children were not followers of their parents' heresy and had disclosed it to the authorities, they were not to be liable to the aforementioned penalties. (11) Inquisitors in the execution of their duties were to receive adequate protection. (12) Heretics were to be detained according to the sentence of the Church. To the Preaching Order had been entrusted the Inquisition, and therefore the priors of the Preaching Order must have authority untrammelled by bishops in the appointment of inquisitors. This Innocent made quite clear at the beginning of his pontificate to the prior of Toulouse, as well as at the end of it, when he even authorized the General to recall those inquisitors, whom the Holy See itself had already nominated, and to substitute others.[1] He saw also the mischief of fanatical Catholicism; within a week of his letter to the prior of Toulouse, he wrote to the bishop of Carcassonne, ordering him to revoke the interdicts which he had laid upon certain places because some individuals therein were merely suspected of heresy.

---

[1] *Layettes*. iii. 4111, 4113.

The Register of Sentences of Bernard de Caux and John de St. Peter (1243–1249) at Toulouse[1] record the condemnation of about 200 persons, of whom 40 were women. The Sentences were pronounced in Acts of Faith, of which there were thirty-seven. Some Acts of Faith comprised a large number of Sentences (e.g. 35 on March 25, 1246). They were held either in the close of the Church of St. Sernin or in the church itself, and sometimes in the town hall. The penalties mentioned in the Register are mostly perpetual imprisonment and confiscation of property. There is one instance of the wearing of the crosses, one of a fine, one of imprisonment for fifteen years (a woman), and one of ten years (a man). There is no instance of the death penalty, but it is incredible that there was none, and perhaps they were recorded in another register now lost.

A curious story was told the inquisitors by Pons Carbonelli, February 21, 1245. One day he received a message that the Count of Toulouse (Raymond VI), wished to dine at his house, the Castle de Faget. Pons at once went home, and found at his door two men, whom he knew to be heretics, cleaning their shoes. He asked them what they wanted, and they replied, 'wait and see.' He ordered them to go away, as he was afraid of the chaplain of the place. They refused, and ordered him to prepare for the count. The next morning the count came with a great number of knights to his house and he entertained them. They then went to a field of the castle where others joined them, and they had a review of their forces, and went on to Lavaur. The count did not see the said heretics, nor eat with them, nor ' adore ' them. About twenty years before he had seen in a field outside Auriac (Haute-Garonne) a heretic preaching, and many soldiers and others were listening to him. His father and mother were both heretics, and he had

[1] *Nat. Lib. Lat.*, MSS. 9992.

himself ' adored' heretics by bending the knee three times and saying ' Benedicite.' He said his father had left the heretics about forty years before. [1] Another noteworthy victim was Alaman de Roaix. [2] He was of noble birth, and members of his family were famous for their support of heresy, and he himself was probably one of their ' bishops '. Condemned for contumacy (January 19, 1248) in the presence of the Bishop of Toulouse, Raymond VII and Peter de Cella, Prior of the Preaching Friars, he existed as a highwayman, and the citizens of Tarrabel and Fourquevaux (Haute-Garonne) admitted that they had supplied him with food and a horse.

Raymond VII died in 1249, the last of the Counts of Toulouse, whose line had existed for exactly four hundred years, the rank having been created by Charles the Bald in 849. Just before he died he caused eight heretics near Agen to be burnt, after they had confessed. By this holocaust he prevented them from lapsing, and himself from suffering the same posthumous indignities from which he had endeavoured in vain to protect his father.

He was succeeded by Alfonse, his son-in-law and brother of the King of France. As Louis himself and his brother Charles had married sisters, daughters of the Count of Provence, the whole of the south of France passed into the power of the French Court, and the silken cord of matrimony strangled whatever of patriotism had vitalized heresy. At the death of Alfonse, the whole of Toulouse and its dependencies were absorbed into the French monarchy. Raymond's lukewarmness and vacillating help for the Church was of indirect assistance to her opponents ; his tenure of the countship kept alive the memory of better days. His death removed the pivot—though now but

---

[1] Vaissete, viii, 1147. For ' adoration ' (*melioramentum*), see vol. i, p. 84.

[2] v. *supra* p. 148.

nominal—of the Albigensian movement, while it cleared the way for the Church to make direct and personally interested appeals to the strongest and most Catholic monarch in Europe, Louis IX.

It would be purposeless and wearisome therefore to endeavour to describe the suppression in the different places where heresy still survived. The Inquisition now attained such cohesion among its several stations and uniformity in procedure that to describe the proceedings of one station would be to describe the proceedings of all. The details of the hundreds of cases recorded may be summarized : the differences were due to the different temperaments of the inquisitors, not to different principles.

BEFORE describing the procedure and penalties of the Inquisition we must endeavour to define the relationship of the office of inquisitor to that of bishop.

It is fundamental to a right understanding of that relationship to bear in mind that the Preaching Order and, still more, the Inquisition which sprang out of it were never intended originally to be permanent parts of Church organization. Preaching against heretics was begun spontaneously by the Bishop of Ozma. At the sight of the wide prevalence of heresy and the impotence of the Church, Diego's heart was hot within him and while he was thus musing the fire kindled, and at last he spake with his tongue. Resignation of his see to devote himself wholly to the eradication of heresy was refused him, and only temporary leave of absence granted him. The crusaders were assembled to destroy the heretics with the sword of steel: the preachers by the sword of the Spirit. The crusaders came with their own officers and owed no obedience to the counts of the south: so the preachers had their own officers and owed no obedience but to the pope. The military and spiritual forces without combined with the military and spiritual forces within, each to each, but there was no subordination of military to military, or spiritual to spiritual. When the conquest had been won the forces which the crisis had called together would disperse, and Church and State resume their normal conditions. The letter in which Gregory IX notified the bishops of the appointment of the preaching friars, bidding them receive them kindly because they (the bishops) could not cope with the emergency,[1] might, *mutatis mutandis*, have been sent by Innocent III to the Catholic counts of the Midi. It was no new experience for bishops to have their diocesan autocracy overruled in times of emergency by papal delegates. The more effectually to discharge their commission the delegates might consult with the local bishops, but were in no respect bound to do so. A legate might be a plenipotentiary, in which case it would be futile to refer the dispute to the pope.

Now the inquisitors were elected from the preaching friars by their provincial prior, and the preaching friars came, as we have seen, to be, through Dominic's insistence, a distinct Order. It was established to meet a certain need, and the importance of its work would rise or fall according to the pressure of that need. That need might vary, but not the authority to meet it. In a tract on ' The Agreement of Bulls '[2] the point is raised whether the Preaching Order is exempt from episcopal jurisdiction, and the answer in the affirmative is based upon (*a*) Constitution II of Honorius III : ' we take the Order and its possessions and rights under our guidance and protection ; ' (*b*) Constitution XXXV of Urban IV : ' All the liberties and immunities conceded by the Roman Pontiffs, our predecessors, we confirm to you and yours by the same authority ; ' (*c*) the endorsement of the same by Clement IV.

It is doubtful, however, whether this independence was implied or perceived by Honorius ; certainly it was not achieved without fluctuation and friction. After all, the office of a bishop—an overseer—is primarily the eradication of error and the dissemination of truth. In this duty every bishop must ' magnify his office ' and to let another take his office is a betrayal of his trust. The pope himself was but a bishop, though, as alleged, the supreme one, and

---

[1] Ripoll, i, p. 47. [2] *Ibid.*, viii, p. 255.

for others not bishops to decide what is heresy might be so interpreted as to invalidate the theory of apostolic succession. Gregory IX ordered his ' beloved sons of the Order of Preachers to pay due and devout obedience to their bishops, saving the institutions of their Order,' but those institutions were important and far-reaching ; for the priors could absolve any excommunicated person who wished to enter their order and labour for the apostolic see, provided that such person compensated the injured party to the satisfaction of the master-general or prior ; only grave offences were to be remitted to the pope. They could hold services during an interdict and grant free sepulture in their churches.[1]

In May, 1232, when the Inquisition was introduced into Aragon, Gregory left its direction to the bishops, commanding them that by themselves, by preaching friars and by others whom they knew to be qualified, they should make diligent search (*perquiratis*) for heretics. In his letter of 1233, commending the friars to the prelates of France, the preachers were to *share* the burden of exterminating heretics with the bishops, but the bishops had nothing to do with their appointment. Gregory, by his mandate of July 15, 1233, ordered the provincial prior to elect several learned friars to proceed against the heretics[2]—a mandate confirmed by Innocent IV, exactly ten years later (July 10, 1243). When the headquarters of the order were removed from Toulouse to Paris, the same Pope (October 24, 1253) authorized the prior of the preaching order at Paris to appoint inquisitors for *all* Poitiers and Toulouse (the domains of Alfonse).[3] Inquisitors sometimes, e.g. Bernard de Caux (1246–1248) issued sentences in absolute independence of a bishop, although theoretically they were not to sit

[1] Ripoll, i, pp. 20, 24, 25.   [2] Potthast, 9263.
[3] *Layettes*, iii, 4111.

alone or impose a penalty without consulting the bishop of
the diocese, and the sentence was to be published in the
bishop's name.[1] The Council of l'Isle (Venaissin) even
declared (1251) that: ' The said inquisition may be made
by any bishop whatsoever (*quolibet*) in his own diocese,
and documents already existing may be called for from
preachers or others who have them,' thus restoring the
bishop to his proper functions.[2] The Register of Carcassonne (1250–1255)[3] exhibits the bishop (William Arnauld)
in that capacity from preliminary inquiry to final sentence.
The Archbishop of Narbonne acted at once in accordance
with the Council of l'Isle, for, the same year, he sat in his
Cathedral Church with a precentor, an abbot, and an
archdeacon, and condemned to perpetual imprisonment
two female heretics.[4] In the following year the Bishops of
Toulouse, Agen, Albi and Carpentras at a council held at
Riom, at which Alphonse presided, only accepted Innocent's
commission to the friars functioning in their respective
dioceses on condition that they proceeded in accordance
with canonical law, and the bishops themselves authorized
two ecclesiastics, who were not friars, to conduct an
inquisition.[5] And even this modified recognition was dis-
regarded by the Council of Albi (1254) which by its first
canon decreed : " The archbishop and bishops shall appoint
at once in each parish one priest and one layman of the place,
of good report, who shall seek out (*inquirant*) heretics by
examining each house, and if they shall find any heretic

---

[1] Potthast, 12743 (July 13, 1254), 15804 (April 15, 1255), 18389
(August 4, 1262) Molinier, *Etude*, pp. 112-116.
[2] Harduin, *Councils*, vii, 433 ; Tanon, p. 178.
[3] Clermont Lib. MSS., 136.   [4] Vaissete, viii, 1272.
[5] *Ibid.*, iii.496. Alfonse, who was no warm admirer of the Inquisition,
issued in June, 1254 a curious ordinance in which he drew up a sort of
plan for persecuting heretics, with a view to submitting it to the pope.
On the back is a design representing a man on his knees, bound to a
stake, with his hands pinioned behind him and delivered to the
flames. Boutaric, *St. Louis et Alphonse de Poitiers*.

they shall with all speed inform the archbishop and bishop and lords of the place that they may receive due punishment '—no preaching friar is mentioned. Seven years before this, the Bishop of Albi, Durand, had obtained special sanction from the pope to exercise inquisitional functions, and drove a thriving trade by selling commutations for confiscations.[1] Yet sometimes the bishop acted in conjunction with the inquisitor, e.g. Nicholas d'Abbeville or his lieutenant, Fulk de St. George.[2] So too did the Bishop of Pamiers, James Fournier (afterwards Benedict XII) with John de Beaune, Inquisitor of Carcassonne.

Even a legate's authority could not override an inquisitor's. Zoën, Bishop of Avignon, on the strength of being appointed a legate, set up an inquisition in the territories over which his legatine commission extended; but on a complaint being lodged by the Inquisitor of Languedoc, the Pope, Alexander IV, promptly stopped him, pointing out that his position as legate gave him no right to act as inquisitor, although, as *bishop*, he might act as inquisitor in his own diocese.

As the provincial with the authority of the pope nominated them, so by the provincial they could be withdrawn, according to the ruling of Innocent IV in 1244, 1248, and 1254, and their commission did not cease with the death of pope or provincial.[3] But during the exercise of their office, they were independent of their provincial, and though Alexander IV exempted them from a liability to be recalled by their provincial, they owed obedience to him as friars, not as inquisitors: ' If perchance a master or minister-general and other priors enjoin you or any one of you to desist from the same business (the inquisition) for

---

[1] Doat xxxv, 83, Potthast, 1274.
[2] Nat. Lib. MSS. lat. 1147.   Vaissete, xiv, 17.
[3] Eymeric *Direct*. Pt. iii qu. 7 and 8.

the time being in respect of certain particulars or persons, we forbid you to obey them ' (Dec. 11, 1260).[1]

A punishment once imposed could not be commuted for another except by mutual agreement of inquisitor and bishop. But sentences were always subject to revision by the pope. Thus Innocent IV permitted Durand, Bishop of Albi, to release certain heretics in his city and diocese condemned to prison by the inquisitors, provided they offered an adequate recompense.[2] Similarly he orders William Raymond and Peter Durand, inquisitors, to absolve William Fort, a citizen of Pamiers : charges the Archbishop of Narbonne to punish six heretics as enjoined by the inquisitors : sets at liberty several heretics whose punishment he considered had been sufficient : orders the Bishop of Albi and the Abbot of Candeuil to re-instate into the communion of the Church John Ferrassa of Albi, and Arsinde his wife, condemned by the notable inquisitor, Ferrier ; orders to be sent back to prison several heretics whom the legate had released against the will of the inquisitors. When the Count of Poitiers [3] complained of the slackness in condemning heretics, living and dead, Innocent extended the jurisdiction of the Bishop of Agen over all the count's territories with a view to his instituting prosecutions therein with the advice of the bishops and inquisitors, and if necessary replacing the supine inquisitors by others more zealous (April 29, 1248).[4] On another occasion he notified the same bishop that he had commissioned the archbishop of Auxerre to commute imprisonment and wearing the cross into personal military service in the Holy Land ; but that as the archbishop could not attend to the matter, he, the bishop, was to do so (April 30, 1248). Louis IX, too, often restored to wives property which had been confiscated from their husbands.[5]

---

[1] Ripoll 1, p. 402. Eymeric *Direct*. Pt. III qu. 2.
[2] Potthast, 12774.   [3] Vaissete, viii, 1241.   [4] Potthast, 12774.
[5] *Ibid.*, 12914, Vaissete vii, 1240 ; Mahul, *Cart. de Carc.*, p. 628.

CHAPTER VI

THE Court of Inquisition might be held with or without notice. A sudden descent upon a town prevented the people from taking concerted measures to outwit it. On the other hand, the proceedings were prolonged, because all the machinery had to be set up, notice of attendance sent to all officials, and accused and accusers summoned. All the inhabitants above fourteen years of age, whether attainted of heresy or not, had to attest their faith before the inquisitor.[1] At first the inquisitor used a town as the centre, and summoned to his tribunal anybody, whether an inhabitant of the town or not; but this procedure the legate, John de Vienne, prohibited.[2] But later, when the lives of the inquisitors were in danger, the Court was set up in some safe place, and refusal to attend however great the distance, was regarded as an admission of guilt. Bernard Gui gives a specimen form of citation: ' Brother . . . Inquisitor . . . to the Chaplain of . . . or his *locum tenens*. By apostolic authority whereby we act, we command you to cite on our behalf such a parishioner of yours: that on such a day at Toulouse at the house of the inquisition next to the Castle of Narbonne he appear personally before us to answer concerning those things which pertain to the Faith and the office of the inquisition. As a sign of our mandate having been received and fulfilled, you shall attach your seal to these presents.' [3]

Whether notified or not, the advent of the inquisition

---

[1] Tardif, *Nouv. Rev. Hist.*, p. 673, Tanon p. 331.
[2] W. de Puy-Laur., 43 ; Potthast, 12766 ; *Layettes* iii, 4111, 4113.
[3] *Practica*, Pt. 1, p. 3.

filled the whole town with consternation. All municipal business was suspended ; all municipal law was subservient to inquisitorial requirements. All barons, counts, bailiffs and other secular officials had taken an oath, renewed every three years, to aid to the uttermost of their power.[1] Negligence was construed as complicity. In every parish a cleric and a layman (sometimes more than one) had been appointed to watch for indications of heresy ; private houses were not secure against search. Discoveries or suspicions were to be reported at once to the bishops.[2] Rewards were given for arrests.[3] No one felt safe. St. Matthew x. 35, 36 was everywhere illustrated, and delators received papal congratulations.[4] A debtor, pressed for payment, would retaliate by accusing his creditor of heresy. By the same channel would a husband or wife seek release from the bonds of matrimony. Fear of being accused engendered counter-accusation as the best means of protection, and thus malice begot mendacity.

The inquisitor was the presiding, not the sole judge. With him sat the bishop and others, ' good and skilful men,' chosen from clergy and laity. The chief official, next to the judges, was the notary, whose full title was : ' by the authority of the Apostolic See, notary public of the office of the Inquisition.'[5] The inquisitor could not *create* a notary, but must appoint one *ad hoc* who was already an

---

[1] *Rec. des ord.*, I, p. 51. Greg. IX. *Decret.* 13, Council of Albi (1254), canon 20.

[2] Long lists of suspects are preserved in the Nat. Lib. MSS. 4269 and 11847.

[3] One mark according to *Rec. des Ord.*, I. p. 50. Renewed in Statutes of Toulouse (1233) and the Council of Albi (1254). Sometimes they were paid in other coin, as when ' Bortha, Knight, hanged two servants who had arrested the mother of a certain Raymond and six other women ' (Lib. of Toulouse MSS. Lat. 155).

[4] Ripoll, 1. p. 56.

[5] Nat. Lib. MSS. Lat. 4269.

official notary either of a bishop, the town, a temporal lord or the king.[1]

The notary might be a cleric, a layman or a monk, provided this last had been a notary before he became a monk. If the Inquisitor could not obtain a notary public, he was to choose two fit persons to act as notaries, and the inquisitor could compel any fit person to act.[2] According to the same pope, notaries could only be excommunicated by the pope. In some respects they acted as a check upon the inquisitor; if the latter, for instance, extorted money or accepted bribes or appropriated to himself goods confiscated from heretics, it was the duty of the notary to inform the pope or the master-general of the order. Notaries of bishops took the oath before the inquisitor, and notaries of the inquisitor before the bishop.[3] His duty was to make and keep a record of all the proceedings of the Court, take down all the questions and answers, whether made with or without torture, at which he had to be present; [4] draw up a précis of the charges, and, at the direction of the Court, supply the accused with a copy: tabulate and index all documents: translate vernacular answers into official Latin: draw up abjurations very carefully, read them to the defendant in the vulgar tongue, who was to repeat them in a loud voice.[5] Under him would be scriveners (*scriptores*) or clerks to make copies, which, however, had to bear his signature as being correct, for sometimes only rough notes would be made at the trial, which would afterwards be put in order and carefully transcribed.

The precincts of the Court would be alive with 'familiars', or bodyguards of the inquisitors; these also acted as

---

[1] Eymeric *Direct.*, Part iii, qu. 18.
[2] *Ibid.*, qu. 19, (quoting letter of Urban IV, 1262).
[3] Eymeric *Direct.*, Part iii, qu. 60.
[4] *Ibid.*, 156 'Quomodo questionatur, de quibus interrogatur, et quomodo respondetur.' [5] *Ibid.* 190.

attendants at autos-da-fé, secret agents and spies, messengers, retainers and servants of all kinds. Their number and expense became so scandalous that Innocent IV ordered them to be reduced to strict requirements (May 12, 1249). The trial might be held in the bishop's house, monastery, church, or other convenient building, but the sentence was always published in church.

According to the order of Peter of Collemezzo, authorized by Innocent IV to be followed throughout Languedoc, [1] the proceedings, as we have seen, opened with a general summons to *all* the inhabitants over fourteen years of age to present themselves and take an oath, under penalties, of abjuration of heresy. Absentees were allowed time to present themselves, after which their citation was published three times in church, or there was one 'peremptory' citation. If this failed to induce a voluntary appearance before the tribunal, persons so cited were excommunicated. If a person's guilt was obvious, or he had avowed heresy, condemnation could follow at once, without the year's grace granted to the contumacious. Goods were confiscated, but returned if the absentee surrendered within the year, but not afterwards. [2] Guarantees up to £100 had to be entered into against contemplated flight. [3]

But taking the oath of orthodoxy, whether before or after formal citation, did not protect a person from definite accusation. Whether the offence alleged were of recent or remote date, time did not efface or affect *pravitas hereticu*. Guilt could be established not only by direct but indirect connection with heresy, even by helping it unwittingly. A heretic could be detected if he (*a*) secretly visited a convicted heretic or had any connection with him ; (*b*) lamented

---

[1] Doat xxxi, 5.

[2] Council of Béziers (1246) Canon XX, Martene and Durand, *Thes.*, V. *Tractatus de Haer. Paup. de Lugd.* (date after 1250).

[3] Clerm. Lib. MSS. 136, Inq. of Carcassonne.

another's punishment; (*c*) complained that another's conviction was unjust; (*d*) frowned at or opposed an inquisitor : (*e*) collected the ashes of a burnt heretic. A woman was dragged before the inquisition because in the pangs of childbirth she cried, not ' O Jesus Christ ' or ' O blessed Virgin ' but ' O Holy Spirit, help me ' ; also a son, because he had given his mother food, who was suspect.[1]

There were what Eymeric calls secret heretics, i.e. those who held error in their mind and were obstinate but did not reveal it in word or deed.[2] Others, according to the same writer, were (*a*) ' affirmative,' i.e., those who held error in their mind and were obstinate and revealed it in word and deed ; (*b*) 'negative ' i.e. those who had been convicted of heresy, but who nevertheless professed the Catholic faith and detested heresy, and, while acknowledging having committed the offences, protested that they did so under compulsion ; (*c*) ' penitent' i.e. those who had once been obstinate of mind, word, deed, or will, but had recanted and abjured heresy, and had satisfied bishop and inquisitor of their genuine repentance, (*d*) ' relapsed ' or ' relapsing ' after abjuration ; (*e*) ' impenitent ', sometimes called ' perfect ' i.e. those who persisted in heresy and modelled their lives upon it. Suspicion was of three degrees : (*a*) ' *levis* ' i.e. mere conjecture ; (*b*) *vehemens*, i.e. strong, where the evidence could be rebutted only by ' great, strong, and forcible arguments ; ' (*c*) ' *violens* ' i.e. very strong, where the evidence ' drives, compels, and forces the judge to a certainty which no shuffling can alter.'[3]

The Council of Narbonne (1243) ruled that ' You shall

---

[1] Doat xxv, 62 Clerm. Lib. MSS. 136.   [2] *v. infra*, p. 171.

[3] Eymeric *Direct.*, Pt. iii. qu. 33 *seq*. Cf. Gerson, ' De protestatione, consideratio 12 : Vehemens suspicio provenit ex signis exterioribus operum vel verborum ex quibus cognitis accipitur argumentum concludens frequenter, et ut in pluribus quod, talia agens vel dicens, est hereticus.'

proceed to the condemnation of no one without clear and distinct (*lucidis et apertis*) proofs, or by confession. For it is better to let a crime go unpunished than to condemn the innocent.'[1] But this principle remained mere theory; there is not a single case of full acquittal in all the two hundred of the Inquisition at Carcassonne.

The accuser might not be available or reliable, but the judge, after secret inquiry, might still order a trial. The accused laboured under two great disadvantages : (*a*) the names of his accusers were not disclosed to him, but only their depositions. 'We do not deviate from common law, except that we do not publish the names of witnesses in accordance with the regulations of the apostolic see made by Pope Gregory and renewed by Innocent.'[2] The reason given for this course was that witnesses might be intimidated, particularly in those places where evidence was most required. Now the great, almost the only, defence, other than an *alibi*, was malice, but the suppression of names of witnesses reduced proof of malice to mere guess-work, and attempts at identifying them entangled the poor wretch more hopelessly than ever in a net of pure conjecture, involving friends as well as foes. A typical case is that of Peter de la Garde who appeared at Villalier before the Bishop of Carcassonne : ' Do you wish to defend yourself against these charges?' ' Yes.' ' Do you wish to have them in writing ?' ' Yes.' ' Have you enemies?' ' Yes.' ' Write down their names.' (He does so). ' Are these *all* your enemies ?' ' No.' ' Then write down the others as well.'[3] Often the charges were purposely vague and

---

[1] Canon III.
[2] ' *Little Manual of the Inquisition*' (1245), *Nouv. Rev. Hist.* (1883), p. 673 by Tardif. There is no record of any such rule by Gregory, but there are two Bulls of Innocent (Ripoll 1, p. 241.) See also Eymeric *Direct*. Pt. ii. p. 81, Bernard Gui, *Practica*, iv, p. 229 (Douais).
[3] Clerm. MSS, 136, Pt. 1. f. 36.

difficult to meet, in order to trap the accused into the dis-
closure of particulars of which neither accuser nor judge knew
anything. Names of alleged witnesses, when given, were
sometimes fictitious or so common as to defy identification.

(*b*) The accused was not allowed an advocate;[1] and,
indeed, it was a thankless as well as a dangerous task.
The more powerful and clever his pleading, the worse for
the Faith, and the worse for himself. In the former case
he might present heresy in such a form as to make it
attractive to catholics ; in the latter, he might show himself such a master of the subject, and so zealous in its
defence as to furnish presumptive evidence of being a
heretic himself. Moreover, he could be forced to disclose
all conversations with his client, and all documents, however
confidential. (*c*) A judge might pretend that he had other
business, and if the examination were not concluded at
once, by the full and frank confession of the accused, the
latter would be detained in prison, and the judge could
not say when he would be at liberty to resume. He would
therefore be satisfied with a simple Yes or No. Or he
might profess sympathy with the accused in his trouble,
and thus gain his confidence and extract a confession.[2]
Neither age, sex, class nor character was allowed to affect
the trustworthiness of the accuser ; children not yet in
their teens,[3] excommunicated criminals, accomplices, gave
evidence by choice or compulsion.[4] All evidence was
written down, read over to the one who gave it, and confirmed by him or her. Every means must be taken to

[1] Council of Albi (1254), Canon XXIII. There is only one instance
of an advocate appearing, viz. in the case of 13 women suspected
of heresy (Doat, xxxiv, 217).

[2] Eymeric *Direct.*, Pt. iii, p. 289, gives Ten Cautions for inquisitors whereby they may counteract probable cavils of heretics. It is
too long to quote, but both cautions and cavils are curious.

[3] After the capture of Mount-segur, a child of ten gave evidence
against his father and sister (Doat xxii, 237 ff.)

[4] *Decretals*, Bk. vi. Ch. 5.

secure a confession—bluff, guile, threats, blandishments, imprisonment (even for many years), torture. ' The foxes are cunning, and must be caught by cunning.' A voluntary recantation, however obtained, was a vindication of the Church, whereas an obstinate defiance was a defeat. Even the confessional was not inviolate against the claims of the inquisition : ' In private confession a heretic must be ordered to accuse his associates, otherwise he is not truly penitent.'[1]

Whatever the pressure brought to bear upon the accused, every abjuration was officially published as voluntary : ' If a heretic refused to recant under threat of death or bonds, he was to be thrust into prison, and frightened by the statement that they (the inquisitors) had witnesses against him, and if he were convicted on *their* evidence, nothing could save him from death.' He was to be kept on scanty food ; none of his friends was to see him, lest they should encourage him ; only, now and again, two trusty and prudent persons, who should pretend to sympathize with him and urge him to avoid death by acknowledging his errors, and should show him what the errors were, and promise that he would not be burnt. They should also coax him to confess that he had put faith in those whom he believed to be ' Good Men ', because others much wiser than himself had done the same and been deceived. Thus softened he might reveal what he had heard from these teachers. ' Then he might be cautiously questioned whether *he* believed their teaching to be good and true ; and if he agreed he thereby confessed himself a heretic.'[2] This ' suspended animation ' might be prolonged indefinitely.[3]

[1]Martene and Durand, *Thes.* V. p. 1802; Mansi. *Concil.* xxiii p. 555; Douais, *Inq.* p. 279.

[2] Martene and Durand, loc. cit.

[3] 'Sic vexati et pluribus annis detenti, confessi fuerunt tandem non solum de novis sed etiam de veteribus et antiquis de xxx annis et de xl et supra.' Bernard Gui, *Practica*, Pt. v, pp. 88, 302.

In the face of the three great disadvantages already mentioned, the facilities which the Inquisition offered the accused to prepare his defence were illusory and even perilous. He was, of course, not allowed to be present when the accuser was giving evidence, for he would then be able to identify him. When brought before the court, the charges were read over to him, and he was asked whether he acknowledged his guilt and would abjure his errors. If so, a confession was drawn up and read to him and publicly repeated when his sentence was pronounced ; e.g. ' This confession of the aforesaid Sychard was recited at Toulouse before the Friar Inquisitors, Bernard de Caux and John de St. Peter, which confession she believed to be true, and agreed that the instrument be made public.' [1]   If he wished to put in a defence, he was released—satisfactory bail being forthcoming,—in order to enable him to prepare counter-evidence, produce witnesses, etc., on a fixed day and at a fixed place. He was also asked whether he wished to have a summary of the depositions made against him. The answer was generally in the affirmative. But the extract was of no help to him, and the Popes, Alexander IV and Gregory X, often rebuked the inquisitors for this unfair treatment. On the day appointed the accused would appear with his rebutting evidence and witnesses, almost invariably declaring that the charges were made not by friends of the Church but by enemies of himself. These he would have to name and give his reasons for naming them. These allegations would require investigation—again in his absence, but the result would not be communicated to him. A third time he would be cited, and asked if he wished to add any further names or produce other evidence. If so, a further postponement would be granted, until the judge was satisfied that no more evidence was forthcoming, for or against. If,

---

[1] Lib. of Toulouse MSS. Lat. 155.

however, the judge believed that facts were being suppressed, or that further inquiry would produce further evidence, the accused was remanded into custody, and there might linger, as we have seen, for many years. Saurine Rigaud confessed at Toulouse in 1254, and following her name in the records is a list of 169 persons incriminated by her, all carefully tabulated with their addresses.

A copy of the four Gospels was placed upon the table of the court, ' so that the judgment might come from the face of God, and our eyes see justice.'

CHAPTER VII

SENTENCES passed at the ' Inquisition ' were announced in the chief church of the city with the most impressive solemnities, in the presence of the highest dignitaries of the Church and State, and a great assembly of the people. Attendance was compulsory, absence bred suspicion and evoked inquiry. The sentence would also be repeated in the church of the parish where the condemned lived. Whether they had faced or fled the trial, they were all excommunicated and excluded not only from ecclesiastical but also secular privileges. To the former a heretic would be indifferent, but the latter cut into all his public and private affairs. He could hold no public office, could make no wills, receive no legacy, sign no document, make no affidavit. He was an outlaw of Church and State, and so far as the latter was concerned, this ostracism was entailed upon his children and grandchildren.

Of the penalties, some, e.g. the crosses and the pilgrimages, were inflicted and supervised by the Church : others, e.g. death, by the State : others again, e.g. imprisonment, torture and confiscation, partly by the Church and partly by the State.

A. The Crosses and Pilgrimages

Imposed with or without flagellation. The Decrees of Toulouse (1229), after the example of Dominic, had prescribed the wearing of the crosses for all who had voluntarily abandoned heresy—a mild inconvenience which proved most irksome. This insistence of Council after Council [1]

---

[1] Statutes of Raymond, 1234, Councils of Béziers (Canon IV), 1234 and (Canon XXVI), 1246, Narbonne (Canon I), 1244, Albi, 1254 (Mansi. *Concil.* xxiii).

proves how vexatious the wearers found it. The penitent
had to wear two crosses, one on the breast and the other
on the back, of a colour different from that of his clothes.
If he had been a ' vested ' i.e. ' perfect ' heretic, he was to
wear a third on hood or veil, of good size, and of the same
colour as the others. If he had forsworn or caused others
to forswear, he was to wear on the upper part of the two
crosses a transverse arm.[1] Wearing the crosses, the penitent
was to appear in Church every Sunday, and being stripped,
so far as the season of the year allowed, submit himself to
be beaten publicly by the priest celebrating Mass, between
the epistle and the gospel. He was to do the same in
every solemn procession. The crosses were to be yellow
and the clothes black. Any one concealing or not wearing
the crosses privately and publicly was regarded as a
relapsed, and punished accordingly. A workman who had to
work in his shirtsleeves had to wear them on his shirt, under
penalty of perpetual and ' strict ' prison.[2] But often no
one would employ a crucifer workman, and no man would
marry a girl who was or had been so marked.

So heavily did this, the lightest of all penalties apparent-
ly, weigh upon some, that attempts were made by bribery
to have the crosses removed. We find the following among
the depositions of the Inquisition at Carcassonne : (i) June
9, 1256. Willemetta Bonet swore that she had given three
geese to Berengaria, wife of Morlano, who promised that
she would do her best to have the crosses removed by the
lord bishop. Perhaps Willemetta was moved to bribe
Berengaria by the experience of B. Laissac, who the
same day swore that when the bishop had released him
from the crosses on the previous Palm Sunday, R.
D' Alzan, a monk, asked him for twenty solidi, on the ground

---

[1] Council of Béziers (1246) Canon XXVI, an expansion of Canon I
of the Council of Narbonne.
[2] v. sub, ' Imprisonment.'

that he had helped in this relief, and he gave D'Alzan the money.[1] (ii) April 10, 1257. Bernard de la Tours, a knight said that Raymond Sabatier begged him, knowing that he was the father of the bishop, to intercede for him to be excused wearing the crosses, promising him one hundred solidi (Melgor), and six pence a year as homage for ever. He did his best but failed. He received some of the money and returned some. He said the sacristan, the archdeacon and the precentor of St. Nazaire (Cathedral) urged upon the bishop the same thing, but failed. [2] (iii) At the instance of the Abbot of Montolieu, Raymonde, the wife of Raymond Morel, was excused for a time from wearing the crosses. In gratitude for this concession the husband alleged (on the same day as Willemetta) that he had bought for ten solidi some stone properly shaped to make a doorway which he had given to William Jordan, the abbot's nephew. [3]

Any one molesting a cross-bearer rendered himself liable to suffer the same punishment. A crossbearer was even to be welcomed, because, like Cain, he was under the protection of the Church, fulfilling the Church's penance, and advertizing the Church's authority. [4] There was a sardonic element in this form of punishment. The crusaders took the cross voluntarily ; the heretics compulsorily. To the former it was an honour, to the latter a dishonour. The crusaders thought to uphold the Cross, the heretics to destroy it.[5] Yet a door was opened by which the penitent could pass from a heretical crucifer to a catholic crucifer. Any one could prove the genuineness of his ' conversion ' by taking the great pilgrimage to the Holy Land, and fight against the enemies of the Cross there. Others, in order

---

[1] Clerm. Lib. MSS. 136, f. 38. [2] *Ibid.*, f. 37.
[3] *Ibid.*, f. 38. Fifty solidi (Melgor),=one silver mark. See Ducange sub *Moneta*.
[4] Doat, xxi, 185. [5] Vol. i, pp. 37, etc.

that the degradation might not be mitigated by their living
quietly in an obscure district among friends and neighbours
with whom familiarity with their appearance would breed
indifference or even sympathy, were ordered to go on the
major or minor pilgrimage wearing their crosses. This
would involve the separation of the penitent from his family
for months or years, perhaps for ever, and plunge him and
them into grief and poverty. The minor pilgrimages were
to St. James of Compostella, Rome, St. Thomas of
Canterbury and the Three Kings of Cologne, besides places
in France. Persons were given eight days to start on the
minor, and fifteen days to start on the major pilgrimage.
Even married women were sentenced to these pilgrimages.
Sometimes money was accepted in commutation. Bernard
de Martres and his wife gave ten solidi for their release
(April 9, 1255), and G. Roqua fifty solidi, because old age
prevented him from fulfilling his pilgrimage (April 27,
1256). On the other hand, bribes were sometines refused.
Peter Barte and Bernard Saissac deposed, on June 9, 1256,
that they had offered a certain sum to the Abbot of
Montolieu to have them excused the pilgrimage to which
the Inquisition had condemned them. But the Abbot
declined the money. They affirmed that they then gave it
to the abbot's nephew.[1]

A person might be sentenced to a minor pilgrimage even
for the accidental, unavoidable or involuntary association
with heretics. A man on a boat met and spoke with certain
Waldenses and heretics, but when he heard their opinions
he left them. For this Peter de Cella sentenced him to the
pilgrimage of St. James.[2]

A person who had fulfilled this penance of the cross was
liable to have it re-imposed for any fresh offence. Berengar
d'Arzens was ordered at the Inquisition of Carcassonne on

[1] Clerm. Lib. MSS. 136 f. 38. v. p 176.   [2] Doat, xxi, 230.

St. Luke's Day, 1254, to *resume* the crosses because he had refused to help in the arrest of a fellow-citizen in the market-square of Limoges, when called upon by the magistrates to do so, well knowing that the said citizen was a fugitive heretic. Sometimes, as an act of clemency, perpetual imprisonment would be commuted to perpetual cross-bearing, and sometimes cross-bearing was allowed as a temporary substitute for imprisonment. Thus Raymond Sabatier,[1] condemned to prison, was permitted to wear the crosses instead, in order to look after his father, ill and poor, but a catholic. At his father's death he was to go back to prison.[2]

The cross was sometimes inflicted in cases of doubt. William de la Broue, Archbishop of Narbonne (1245–57), ruled that if a person claimed to have confessed his heresy to another inquisitor, but could not prove it, he was to be detained, and if reported for or suspected of heresy, and there was no evidence that he had submitted to penance, confession must be extorted by ' hard ' prison and bare food, since it was to be presumed that he was concealing the truth. If this failed, he was to be sentenced to perpetual imprisonment or wearing the crosses according to the discretion of the inquisitor. Lapse of time was not to weigh with the production of evidence or infliction of the sentence.

B. IMPRISONMENT

In passing from crosses and pilgrimages, we pass theoretically from ecclesiastical to secular penalties. The condemned were handed over by the Church to the secular power with the condition that ' in its judgment and sentence

---

[1] v. p. 176.

[2] A wily fellow ! he gets out of prison because his father is ill and poor, yet he can offer a considerable sum of money to get out of wearing the crosses, because the sight would worry his catholic father !

it avoids death and mutilation, so far as the canonical Sanctions advise.' [1]

Short of the extreme penalty was placed imprisonment, either temporary or perpetual : the former was very seldom ordered, and it was nearly always indefinite.[2] The prison might be episcopal, but this implied no shortening of the secular arm, for bishops were often barons, and, as such, had their prisons either apart from or in their palaces.

Perpetual imprisonment was inflicted upon credents and associates and helpers of persons excommunicated.[3] Imprisonment was either ' wide' or ' hard', the former being for those who had failed to abjure within the time of grace, the latter for those who had relapsed or connived at heresy, or had recanted only under fear of death. The former was little more than detention, and prisoners were allowed to associate with one another, and even to receive visits and food from friends. Husband and wife were not denied each other.[4]

These privileges, however, led to a relaxation of discipline which had to be corrected. A curious light is thrown upon the condition of prison life by the injunctions which the Inquisitor of Carcassonne and Albi, John Garland, laid upon Ralph, the gaoler, and his wife Bernarde. They were

---

[1] Limborch, *Lib. Sent.* p. 388 ; de Cauzon (*Hist. de l'Inquis. en France,* vol. II, pp. 284 ff) discusses this recommendation, and concludes, against Douais (' *Inquisition* ' pp. 263 ff.), that ' if the secular arm *had* stopped short of death or mutilation, excommunication would quickly have dispelled its naïveté.'

[2] Of over 200 sentences by Bernard de Caux and John de St. Peter, between 1246 and 1248, only two were for definite periods—15 and 10 years. (Lib. of Toulouse MSS lat. 9992.)

[3] The usual form of sentence was : ' ad peragendam condignam penitentiam in perpetuum carcerem retrudi volumus et precipimus ibidem commorari.' Inquisitors also had their prisons either in their own houses or a separate building, for either temporary detention or perpetual imprisonment (Eymeric *Direct.* Part. II qu. 59).

[4] Sit . . . liber accessus uxoris ad virum immuratum et e converso, ne cohabitatio denegatur eisdem, sive ambo immurati fuerint, sive alter.' Council of Béziers (1246) Can. XXV.

forbidden upon oath to have in future any scrivener or
horses in the prison, or receive any gift from a prisoner.   If
a prisoner died, they were not to keep his money or anything that was his, but to tell the inquisitors at once.   They
were not to take out of his cell any of the '*incarcerati et
inclusi*', [i.e. those undergoing the most rigorous kind of
confinement, and for no cause whatever were they to take
the '*immurati*' beyond the first wall of the prison.   They
were not to eat with the prisoners, or join in or help their
games in any way.   They were not to employ on their own
business servitors who had been assigned to other persons,
or send them to another place without the special
permission of the inquisitor.   Penalty : instant dismissal.[1]

Still with all their endeavours to make the best of their
slender resources, the poor food, the cold, the hard ground
for a bed, the hope deferred that maketh the heart sick, the
anxiety as to home affairs, the lack of news in those cases
where the prison was unknown to their relatives and
friends—all this must have made their existence a misery.

But *perpetual* imprisonment was worse.   Solitude, starvation, disease, fetters, frequent examinations, sometimes
torture and threats of it, threats of death by burning, all with
a view to force them to incriminate others on the promise
of relief for themselves, sometimes proved too severe a
strain for flesh and blood, and either robbed the stake of a
victim or a friend of his life or liberty.   At Albi and
Cordes ' many died owing to the small cells, scanty bedding,
starvation and savage torments,' [2]   The cardinals whom
Clement V had sent to make inquiries found *some* in fetters
and *all* in very narrow and dark dungeons.[3]   Some tried

---

[1] Doat, xxxii, 125.   [2] Doat, xxxiv, 4.
[3] *Ibid.*, xxx. 34.   Therefore no improvement in half a century upon
their condition as described in the Annals of St. Louis : ' In aliis
domunculis sunt miseri commorantes in compedibus tam ligneis
quam ferreis, nec se movere possunt, sed subtus se egerunt atque
mingunt, nec jacere possunt nisi resupini in terra frigida et in hujus-

to commit suicide by the only means available—a hunger strike. Thus in October 1309, Amiel de Perles, a well-known Catharist, tried this as soon as he was arrested ; and Peter Raymond did the same the following year. At the sight of the stake he had recanted, but on being taken back to prison he recovered his fortitude and declared that he had lived and would die a Catharist. In each case the Catholic Faith was vindicated by holding the auto-da-fé on a date earlier than the one fixed, and both were burnt at the stake.[1]

A nun of the Convent of Lespinasse in the Diocese of Toulouse, convicted of having seen and worshipped [2] several heretics, listened to their preaching, given shelter and alms to Waldenses, believed them to be ' Good Men,' and denied the Truth contrary to her oath, was condemned to strictly solitary confinement in a small room within the convent ; necessaries were to be passed to her from outside through a little window ; no one was to visit her. The prioress was ordered to see the penalties carried out.[3]

Detention pending inquiries often lengthened into perpetual imprisonment, not as a result of such inquiries, but because the inquisitors were too busy elsewhere, and the case was forgotten. Ten such prisoners at Albi, who had languished in prison eight years, appealed to the pope to be condemned or acquitted. An even more scandalous case was that of William Salavert of Cordes who was remanded into custody for further inquiries in 1300. Not until nineteen years afterwards was he brought before the inquisitors, Bishop Béraud de Forgues and John de Beaune.

---

modi tormentis nocte dieque longis temporibus quotidie perseverant. In aliis vero carcerum locis degentibus, non solum et aer subtrahitur, sed et victus, excepto pane doloris et aqua, quae etiam rarissime ministratur.'
[1] Limborch, *Sentences*, 178–9, 350–1.   [2] vol. i, p. 84.
[3] Nat. Lib. MSS. Lat. 9992 f. 6a.

No fresh evidence was brought against him; the depositions which he had made under torture when remanded he confirmed; he had not relapsed during his long incarceration. But the nineteen years counted nothing in his favour. He was released indeed, but ordered to wear the crosses, and go on certain pilgrimages—a sentence which might have been imposed at first.[1] William Garne was in prison for nearly forty years (1283–1321) on a charge, not conviction, of conspiring to burn the archives of Carcassonne.[2] Many, of course, died in prison uncondemned.

The horrors of this lingering death were so great that sometimes the inquisitors would exercise their discretion and commute it for some other punishment, temporarily, or permanently. Thus the Council of Béziers, (1246) by canon XX ordered: ' The punishment (or penance) of perpetual imprisonment, with the indulgence of the lord pope committed to you in this matter, you may (*poteritis*) mitigate or commute, on the advice of the prelates to whose jurisdiction they are subject.' [3]

Besides appeal to the pope for revision of sentences, appeal was made to the supreme *secular* power. Reynold de Chartres and John de St. Peter, inquisitors, wrote to Alfonse, Count of Poitiers, that under their predecessors the secular arm had burnt certain heretics who had only been condemned to perpetual imprisonment, and such predecessors had made no protest against it. They themselves, however, did protest and had put the facts before the pope for his instructions. Meanwhile they refused to hand over to the secular arm for burning those heretics detained in their prisons, although such refusal might be regarded as favouring heresy and might even destroy the Inquisition itself (1257). Sometimes temporary release was granted a

---

[1] Nat. Lib. MSS. 11847 f. 45 ; Limborch, p. 228.
[2] *Ibid.*, pp. 282–285.
[3] Cf. also Canon xxii and Council of Narbonne (1244) Canon vii.

prisoner on condition that he or she acted as a decoy. On these terms Alazais de Cavanac was let out on furlough from September 3, 1250 to All Saints' Day. Under sentence of death, Arnauld Dominic was respited on promising to arrest eleven heretics. He succeeded in capturing seven, but the others escaped. For this, Arnauld was given his liberty, but soon lost his life, for he was killed in his bed by the friends of those whom he had captured.[1]

But ' quis custodiet ipsos custodes ? ' The power that received appeals *from* inquisitors could also receive appeals *against* inquisitors. The King of France (1291) ordered his seneschal to inquire into complaints made against the inquisitors at Carcassonne for illegal arrests, and, ten years later, against the inquisitor at Toulouse. To correct the many abuses (*fraudes*) of prison management Clement V at the Council of Vienne [2] ordered that the prison should be common to bishop and inquisitor : that there should be two principal gaolers, ' discreet, industrious, trustworthy,' one appointed and paid by the bishop, and the other by the inquisitor. Each gaoler should be provided with a key, and have under him a good and faithful servant. But Bernard Gui, inquisitor, by no means approved of this moderating policy.[3]

It is a relief to come across even a few instances where the suspect was allowed to report himself instead of being detained in prison indefinitely. One suspect was ordered to stand at the door of the inquisitor's house from the breakfast to the dinner hour, and not to leave without the inquisitor's permission.[4]

Another was confined to his house, and another was allowed to move about his town.[5] Another could go

---

[1] Pelhisse, *Chron.* p. 98.
[2] Quoted by Eymeric, *Direct*. Pt. II. p. 70. These regulations were made in response to complaints made by the consuls of Albi and Cordes, 1305.
[3] *Practica*, p. 174.   [4] *Ibid.*, p. 302.   [5] Clerm. Lib. MSS. 136.

anywhere during the day, but had to return to prison at night.[1]

C. TORTURE

Only gradually has the Church come to see the futility of torture as a means to get at the truth. Even St. Augustine approved of torture for heretics—except Manichees, perhaps because he had been a Manichee himself. It is uncertain whether torture is forbidden by Canon Law, for the meaning of the word 'questio' is disputed. Gratian says : (*a*) 'You must not begin a trial with questions.'[2] This is a quotation from a letter of Gregory VII in which 'questionibus' is given as an equivalent for 'questibus.' But 'questio' certainly means 'torture' in Canon Law itself and mediæval Latin. (*b*) 'We have also given command to the judges to place the criminal (*iniquum*) under questions in reason, even binding him with chains if expedient, so that he may be compelled to pay the money.' This is a quotation from a letter of Alexander III, and the meaning of 'tortures' for 'questionibus' is borne out by the letter itself written to the Archbishop of Sens and the Bishop of Paris, in which 'questionibus' is emphasized by the addition 'duris'.[3] Canon Law distrusted rather than absolutely prohibited it : 'Confession ought not to be extorted but rather spontaneous. For it is a very bad thing to judge any one on suspicion or an extorted confession.'[4] Unfortunately for her good name the Church did not persevere in this 'more excellent way,' but, to use her favourite description of a relapsed heretic, 'returned as a dog to his vomit.' Yet not at first, and not, in the Suppression of the Albigensian Heresy, to the extent of the Spanish Inquisition. Not until 1252—twenty years after the foundation

---

[1] Doat, xxii. 172.   [2] *Tit.* xv. qu. vi. cap. 1.
[3] Mansi *Concil.* xxii. 441. See Tanon, p 366.
[4] Grat. *Decret.* xv. qu. vi cap. 1. See de Cauzon's *Hist. de l'Inq.*, vol. ii, pp. 229 ff.

of the Inquisition—do we find torture explicitly ordered, although we meet with isolated instances before that date. In 1243, Arnauld Bordeler de Lauzete was put to the rack, but said nothing, neither could anything be tortured (*extorqueri*) out of him.[1] These exceptions were legalized by Innocent IV in his famous Bull ' *Ad extirpanda* ' (May 15, 1252) which, together with the Constitutions of Frederick II, formed part of the ' standing orders ' in all statute books for the universal guidance of inquisitors.[2] ' Let the podesta or Rector be bound to force all heretics whom he holds as prisoners, excepting the loss of a limb or danger of death, being in fact robbers and murderers of souls and stealers of God's Sacraments and of the Christian Faith, to confess plainly their errors, accuse the heretics of their acquaintance, and disclose their goods, whether credents, receivers, or defenders, just as thieves and robbers of material things are forced to disclose their accomplices and to confess their wicked deeds.'[3] This was confirmed by Alexander IV (1259) and Clement IV (1265). Torture is very seldom mentioned in the Registers, the explanation being, not that it was seldom inflicted but that the notary was less interested in the *means* of obtaining avowals than in the avowals themselves, which outside the torture chamber were recorded as having been made spontaneously. ' William Agassa confessed the aforesaid spontaneously,' although it is expressly stated that he had made the confession ' after he had been put to the torture ' (*tormento*).

---

[1] Doat xxii. 7.

[2] By these Constitutions (1224) every heretic in *Lombardy*, of whatever name, was, when convicted, to be burnt, or if his miserable life was spared as a warning to others, his tongue was to be cut out, because he had not feared to speak against the Faith and God (Pertz, *Leges*, vol ii, p. 252. See also pp. 284, 287).

[3] Volumus . . . ut statuta nostra et alia ecclesiastica et secularia et constitutiones etiam quondam Frederici Romanorum imperatoris, tunc in devotione ecclesiae persistentes edita . . . observari faciant et observent '—Bull, ' *Ad extirpanda.*'

Bernard Gui in his *Practica*,[1] which was the inquisitor's text-book in the later stages of the Suppression and embodied the earlier papal and conciliar rulings, quotes the above bull almost verbatim, but uses the expression '*per quaestionum tormenta*'; and this makes clearer his direction later on : ' such a man shall be (*poterit*) limited or restricted in food or otherwise, in prison or chains or even be tortured (*quaestionari*) with the advice of skilled persons . . . that the truth may be got out (*eruatur*).[2] '*Questio*' had already reverted to its Ciceronian signification of 'torture' even though Eymeric declared that it must be moderate and without effusion of blood.   Youths and old men were to be tortured lightly ; a pregnant woman was to be threatened with torture, but not put to it.

The Register of Bernard de Caux contains only one allusion to torture, and that a doubtful one ; ' All which things having sworn to, he had often denied before us, and afterwards by fear of having them proved (or being made to prove them—*motu probationis*) he acknowledged all the aforesaid things to be true.' (September 7, 1244).[3]

There is no trace of torture in the Inquisition of Carcassonne (1250–1258), and only one in the Inquisition of Toulouse under B. Gui, but this was because it hindered the expeditious execution of the inquisitor's office [4] : ' He (William) confessed the aforesaid, and when placed in judgment before the inquisitor, the notary and " religious "

---

[1] p. 218.
[2] *Ibid.*, p. 284.   In view of these extracts and the fact that Gui resented any modification of torture by papal bulls, it is strange that Bp. Douais should state that Gui is silent on the question of torture. There is only one instance at his Inquisition at Toulouse, but he regards it as an established practice (*Practica*, iv., p. 174).   So also Eymeric, whose *Directorium*, Part III qu, 61 gives special regulations and discusses the signs of the sufficiency of torture.   See also *Scholion*, Part III. 108 of Pegna.
[3] Nat. Lib. MSS lat. 9992 f. 7
[4] *Limborch*, p. 266. *Practica* iv. p. 74.

witnesses, without proceeding to questions and torments. To this confession he adhered for a long time until a violent agitation was kindled by the heretics against B. de Castanet, Bishop of Albi, of happy memory, and William de Morieres, Inquisitor; and then the said William, as well as some others, began to withdraw and vary what he had confessed and to deny that he had confessed anything about heresy, except under compulsion of tortures.' The Register in which there is most frequent reference to torture is that of Geoffery d'Ablis.[1] Specially examined as to her having been submitted to the torture, a woman n 1273 denied that she had even been threatened with it. William de la Broue, Archbishop of Narbonne (1245–1257), instructed inquisitors that, if persons were suspected or reported for heresy, confession must be extorted from them by ' hard ' prison and limited food (*vitam*) according to the rank (*qualitatem*) of the persons, but there is no mention of torture. But whatever obscurity shrouds the torture chamber in the middle of the thirteenth century, none hangs over it at the end. Protests poured in upon pope and king, not only against the cruelty of tortures but against their futility, in that, instead of extracting truth, they extracted falsehood, and thus defeated the very object of their infliction. The Seneschal of Carcassonne wrote to Philip the Fair (1297): ' We are informed by several trustworthy persons that inquisitors punish the innocent and imprison them. . . . and by certain *tortures lately invented* extort many lies about respectable persons, living and dead, and worthy of every confidence.' The king put a stop to what he described as ' impious and utterly inhuman crimes, hateful and horrible procedure by seizures, questions and unthinkable torments.' [2]   Clement V sent two cardinals to

---

[1] Nat. Lib. MSS lat. 4269.
[2] Doat, xxxii, 266 ; xxx, 68.   Vaissete, x, p. 379.

Carcassonne and Bordeaux to inquire into similar complaints and found them justified.[1]   Bernard de Castanet, Bishop of Albi (1275–1308), and William de Morieres, were inquisitors charged with extracting confessions ' by force of torments ', because in 1318 in the inquisition at Albi, Isarn Colli before the bishop and the inquisitor, John de Beaune, withdrew the avowals he had made in 1302–1304 before their predecessors on the ground that he had made them under torture.   The Council of Vienne (1311) ordered [2] that torture must have the sanction of the bishop, and both the bishop and the inquisitor must be present at the torture, thus taking it as established and legal.   The right conclusion, therefore, seems to be that at first torture was rare : that the only form mentioned is the *eculeus* or rack, as avoiding effusion of blood ; that even after Innocent IV legalized it, resort to it depended upon inquisitor or bishop : that towards the end of the century and onwards it became general and systematic, and so cruel that both Rome and Paris intervened for its restriction, though not abolition.

Strictly speaking, a person could only be tortured once, but it was craftily argued that continuation is not repetition. ' If after being properly (*decenter*) tortured, he is unwilling to confess the truth, other kinds of torments shall be exposed to his sight, by saying that he would have to go through all of them unless he revealed the truth ; and if then he would not, he should be consigned to the terror of and the actual torment on the second or third day, for con- tinuing, not repeating, the torments, since they ought not to be repeated unless new evidence against him arise, then they can be and are not prohibited from being continued.' [3] Witnesses might be exposed to torture.   It was admitted

[1] 'Adeo gravantur, et hac tenus sunt gravati, carceris angustia, lectorum inedia et victualium penuria et saevitia tormentorum quod reddere spiritum sunt coacti.'   (Doat, xxx, 4 ; xxv, 34, 68.)
[2] *Multorum*, Ch. I.
[3] Eymeric, p. 69. Part III, qu. 61.

that there was no express law to justify this, but it was argued it was within common law. There is no instance of this in the Registers, but Eymeric [1] declares that he saw such a sentence carried out at Toulouse where a father gave evidence against his son but afterwards withdrew it.

D. DEATH

The terrible fate of being burnt at the stake was reserved for those who obstinately resisted all methods, fair and fierce, to renounce their heresy, or for those recidivists whose repeated recantations were regarded as worthless. Not until the middle of the thirteenth century do we find in France this punishment *specified* in the committals to the secular arm, although it was always regarded as permissible, and we have seen a Bishop of Toulouse order a heretic to be burnt summarily without trial. [2] The *Book of Justice* (1260) speaks of putting a heretic to death without specifying the method ; but the Etablissements of Louis IX are plain ; for the LXXVth of them orders that any one suspected of heresy is to be sent to the bishop, and, if found guilty, is to be burnt and his goods given to the baron. [3] This confiscation of goods tempted both ecclesiastical and secular powers to do away with the owner. Possible release from even ' perpetual imprisonment' would start vexatious endeavours to recover the forfeited property ; detention in prison spelt continuous drain upon the confiscated property which was charged with the maintenance of the prison, or upon the resources of bishop or baron. It was therefore to the material interests of both that the number of the condemned should be large,

---

[1] Eymeric, Part III, qu. 73.   [2] p. 144.
[3] De Cauzon, vol. i, p. 310. The letter of Innocent III to the Magistrates of Viterbo (Epp. ii, 1) in which he says heretics ' ecclesiastica debent destructione praecidi ' *may* mean nothing more than excommunication, but the analogy he draws between heresy and treason gives a strong suspicion of the death penalty.

but that the number should be reduced by death as soon as possible. Hence complaints that many had been burnt who had been sentenced only to imprisonment.

We have already seen that during the War of Suppression hundreds of heretics were burnt, but this was by sentence of military courts. Deaths by sentence of inquisitional courts were much less numerous ; and this is true even of the most zealous inquisitors. Bernard Gui was Inquisitor of Toulouse from January 16, 1307 to the end of 1323. During these seventeen years he pronounced 930 sentences, according to the Register of the Inquisition of Toulouse, but the number of individual sentences was less than 700, 170 being mentioned twice, and eighty-five thrice. The number condemned to the fire was 114, and not ' more than 630 ' as Molinier states.[1] Of these 114 seventy-four were exhumed, and of the remaining forty who were burnt alive, nine were impenitent, and thirty-one had relapsed.[2] At an auto-da-fé held at Toulouse from Sunday, April 5th, to Thursday, the 9th, 1310, Gui sentenced twenty-five to wear the crosses and go on pilgrimage, sixty-five to perpetual imprisonment, of whom three were to be put in chains, and eighteen were to be burnt. Exactly two years later the same inquisitor sentenced fifty-one to wear the crosses, eighty-six to perpetual imprisonment, ten who had died during trials to have their properties confiscated, thirty-six to have their bones exhumed and burnt, five to be imprisoned for contumacy as soon as they could be arrested, and only five to be burnt. The earlier Register of Bernard de Caux shows no case of burning, but it does not follow there was none, for he had the reputation of being very severe, and the Register is confined to the contumacious and penitent.

---

[1] *Inq. dans le Midi*, p. 207.
[2] By the Council of Narbonne (1244) Canon XI, relapsed were to be put to death even after they had recanted.

It was not to the *spiritual* credit of the Church that a heretic should be put to death. ' While there is life there is hope ; ' and the Church hoped that the terrors, direct and indirect, of incarceration or the very sight of the stake, would bring about the ' conversion ' of the soul.[1] But the public cremation of a defiant heretic was an admission and an advertisement of the Church's impotence. As the sentences were published in the largest church, so the executions were carried out in the largest space, where, before the secular arm put the torch to the faggots, a Sermon (which often gave its name to the whole ceremony) was preached to the vast assembly, justifying the penalty, and warning the spectators ' lest any man fall after the same example of unbelief.'

Why was not a heretic despatched by a more expeditious and humane method ? The answer is that the Church must destroy not only the life but the body of a heretic. Any other means would have necessitated burial, and the dead heretic would contaminate the dead saint. Hence the exhumation and cremation of the remains of a discovered heretic, even after many years since the interment. If heresy was to be destroyed, every vestige of the heretic must be destroyed also. An exhumation was not only a public insult to the memory of the heretic, it was also the removal of a clandestine insult to the memory of the saints. It signified that in death he had not escaped the penalty to which he was liable in life. In 1236, the Inquisitors, Peter de Cella and William Arnauld, on the evidence of only one witness, and him an Italian, condemned a large number of persons dead and living. The dead were exhumed and their putrid remains were dragged through the streets and at the crossroads, preceded by a town-crier with a trumpet

---

[1] Stephanie de Proaudo recanted ' when she saw the punishment of the fire prepared for her.' Limborch, *Sentences of Toulouse*.

shouting : ' qui aytal fara aytal perira.' [1] (A like fate for like offenders). The bodies were burnt in the presence of the Count of Toulouse. The Seneschal of Carcassonne (1270) ordered the bodies of several heretics to be handed over to the Lord of Mirepoix ; if the bones had perished, then bags full of their dust to be delivered to him. A woman, Ricarda, and a man Yfarni, both dead, were condemned by Bernard Gui for having been hereticated by Peter Autéri and Améli de Perles on their death beds. The sentence the inquisitors passed on them was : ' As a mark of perdition, the bones of each, if they could be distinguished from the bones of the faithful, were to be exhumed and burnt outside the cemetery.'

An order for exhumation and cremation was subject to appeal. Pons de Pouget, inquisitor, having issued such an order against the remains of Peter de Fenouillet, knight, of the diocese of Narbonne, an appeal was entered, and the hearing opened in the chapter hall of the Preaching Friars at Montpellier (1306). It was not finished until 1309. The sentence against Peter himself as a heretic had been launched as far back as 1262, and yet half a century afterwards his R.I.P. was disputed.[2] Any clerk who had officiated at the burial of a heretic was excommunicated, as well as all who attended it. The bodies of favourers of heretics were exhumed but not burnt.

This outrage upon the tenderest of human feelings, of course, did not always pass without disturbance. According to the eye-witness, William Pelhisse,[3] William Arnauld, the Inquisitor, only just escaped being thrown into the Tarn at Albi for merely ordering the body of a woman to be exhumed from the cemetery of St. Stephen (1234).[4]

---

[1] Pelhisse, *Chron*. 110.   [2] Doat. xxxii, 112.
[3] *Chron*. 113–116.
[4] Exhumation of the excommunicate was in accordance with canonical law (v. Gratian's *Decretals* Bk. I. Tit. 28, Ch. 12).

E. Confiscations, Fines, Compensations

As the Inquisition was declared to have originated in the Garden of Eden, so confiscation was traced to man's expulsion from it. That action of God, it was contended, established the principle that all property is held in trust for God, and that when man misuses it, the powers that are ordained of God have the right to confiscate it and give it to others who will put it to better purposes. Now no more ungodly use of property was conceivable than in the furtherance of heresy. Hence condemnation for heresy carried with it the confiscation of the heretic's property.

But we are bidden to ' render unto Cæsar the things that are Cæsar's, and unto God the things that are God's.' The practical interpretation of this dictum would have been that all property of lay heretics should be handed over to the State, and all property of clerical heretics to the Church. But this division was by no means as simple as it looks. For a bishop in his capacity of baron would seize property which was claimed by a count. An ecclesiastic might possess property by personal inheritance and not by official right, and this private property might be seized by the count against the bishop. Hence the endless disputes between Church and State over the spoils. The practice in the Empire was laid down by the several Constitutions of the Emperor Frederick. By those issued at Worms (1231) heirs enjoyed possession of the goods and patrimonies of the condemned, but the benefices returned to his overlord, and the expense of the burning of the condemned, living or dead, including a reward to the count for executing it, was paid for out of the goods of the condemned.[1] But eight months later (February 1232) the law was made even more severe. Goods were confiscated and not returned even to their sons, ' since it is far more serious to offend

---

[1] Pertz, *Leges* ii, p. 284.

the eternal than the temporal Majesty.' If the proper officials were remiss in suppressing heresy, Catholics could attack the land, possess it and preserve it in the Faith, saving only the rights of the suzerain. [1]   These Constitutions were renewed in May 1238, but in a modified form ; ' children who were not themselves heretics, and who disclosed the latent perfidy of their parents ' were not to be punished, being innocent.   The notice of the preaching friars was particularly called to this order. [2]   In France Louis IX as early as 1228 ordered his bailiffs to seize the goods, mobile and immobile, of the excommunicated, and not to restore them until they had recanted. [3]   But these officers were in no hurry to hand over that part of the spoil which was due to the Church.   Hence Gregory IX, in 1238 addressed a sharp rebuke to the king and his mother, pointing out the illegality of the detention of the goods of heretics in the domains and fiefs of the Church in the Dioceses of Albi and Narbonne, and insisting on their restitution.   They had also seized the dowries of Catholic women whose husbands had been condemned for heresy, as well as their loans deposits and other securities given them by Catholics. They had also declined to give particulars (*census*) of the possessions of the condemned to the Catholic lords from whom the condemned held them, to the injury of peace and faith. [4]   The letters also which Innocent IV sent to prelates ranging from Bordeaux to Narbonne prove how widely prevalent these malpractices were, nine years later (1247).

If the confiscated property were held on feudal tenure, it was sold to the mutual profit of the suzerain and the immediate lord, on condition that the purchaser discharged the services inseparable from it.   Where properties were

[1] Pertz, *Leges* ii, p. 287.   [2] *Ibid.*, p. 326 ff.
[3] *Rec. des Ord.*, vol. i, pp, 50,61 ;   Isambert I, pp. 232, 257.
[4] Vaissete, vi, 839.

not subject, the suzerain could take possession of and sell them, reserving, however, the payment of quit rents and other revenues. This arrangement was made by Louis IX with the Bishop of Albi (1229), the Bishop of Agde (1234) and others.

When Alfonse succeeded to the territories of Raymond, Count of Toulouse, he, following the example of Louis, ordered his seneschal to seize and confiscate to himself all the real and personal property of heretics sentenced to death or perpetual imprisonment. [1] But in his rapacity he checked the supply. For if a bishop as an inquisitor condemned a heretic, he might lose his own property when the condemned held it of him. Hence it was agreed (1264), that forfeited property should be equally divided between the king (or prince) and bishop, but that the bishop should have the option of buying out the royal share within two months at arbitration price. If the bishop declined, the bishop (or prince) was to transfer the lands within a year and a day to some one of the same standing as the former owner, to be held under the same terms of service ; but all personal property belonged to the Crown. Thus Church and State became very rich, and persecution was sordidly encouraged. [2]

Confiscation was swift : restitution tardy. The *Correspondence d'Alphonse* [3] contains many complaints of illegalities, and corresponding orders to his seneschals to sit with inquisitors to inquire into these complaints ; but complaints had to go to Paris, and the aggrieved parties often wisely refrained altogether from complaining, and so cut their losses.

---

[1] Potthast, 12743.

[2] Bertrand de Castanet out of such spoils built the gaunt Cathedral of Albi, part church, part fortress (Doat, xxxiv, pp. 131–133).

[3] Edited by Molinier, vol. i, pp. 263, 805, 806, 832 ; vol. ii, pp. 1400, 2118.

In theory the acceptance of pecuniary fines by the inquisitors was a violation of the vow of poverty ; and hence the Provincial Chapter of Montpellier (1242) strictly prohibited inquisitors from imposing money penalties on dead or living, or receiving any. Yet the stream of gold which flowed so easily into the coffers of the Church tempted some of the inquisitors to succumb to extravagance and easy travelling. Hence the same Chapter forbade an inquisitor to ride unless pressed for time, or there was danger in walking, or he was ill, and then only by permission of the bishop. He must not carry money or contract a debt. Horses and other expenses must be provided by others. So Alfonse threatened to have the Inquisition removed from Toulouse to Lavaur or other suitable place if the expenses were not cut down. All accounts were to be sent to Paris.[1]

The immense sums thus raised were used (i) for the expenses of the Eastern Crusades, (ii) for the general expenses of the Inquisition. By an Ordonnance of St. Louis (1258) the expenses of the Inquisition had to be met by the lords to whom fell the confiscated property. These expenses were swollen, not only, as we have just seen, by the personal extravagance of the inquisitors but by a host of subordinates with large salaries and little work. Innocent IV (May 12, 1249) [2] ordered the inquisitors to reduce their staff of scriveners and familiars to strict requirements, pointing out the scandal which these grave exactions generated, as well as the risk to their own reputations, (iii) For the building, enlargement and maintenance of prisons. The sudden increase in the number of prisoners far exceeded the accommodation. By the above Ordonnance, Louis ordered ' barons, prelates and landlords (*terrarii*) ' to provide adequately for the needs of the

---

[1] *Correspondence*, vol. i, pp. 948, 415.   [2] Doat, xxxi, p. 106.

incarcerated and immured in their own territories. At Carcassonne and Béziers he ordered more prisons to be built, and here he bore the cost of their maintenance himself.[1]

Alfonse had to do the same at Toulouse, and bishops at other centres. William Arnauld, Bishop of Carcassonne, with grim humour ordered as part penance that a heretic should provide bricks, lime and sand for building prisons. So R. Autéri and R. Améli stood guarantee for Arnauld of Narbonne in a bond of £20 that on the day after his being let out of prison he would go and work as a mason for certain nuns for two years : and if at any time he could not work, his guarantors would provide an efficient substitute (1252). (iv) For the building, enlargement and beautifying of churches aud monasteries.

Sentences were commuted for money for these purposes : one hundred solidi for the upkeep of an altar at Alzona, £6 for the shrine of the blessed martyr, Antonine, at Pamiers. The huge church of St. Cecilia at Albi, was, as we have seen, built by confiscated money. At Lavaur twelve of the principal citizens were allowed to commute their sentences for money sufficient to build a church there— afterwards the cathedral. At Cordes the Bishop of Albi ordered the people who had been excommunicated *en bloc* to build a church for the preaching friars, and at the entrance to place statues of two inquisitors who had been killed. The people completed the church, but demurred to the sacred commemoration of men whom they regarded as murderers and not martyrs. But the Bishop was adamant, and the distasteful task had to be carried through 'to the uttermost farthing' before he would remove the ban.[2]

---

[1] The payment to the gaoler was about £12 per annum per prisoner.

[2] Doat, xxxv, pp. 122–129.

The Castle of Béziers was confiscated and given to the Preaching Order for a convent by Louis IX in 1247, although it was not until 1252 that Peter of Arles and Bernard of Roscazels took possession of it. A royal gift, it was always under royal patronage.[1] (v) For the enrichment of the hierarchy and nobility. Bishops and barons, who, owing to their ceaseless petty wars, were short of money, found an abundant source of replenishment in the property of heretics. Many heretics belonged to the commercial class, whose wealth consisted less in land than in splendid houses, costly furniture and ample capital.

Fulk, the ex-troubadour bishop of Toulouse, was always begging, yet in less than a century, *half* of the diocese had become an archbishopric, comprising six dioceses, the other half being formed into the see of Pamiers, all richly endowed. We have already noted the rapacity of the Bishop of Albi. In the accounts of the royal proctors of Carcassonne we constantly find the confiscations of Albi shared by the bishop.[2]

Confiscation was not limited to property, it extended to offices. Even innocent heirs were visited with the sins of their fathers and grandfathers. A son or heir of a man condemned for heresy, because he had, when dying, asked for the Consolamentum, could not defend his right to succession to the property by pleading that the testator was not of sound mind, if it could be further proved that the said testator was suspect when in health. By an Ordonnance of Louis (1258) neither children nor grandchildren of a man only suspect could hold or be appointed to any public office.[3] At Albi (1306) the king's vicar sup-

---

[1] Granier, *Preaching Orders in Béziers* in *Mélanges de littérature et d'histoire religieuse*, vol. i, 1899.

[2] Doat, xxxv, v. 63.

[3] A confirmation of the Bull of Alexander (April, 1255), Potthast, 15805.

ported the people against the inquisitor; but the latter found that the vicar was a grandson of a condemned heretic, and therefore was disqualified from holding any public office.

The harshness of this law of heredity was sometimes mitigated in the interests of the Church. Sancho Morlano, Archdeacon of Carcassonne, turned heretic, and attempted to utilize his office by stealing and burning the books of the Inquisition. His two grandsons, Isarne and Sancho Morlano, however, so far from following in the erring footsteps of the archdeacon, were not only Catholics, but the former became Arch-priest of Carcassonne and his brother a parish priest. From those very books the dreadful secret of their grandfather was disclosed; but on petition to Nicholas IV, the pope regularized the situation by sanctioning their appointment to all their ' orders, charges and dignities.'[1] Archion of Spoleto, complained to the Pope, Honorius IV, that in spite of his father having been absolved by the Inquisition, and dying with the sacraments of the Church, he (Archion) and his sons had been deprived of their property and their offices by the podesta and commune. Honorius granted them restitution of all secular offices and ecclesiastical privileges, as well as their property (November, 1286).[2]

[1] Doat, xxxii, p. 136 ; Potthast, 22548, 22840.
[2] But this was in the Papal States. Cocquelin, iii. p. 285.

CHAPTER VIII

WITH inquisitors established in the great towns and controlling thence the centres of smaller populations, with an authority independent of legate, bishop, or king, and responsible, as their title *a sede apostolica deputati* showed, only to the pope, with the secular arm as their obedient servant, with rules and regulations to cover every contingency in life and death, with life, liberty, person, property, office, succession, all subjugated to their jurisdiction, the Church had every reason for thinking that the suppression of the Albigensian Heresy would quickly be accomplished.

That no one in authority should plead ignorance of the laws affecting heresy, Urban IV (November 3, 1265) called upon all magistrates, provosts, etc., to include such laws among their municipal statutes. All these laws were to be included in four uniform volumes, one of which was to be kept by each city, one by the diocesan, one by the preaching friars, one by the minorite friars.[1] These would contain not only bulls, but case law, i.e., papal decisions of intricate cases referred to the pope. Thus Clement IV (1258) answered several questions put to him by the minorite inquisitors : *Question* (1) : If a man has abjured heresy, but is subsequently found never to have been a heretic at all, can he be said to have *re*-lapsed, if after such abjuration he actually falls into heresy, and can he be punished accordingly ? *Answer :* By a certain fiction of law he should be regarded as having *re*-lapsed. But if the suspicion of his relapse is slight, he is to be given the

[1] Ripoll.

benefit of the doubt and not punished. *Question* (2) : If a man after abjuration receives or conceals or associates with or visits heretics only once, or gives or sends them food but never *adores* them, can he be said to have *re*-lapsed ? *Answer :* Yes ; his conduct after his abjuration is proof of his conduct before it. *Question* (3) : If a man swears falsely about himself or his associates, not by hatred or bribery but by fear of death, and then tells the truth about himself and his associates, what must be done ? *Answer :* If the second attestation is made not by fickleness or hatred or bribery, but by zeal for the faith and real repentance, it should be accepted. *Question* (4) : Are divination and sortilege to be punished ? *Answer :* These are no concern of the inquisitors unless they savour of heresy. *Question* (5) : Are heirs to make good the fines which the defunct have failed to pay in whole or in part ? *Answer :* Yes. *Question* (6): Are inquisitors to adjudicate in disputes about loans ? *Answer :* No, unless the loan has been contracted in satisfaction of a penance. *Question* (7) : Can heirs be compelled to make satisfaction for those who died before their punishment had been pronounced, especially seeing that such, when alive, had pledged their goods to the inquisitors to do penance ? *Answer :* No, at their death, the charge was extinguished, seeing that they did not die heretics, but were still incorporate in the unity of the Church. But if, after their death, sentence is pronounced against them, the confiscation must proceed. Other points were : that a cleric condemned for heresy must be unfrocked first ; that clerics impeding inquisitors in the exercise of their duty must be treated as favourers of heresy and treated more severely than the laity.[1]

Thus armed and prepared in every point, so little did the Church expect any recrudescence of heresy that at the

---

[1] Ripoll. Doat, clv, p. 235.

Council of Lyons (1274), regarded by some as the Fourteenth General Council, the heresy at its very doors was passed by without comment. Yet scarcely had its members dispersed before the whole of Southern France was once more ablaze, and it was another half century before the fires were extinguished. This was due partly to the political situation, partly to the jealousy between Dominican and Franciscan Inquisitors, partly to the reaction of human nature, and partly to the indomitable zeal of one family, the Autéris.

The political situation can be only briefly described. For nearly thirty years there was a rapid succession of popes, including an Interregnum of nearly three years, which caused unsettlement and weakness in papal policy, especially as these thirty years were followed by the 'Babylonish Captivity,' beginning with the King of France's own nominee, Clement V. After the death of Alfonse, the whole of the territories of Raymond VII, according to the Treaty of Paris, were united to the French Crown, and Philip le Bel, whose long reign of forty-six years contrasted with the many short reigns of the popes, had no wish to sacrifice the peace and prosperity of the Kingdom of France to the aggrandizement of the Church of Rome. With him the Kingdom came first, the Church second. He first taught Europeans, what the Emperor had in vain attempted, that Roman Bishops could be vanquished in spite of their pretensions, and laid under restraint. With Philip, pro-heretical only because anti-papal, and that solely on political grounds and for political purposes, appeals against inquisitors found ready acceptance. Four times in ten years—1291, 1297, 1299, 1301—he ordered inquiries into their proceedings, and on each occasion decided against them. For instance in 1297, as we have seen,[1] he described

[1] p. 187.

their crimes as ' impious and inhuman.' Matters not im-
proving, he passed from words to deeds. He deprived the
Bishop of Albi, Bernard de Castanet, of his temporalities
and mulcted him in £2,000. Even the bishop's father
Peter, who was of consular rank, and his own officers
opposed him, and when the chief citizens of Albi went with
the King's Reformers to the Court of Senlis to support the
official report of the bishop's malpractices, the bishop's
father went with them (1301).[1]   The king further demanded of the master-general of the preaching friars that he
should recall Fulk, the inquisitor, from Albi; and on his
refusal, he forbade his seneschal to carry out the inquisitor's commitments to the secular arm.   Thus for a time
the whole inquisition in France, so far as its more severe
sentences were concerned, was brought to a standstill.
Clement V, the King's nominee, under his eye and power,
nolens volens pursued the same policy.   The consuls of
Albi and Cordes (1305) complained that the inquisitor
condemned the innocent and thrust them into dungeons
that were veritable death-traps.[2]

The report of the two commissioners, Cardinal Taillefer
and Bishop Beringar Frédol, upheld the consuls and
implicated the inquisitors.   The commissioners, as pleni-
potentiaries, ordered certain reforms, such as that the
prisoners should be removed from the subterranean dungeons
to the higher and better lighted prisons; but Taillefer
was over a hundred years of age, and, as far as we know,
no improvement was made.

We have already seen how the Church of Carcassonne had
nursed in its bosom a viper in the person of its archdeacon.

[1] In one year (1299) twenty-eight sessions were held in his palace.
Of the twenty-five defendants, six were lawyers and of these one,
Raymond Constans was the bishop's notary, and another, Raymond
Calviére, a notary, of the King's Court.   None was of knightly rank.
(*Nat. Lib.* MSS. Lat. 11847).
[2] Doat, xxxiv, pp. 42–80.   Compayré, pp. 240–245.

He was imprisoned, but easily escaped, probably to Lombardy, with many others. At this time the importance of the inquisitions at Carcassonne and Toulouse may be gathered not only from the registers but from the description given them by the pope in the letter which he sent to the inquisitor of the March of Treviso. For, having heard that great numbers of heretics from France were living in the diocese of Verona, he informed the inquisitor of the March that a special messenger would be sent to him from ' the inquisitors in the Kingdom of France ' to whom the heretics were to be delivered. That this title meant the inquisitors of Carcassonne and Toulouse is clear from the original bull preserved in the archives of Carcassonne.[1] Yet their eminence weighed little against the popularity of heresy. When in 1296 Nicholas d'Abbeville, the inquisitor at Carcassonne, condemned two notaries, Garrici and Bruneti, as heretics, the whole city rose in their defence. Nicholas was driven out of the city and the convent sacked. The consuls combined with those of Castres in an appeal to both pope and king to redress their grievances. Philip prohibited imprisonment on mere suspicion, but in the main upheld the inquisitor, and the dispute ended in a sort of compromise, the people undertaking to build a chapel in the convent in honour of St. Louis (1299). The chapel was built the following year.

Among the heretics residing in Lombardy whose numbers and strength drew forth the command of Pope Nicholas IV, to the inquisitor of Treviso, was the celebrated Peter Autéri, and his family history and career throw a strong light upon the activities of the heretics at this time.[2] Peter Autéri was a native of Ax in the County of Foix, a town of some commercial importance, which by its geographical situation

---

[1] Douais, *Arch. de la Gasc.* viii, pp. 384, 446. Bernard Gui succeeded Odo as prior in 1297.
[2] Nat. Lib. MSS. Lat., 4269.

and natural features long resisted crusaders and inquisitors, and provided a refuge for those heretics who had escaped both. Peter came of a family noted for its sturdy adherence to Catharism ; his father, R. Autéri, a man of means, had stood guarantor for a heretic [1] Peter himself had been a notary in his native town, but through the study of the Bible he and his brother William were converted from Catholicism. This meant the sacrifice of a lucrative and honourable profession ; but counting it as nought for what he believed to be the Truth, he left his native town with other members of his family, e.g. his daughter, Matilda, and her husband, and went to Lombardy, all his property being confiscated to the Count de Foix (1296). In Lombardy there were many ' perfects ', and Peter Autéri may have become their ' bishop ', to whom Pope Nicholas referred particularly in his letter to the inquisitor of the March of Treviso. Communication between Lombardy and Ax was easy, and often Peter and members of his family returned to Ax, where they were warmly, if secretly, welcomed. Peter, who was affectionately known as the ' Veteran,' was indefatigable, in spite of his advanced years, travelling great distances in Aude, Limoux, the Garonne, Toulouse, and elsewhere,[2] and joyfully ' enduring hardness.' Everywhere he had his scouts to give him notice of danger, and the faithful notice of his arrival. In the spirit of the *Pater noster* which, as we have seen,[3] was held in special honour in the Albigensian ritual, Peter ' consoled ' the very man to whom by law his property had been forfeited, Roger Bernard, Count de Foix (1302). His son, James, actually held in the Church of St. Cross at Toulouse a service for women credents, a fact which proves the audacity of the leader and

[1] p. 197.
[2] For places and dates v. Molinier, *L'Inquis.*, *Etude*, p. 151, note 2.
[3] Vol. i, Index, s.v.

the popularity of the heretics (1305), under the very eyes of 'the inquisitor of the Kingdom of France.' Their organization, too, was strengthened, for Peter as 'bishop', ordained 'perfects', e.g. Pons d'Avignon and Pons of his own native town (Ax) in the house of Arnauld Issaure at Larnat (1303). His fervent zeal, persuasive eloquence, legal knowledge, undaunted courage and utter self-sacrifice, with the devoted support of his numerous family, put new heart into heresy, so that Geoffrey d'Ablis, who had succeeded Nicholas d'Abbeville in 1303,[1] and to whose Register we owe most of our knowledge of Peter, admitted that he could make no headway against it. Peter was particularly active in the Ariége, and, it was alleged, not always creditably. The women of the district were said to be frivolous, a trait of which the propagandists took advantage. The women were asked if they would like to see some handsome men, and thus were introduced to heresiarchs and enticed into talks on heresy. Children also were given presents.[2] In this way heresy entered the home and stole away the heart. Alarmed at its progress, the Inquisition marshalled all its forces against it. Bernard Gui wrote letters (1303) to all the officials, ecclesiastical and secular, of Carcassonne, Toulouse and Albi, urging them to the strictest vigilance as regards heretics and their supporters. Peter Autéri is not named, but doubtless he, more than anyone else, was in the inquisitor's mind.[3] James, his son, was at last captured (1306), but escaped ; a year later he was re-captured, together with a colleague, Prades Tavernier, through the treachery of a pretended credent. He was imprisoned at Carcassonne, and was still there when his father was captured. The very sight of an Autéri carried, in the mind of the Church, infection. Pons Améli de Garda confessed that he had often

---

[1] For date see Molinier, p. 126, note.   [2] Molinier, *Etude*, p. 118.
[3] Doat, xxxiii, 143, 147.

seen Peter and James Autéri in Toulouse, and had heard them preach, and had 'adored' them on bended knee about three years before, i.e. 1304. On the same date March 3, 1307, first Sunday in Lent, in the Church of St. Stephen where the Inquisition was held, witnesses declared that Ricorda and William Yfarni had been hereticated by Peter Autéri and Pons Améli in their last illness. In fact Peter appears on every page of the Register. He not only fanned into flame 'the smoking flax', but took measures to keep it burning after his own course was run. He thought this could be best done by the purchase and circulation of the Bible, and particularly the Gospels and the Epistles of St. Paul, in the vernacular. For well-bound copies he was prepared to pay a good price. So testified William d'Ablis in his examination : 'They shewed me a book in the best Bolognese lettering and beautifully illuminated which was the Gospels and the Epistles of St. Paul in Romance.' Also Peter de Luzenac said : ' James (Autéri) asked me to buy him, when I returned to Toulouse, a complete Bible, if I could find one, up to £20 in price. I said : ' I did not think I should return to Toulouse for a whole year, but I would send the said Bible from Montpellier, where there were plenty.'[1]

The capture and imprisonment of his son in no way daunted the 'Veteran', and he had many narrow escapes. When staying in the village of Montaillon, where all were heretics except one, all the people were arrested and taken to Carcassonne ; but Peter was too slippery, and got away. For eight months (September 1308–May 1309) he had to lie low in one place. His enemy at last discovered his hiding-place and raided the house. Peter's host and hostess were seized, but once more he himself slipped

[1] Nat. Lib. MSS Lat. 4269, 64. Limborch, *Sentences of Toulouse*, pp. 50, 84, 300.

through their hands. This second escape, which in Bernard
Gui's view could only be due to apathy or collusion, evoked
from him a flaming appeal : ' Gird you, sons of God ! With
me arise, soldiers of Christ ! against the enemies of His
Cross, corrupters (MSS. corruptions) of the truth and purity
of the Catholic Faith, even Peter Autéri, the heresiarch,
and Peter Sanchi and Sanchi Mercatier, co-heretics and
co-criminals . . . lurking in secret places and walking in
darkness' (August 10, 1309.)[1] Meanwhile Bernard was
carrying on the Inquisition with a scientific precision never
before equalled. Between May 10, 1308, and September
27, 1309, no less than forty-one sessions were held, of which
thirty-six took place at Carcassonne. Most of those arrested
confessed at once, and made a public reconciliation,
swearing that neither tortures, nor threats nor entreaties,
nor money nor fear, nor hate nor affection had forced them
to their confession. They threw themselves unreservedly
upon the mercy of the Church and promised in turn to persecute heretics and their supporters. The longest document in
the Register (4269) deals with William de Rodez, a nephew
of William Autéri. ' A man's foes shall be those of his
own household,' even of the household of faith. Under
the minute examination of the inquisitors full particulars
of Peter's movements and methods would be extracted
from those who to save themselves imperilled their leader.
In the Inquisition Courts was woven the net that slowly
yet surely closed around the redoubtable heresiarch. He
was at length betrayed into the hands of the enemy by
Peter de Luzenau, a fellow-notary without money and
without honour, at the house of Perrin Maurel. Two
members of the Maurel family, husband and wife, had
been arrested in 1308, and their disclosures had forced
their son to flee. He went north, and came to lodge at

[1] *Practica*, p. 4 (Douais).

a farm belonging to a relation, Perrin Maurel, where Peter had also sought an asylum (June, 1309), and where he had been with his daughter for five weeks. The arrival of another fugitive at a house strongly suspected of heresy spelt danger to Peter, and he hurriedly left, but his enemies had the scent, and he was caught as stated above. He was condemned to death, but was kept in prison in the hope that the Church would gain the famous victory of the ' veteran's ' recantation. His sentence bears not his name, but the note in the margin of it tells us that *ipse* is Peter Autéri.[1] He is described as ' a certain obstinate Manichean heretic.' The execution was postponed in the usual form : ' The same being reserved and retained, that if hereafter he wishes to be converted and to return to Church unity he may be preserved (*conservetur*) for life. In which case we reserve to ourselves the full and free power of imposing on the same a salutary punishment and penance for deeds committed in the crime of heresy.' But the Church was baffled by the bravery of the ' veteran'. He was taken from prison and burnt at Carcassonne on April 9, 1311, in the presence of a vast concourse of people to whom his last words were : ' If I had been allowed to preach to you, you would all have embraced my Faith.'

The interrogations of Peter before the Inquisition have unfortunately not survived.

[1] *Practica* by B. Gui, p. 129 (Douais), Limborch, *Inq.* 110. Molinier, *Etude*, pp. 159 ff. ; Prof. Vidal, *Revue des quest. hist.*, January 1906.

CHAPTER IX

A NOTHER powerful, if oblique, stimulus to the recrudescence of heresy came from the very midst of its
enemies, viz. the jealousy which existed between Dominicans and Franciscans. The rise and cause of that jealousy
is a matter outside our own subject, but it was the obvious
policy of the heretics to use these dissensions for their own
advantage.

The Dominicans had never been very acceptable to the
archbishops of Narbonne, and the archbishops had for the
most part been their own inquisitors. On the other hand
there was in the city of Narbonne a large Franciscan convent, and of this the famous Bernard Délicieux became a
member (1301). He had joined the Order in 1284, and,
endowed with great oratorical gifts, he had travelled about
as a Reader from convent to convent at a time when the
whole country was in a ferment owing to the excesses of
the inquisitors. Délicieux, the Franciscan, reached Carcassonne at a time when the whole city was incensed against
the inquisitors for their outrageous treatment of one of its
most respected burgesses, Castel Fabri. He had been
condemned for heresy *in contumaciam*, excommunicated,
and his goods confiscated. But the Franciscans defended
him, and vouched for his orthodoxy ; and when he died, he
died in their arms, and was buried in their cemetery. As
aiders and defenders of a condemned heretic, therefore, the
Franciscans themselves became liable to excommunication
and other penalties. Dominicans and Franciscans, Preaching and Minorite Friars, both having inquistorial powers—a
dispute of this nature struck at the very root of the Inquisition itself, and could only be dealt with, the pope excepted,
by a General Chapter of the Preaching Friars. This met

at Marseilles, and before it appeared Délicieux, famous already for his eloquence as an advocate, with the authority of his provincial, Arnauld de Roquefeuille. He was refused a hearing, and when he called the next day at the lodging of the inquisitor, Nicholas d' Abbeville, the door was shut in his face. But he nailed his ' Instrument of Appeal ' to the inquisitor's door—a long and somewhat wordy document,[1] in which he declared : ' The said Castel Fabri all his life was reputed by men and women of the diocese of Carcassonne and other dioceses near and far to be a true Catholic Christian, and there never was the slightest breath of suspicion against his Catholic Faith. He was liberal to widows, the poor, the Preachers, the Minorites, and other religious orders.' The issue of this dispute does not come within the limit of our subject, except that it does not appear that the Dominicans recovered the body of the condemned Fabri for exhumation and burning ; but the body of his wife, Rescende, who had also been condemned for heresy, but could not receive the protection of burial in the Franciscan convent, was exhumed and burnt (1328).[2]

From Marseilles Délicieux went to Albi, and joined the united deputation of Albi and Carcassonne to the King. The Report of the royal commissioners, together with the forensic eloquence of Délicieux, so impressed the king that he ordered that all commitments of the inquisitors must have the sanction of his seneschal and the bishop. If they disagreed, the case must be submitted to a commission of four, consisting of two Dominicans and two Franciscans (1301). Two years later, B. Délicieux was back again at Carcassonne where his fiery denunciations of the Dominicans inflamed the people to attack those consuls who had sided with the inquisitors, and drive them out of the city. News of the disturbance reaching Albi, malcontents of the

---

[1] Doat, xxxiv, 123 ff.   [2] *Ibid.*, 236. 241.

city hastened to Carcassonne and forced the vidame to transfer the prisoners from the prison of the inquisitors to the citadel. For this the vidame was excommunicated by the inquisitors, and on appeal, his defence was readily undertaken by Délicieux. We get some idea of the enormous expense of these appeals when, even with a friend for advocate, Carcassonne subscribed £1,500, Albi £1,000 and Cordes £500. Délicieux, to strengthen his client's appeal, endeavoured to enlist the support of the queen, whose confessor was a Franciscan. He was so far successful that the king, taking a grave view of the disturbances, determined to investigate them on the spot, and himself came south to his sub-capital, Toulouse, accompanied by the queen and their three sons. Before the Court Délicieux candidly avowed himself opposed to the Inquisition as such, and called for its abolition. He claimed that it was no longer needed. There had not been a single heretic in Albi for a long time ; even the provincial of the preachers themselves, William Peter, had acknowledged only a few days previously that there were not more than forty or fifty heretics in Albi, Cordes and Carcassonne put together. The faith of the preachers had degenerated into fanaticism ; even Peter and Paul would have been hard put to it to clear themselves of heresy. Philip le Bel was not deceived by the exaggerations of the advocate, and gave a fair judgment. He confirmed his letter of December 8, 1301 : the Inquisition was established for the confirmation of the Faith : it rested with the pope, not him, whether it was still needed. But the conduct of the inquisitors was a different matter ; they had long scandalized everybody, and it must stop. There must be no more torture or the deliberate infliction of suffering : prisons must be conducted on humane lines : they were *ad custodiam, non ad poenam.*

It would have been well for the fair name of Délicieux if

he had stopped here, or used his forensic abilities in the exposure of abuses and defence of the abused. Unfortunately he allowed himself to become mixed up in a plot which had for its object the dethroning of James, King of Aragon, a feudatory of the King of France. Into its details we cannot diverge. Délicieux's part was a minor one, practically nothing more than that of a messenger, but it afforded his enemies, the inquisitors, a fulcrum sufficient to shift him out of the way. The king soon forgot his misdemeanour, not so the Inquisition. Sixteen years afterwards (1319) he was arrested on three charges : (1) he had opposed the Inquisition : (2) he had conspired against the King of France : (3) he had attempted to poison the Pope, Benedict XI, by sending him a box of poisoned medicines and powders, with a letter to the pope's doctor, written in his own hand, explaining how the said preparations were to be given to the pope. His judge was the *Archbishop* of Toulouse,[1] John Raymond de Cominges, assisted by the Bishop of Pamiers (the celebrated James Fournier, afterwards Benedict XII)[2] and the Bishop of St. Papoul. The last charge failed, but he was found guilty on the other two counts. In Carcassonne, in which and for which he had won his greatest triumphs, he was publicly degraded, and in its prison he languished till his death, bound in chains, and fed only on bread and water.

[1] Made such two years before.

[2] His register of sentences is enormous. Douais observes: ' of all the Bishops of Languedoc he displayed most zeal as an inquisitor —a zeal which brought him the Pontificate.'

THE blood of the Albigensian martyrs, Peter and James Autéri, was not the seed of the Albigensian Church. No phœnix sprang from their ashes. The cohesion which their zeal gave to heresy was but transient, and their deaths were followed by disintegration and weakness of the cause for which they had lived and died.

The last act, practically, of the tragedy took place at Albi. For a century the bishops of Albi had successively and successfully exerted themselves less to suppress heretics than to possess their property. Simon de Montfort handed over to the Bishop of Albi the Castles of Marssac and Rouffiac (1212).[1] Under the Inquisition the bishop complained to the pope, Gregory IX, and the pope to the king and queen, protesting against their bailiffs at Albi retaining possessions of the condemned heretics in the domains of the Church (1238). La Garde, the property of Ozilis de Morlhou and Saure, his wife, was seized by Bernard de Castanet. This was exchanged by confirmation of Philip le Bel for the Castle of Montirat, and in the same letter the king donates to him properties in Monastiés which had been confiscated from Vierna and Pons Bernard, her husband, for heresy.[2] Over these spoils there were frequent disputes between bishops and counts, particularly the Counts de Castres. Bishops worked hand in hand with inquisitors, tne latter for suppression of heresy, the former for possession of their property. But attack on religion and attack on pro‑ perty will evoke a corresponding resistance each to each, and these counter-attacks will combine for mutual support. Hence the Count de Castres took under his protection

[1] *Compayré*, lv.   [2] *Ibid.*, lxxxv.

heretics with whose doctrines he had no sympathy, but through whom he could vex his adversary ; and the heretics availed themselves of the quarrel to push their religion. They met in the Church of St. Vincent at Castres, and before the altar of St. Peter under the leadership of Raymond Duval were sworn to secrecy as to his movements, and received the new passwords and signs of recognition. This league was extended so as to embrace Albi, Cordes and Carcassonne under the same leader, with one Didier as deputy. These hid in the country during the day, but slipped into the towns during the night to hold meetings. With his flock in revolt, with a notary even of his own Court in secret, and a notary of the king's Court in open sympathy with the heretics, with the Count de Castres in active hostility to him, the Bishop of Albi found his episcopal throne no easy seat, and more than once was he driven out of the city, followed by cries of : ' Traitor ! ' At the last flight he was away for five years, and returned only just before his death.

But in all this there was much of the earthy. These material interests withdrawn, the heretics had no inherent strength, no force in reserve. It had been more a fight for heritages than for heresy. On the death of B. de Castanet the storm abated. The heretics slunk away and the populace made their peace with their new bishop. Assembling in the cemetery of St. Cecilia at Albi (1320), the Bishop of Castres preached a sermon ; after which all the inhabitants and consuls repudiated all their former conduct, promised reparation for all torts done to the late bishop Bernard de Castanet, and as compensation and memorials for their misdeeds and gratitude for canonical absolution, undertook to build a chapel in the church or cemetery of Cecilia, and a porch to the church of preaching friars. They were also to erect two monuments, one upon the tomb of Geoffrey d'Ablis at the convent of the preaching friars at Lyons, and the other at the tomb of Fulk de St. George at their convent at Carcassonne. Henceforth the Albigensian Heresy with its scattered groups and isolated individuals carried on a guerrilla warfare, which was quickly suppressed before the trained, disciplined, and organized forces of the Church Militant. Driven into Piedmont and Lombardy and refined in the furnace of affliction they were melted and moulded into the nobler and purer community of the Vaudois.

EPILOGUE

The Albigensian Heresy has ceased to be, but the methods of its suppression remain and generate divergent opinions as to their ethical and religious character.

The Albigensian Heresy was contemporary with the strenuous endeavour of the House of Capet to extend its kingdom from the Channel to the Mediterranean. The summons of the pope to come to the help of the Church, robed its earthly ambition in the vestment of a spiritual duty. Ostensibly rendering a service to God, the kings of France rendered a still greater service to themselves. Cautiously they felt their way, and, ere the House of Capet came to an end, the Kingdom of France had absorbed all those splendid provinces of the South which had been infected with heresy. Against the might of the North, the slender military resources of Tolosan patriotism proved unavailing. The marriage laws, too, which prohibited wealthy widows and heiresses of the South from marrying within ten years of the death of the heretic except with the nobility of the North, consolidated socially that union which had been brought about politically. Simon de Montfort, Count of Leicester, the Champion of the Church, who fell for her in battle, gained nothing for his descendants ; all the spoils went to the State or the Church.

The Albigensian Heresy was also contemporary with the

strenuous endeavour of the papacy to retain and strengthen its grasp upon the ' Two Swords ' of St. Peter—the spiritual and the temporal power. Never has the Roman Church had such a *succession* of able Popes as she had in the thirteenth century. The codification of Church Law by the Canonists and of Church Doctrine by the Summists presented to that uncritical age no crack or loophole through which an opponent could shoot the arrow of truth. The Church disarmed her enemies by compelling them to hear and not to argue ; and by making it criminal for any layman to possess any part of the Bible in the vernacular, the heretics were dependent solely upon memory in the conduct of their services, the instruction of their members and the propagation of their religion. The inquisitors formed but a small proportion of the preaching orders. As their official title implied, they were commissioned to preach, and preaching and teaching went on everywhere incessantly. The preachers became expert not only in the laws and doctrines of the Roman Church but in conveying that knowledge to the people in their own language. The Catholic persecution of heresy, too, was more comprehensive and more incisive in the thirteenth and following centuries than the Pagan persecution of the Catholic Church in the first centuries ; it punished the dead as well as the living, and the innocent descendants as well as the ' guilty ' parents. Giving to ' faith ' in Pauline theology the concrete sense of ' creed,' Innocent III maintained that ' he who takes away faith takes away life, for the just lives by faith.' [1]

Against this ceaseless, merciless erosion the rock of the Albigensian Heresy was worn away. It had nothing of that ' first love ', and purity of Gospel truth which inspired and strengthened the early Church to triumph over its persecutors and lead captivity captive.

[1] Qui fidem adimit, vitam furatur, justus enim ex fide vivit. *Regesta*, i. 93.

For the Catholic Church to call heretics ' coiners ', ' robbers,' ' murderers,' was no mere figure of speech. The Church sincerely believed and taught that all who diverged from the Roman Faith were as great a menace to the peace and stability of Christianity as those to whom such names are generally applied are to society.

It would be a philosophic anachronism to judge the Suppression of the Albigensian Heresy of the thirteenth century by the standards of the twentieth ; but it is incredible that any one who professes to have ' the mind of Christ ' should, by stressing Rome's claim to be *semper eadem*, be found to justify it to-day. Yet an eminent cardinal revered throughout the whole Roman Church could write in the latter part of the nineteenth century : ' he (a heresiarch) should meet with *no mercy* ; he assumes the office of the Tempter , and so far as his error goes, must be dealt with by a competent authority, as if he were an embodied evil. To spare him is a false and dangerous pity. It is to endanger the souls of thousands, and it is uncharitable towards himself.'[1]

Had preachers not been commissioned by pontiffs to turn persecutors but had kept themselves to the original purpose of their order, the task of defending ' the faith which was once for all delivered to the saints ' would have been completed more quickly and more creditably ; and, ' looking unto Jesus, the Author and Perfecter of our faith,' the true ' crucifer ' would have found then as always, that the victories of the Church are won, ' not by might nor by power, but by My Spirit, saith the Lord.'

---

[1] Newman's *Apologia pro sua vita* ch. 1.   On the whole subject see Coulton's *Mediæval Studies, No. 18.* ' *The Death-Penalty for Heresy :* ' ' During at least seven centuries, Rome has consistently asserted *in principle*, a disciplinary and punitive power over all baptized Christians.   She only ceased to assert this in practice when she found herself deprived of the necessary physical force.'   p. 40.

APPENDIX

So long as the Church insisted that the Christian Faith could only be preached and read in the Latin tongue, she went into the fray against the Catharists with the sword of the Spirit sheathed. Heresy made its way because from the beginning it was preached in a language understood by the people—viz. the Romance language.

Authorities differ as to the extent and character of the Romance language. Some [1] hold that it was a corruption of the Latin, and that it was common to all the countries of Europe in which Latin had been spoken, and was preserved in a pure form in the poetry of the Troubadours. Others [2] maintain that the language of Southern France and Catalonia was only one of the many dialects of the Romance.

The name is derived from Romania, the general name for the Roman provinces in Gaul, Spain, and Italy. In proportion to the pride with which a person regarded Latin as an imperial and a sacred language would be the contempt with which he would regard a dialect which was a corruption of it. On the other hand, a preacher, however good his ' matter ', struggling with a strange language, constantly making errors in grammar and meaning, would only arouse the ribald laughter and contemptuous retorts of his audience, and specially so when that ' matter ' was actually controversial. Again : as with the spoken so with the written word. The Albigenses, and still more the Waldenses, of whose labours in this respect the former availed themselves, spared no pains or expense in putting the Scriptures into the people's hands in a language they

[1] Raynouard, *Choix des Poesies originales des Troubadours*.
[2] Lewis, *Origin and Formation of the Romance Languages*.

could understand, and in a complete form. Where will be found so early and so complete a vernacular version of the New Testament in Western Europe, as the Romance—the four Gospels, Acts, Apostolic Epistles, Apocalypse? Against this we can set only the four Gospels in Anglo-Saxon, and the four Books of Kings in old French. Moreover the copies which have survived are handy in size, and simple in decoration, cheap and portable, and so compare favourably with the splendid and cumbersome folios of the Vulgate. Many are of the twelfth and thirteenth centuries and therefore contemporary with the rise and fall of the Albigensian Heresy. In the will of an Englishman who died 1345 a Romance Bible is expressly mentioned among his effects; ' *Etiam Bibulam (Bibliam) in Romanam Linguam translatam.*'[1] Archbishop Usher had several copies in his Library at Dublin; [2] ' The New Testament with the Books of Proverbs, Ecclesiastes, Cantica, Wisdom, and Ecclesiasticus, in the Romance or Waldensian dialect.' In the same Library were other documents, called Waldensian, of the twelfth century, e.g. the metrical pieces of La Nobla Leyezon and la Barca.

It is significant that the version is called Waldensian and not Albigensian. This is due partly to the fact that the Waldenses survived but the Albigenses perished; but still more to the fact that it was the Waldenses who first made and promulgated the Bible in the Romance vernacula.. The pioneer was he from whom the Waldenses received their name, Peter Waldo of Lyons. Stephen de Bourbon, whose account is generally accepted [3] says, ' They were

---

[1] Surtees Soc., *Publications*, vol. i, 1836.

[2] Six copies of the N.T. alone are mentioned—Dr. Todd, *British Magazine*, vol. xix, pp. 393–6.

[3] Quetif and Echard, vol. i, p. 192 : Ricchini in his Dissertation ' de Valdensibus ', prefixed to his edition of Moneta Stephen de Bourbon, was a Dominican and composed his ' De septem donis Spiritus Sancti,' 1225. The quotation is from Part IV, ch. 30.

called Waldenses from the first author of this heresy, named Waldens. They are also called " the Poor Men of Lyons " because they started there by professing poverty ; but they called themselves poor in spirit because the Lord said in Matthew v, " Blessed are the poor in spirit." . . . Now that sect began in this way, as I have heard from many who saw their forefathers, and from a certain priest who was highly honoured and wealthy in the city of Lyons, and a friend of our Friars, called Bernard Udros. When he was a young man and a scrivener, he wrote for the said Waldens some rather old (*priores*) books in Romance (that is, Gallic), Stephen de Ansa translating them and dictating them to him. This Stephen was afterwards beneficed in the great Church of Lyons, but was killed by falling from the balcony of a house he was building. I have often seen this man myself. The said Waldens, a rich man in the city, heard the Gospels, and not being much of a scholar, (*literatus*) but eager to understand them, made an agreement with the said priests, the one to translate into the vulgar tongue, and the other to write it at his dictation. They dealt in the same way with many other books of the Bible, and many Authorities of Saints which they called " sentences grouped under heads." '

The following account taken from the anonymous Chronicler of Laon does not necessarily contradict Stephen de Bourbon, but may be the explanation of Waldo being ' eager to understand the Gospels.' ' In the year of the Incarnation 1173 there was at Lyons of Gaul a certain citizen named Valdesius who by tricks of trade (*per iniquitatem fenoris*) had amassed enormous wealth. On a certain Lord's Day he turned aside to a crowd which had gathered before a jongleur, whose words so pricked him to the heart that he took him home and heard him with the closest attention, for his story was how the blessed Alexis had died the death of the righteous in the house of his father.

The next morning the said citizen hurried to the School of Theology to seek spiritual advice. On being taught many ways of coming to God, he asked the Master which of them was the most sure and *perfect* way. The Master quoted the Lord's saying : " If thou wouldst be perfect, etc." Going home he offered his wife the choice between his personal and real estate (*mobilia sive immobilia*)—lands, waters, meadows, woods, houses, rents, vineyards, mills and kilns. At first overcome with grief, she stuck to (*haesit*) the real property. He then sold his personal property, gave a great part of the money thus realized to his two little girls whom, unknown to their mother, he handed over to the Order of Font-Everard, and the largest part he spent on the poor.'

In this way, 'the poor had the Gospel preached unto them,' for Waldo took the initiative in and bore the cost of having translated and distributed the Bible in the vernacular.[1] What was its base ? For the most part the Vulgate of Jerome, but by no means a servile rendering of it. Thus in the Lord's Prayer which had a supreme place in their services, ' daily bread ' was rendered ' *nostre pa qui es sobre tota causa.*' Guiraud [2] charges the heretics with a deliberate perversion of the text in the interests of their tenets, because, as ordinary bread was material, it was evil, being made by the Devil. The petition therefore was to be understood mystically. And yet Jerome himself gives *panem superstantialem* which the Vulgate retains, and the Fathers were in favour of *consubstantialem*.

Least of all was it a translation based upon the Textus Receptus of the Vulgate current in the learned University of Paris. To the great scholar, Roger Bacon, is usually

[1] Cledat has published the N.T. in Romance, and proves that it was made by the Catharists and used in the region comprised of Aude, Haute Garonne, Ariège and Tarn.

[2] *Cartulaire de Prouille*, Introduction, p. cxxii, Lightfoot, *Fresh Revision of N.T.*, Appendix.' See also vol. i, p. 12.

given the credit for first calling attention to the corrupt state of that text. ' For forty years many theologians and Paris book-sellers have been copying and selling a corrupt text. A great number of careless scribes have added to the confusion by making changes of words, etc., according to their own judgment. Theologians have no means of examining the text critically, and so rely upon it as correct. Later, when, perhaps, they became conscious that there was something wrong or unsatisfactory, they wished to change what they imagined had been wrongly translated. But because they had not the ability, each one made what corrections he pleased.'[1] Bacon's ' Forty Years ' would take us back to 1227. But that there were textual critics nearly a century before the complaint of the learned Franciscan is proved by the extant copies of the Romance Bible. Such critics the ex-merchant of Lyons summoned to co-operate with him in giving the poor as pure a text as that age, largely ignorant of Greek and wholly of Hebrew, could produce. In eighteen places, for instance, in St. John's Gospel alone, it agrees with the Itala as against the Vulgate, and in three notable places with Codex D. which at one time was in the Church of Irenaeus at Lyons from which the Romance version issued.[2]

On the other hand, the Waldensian translators, in the supposed interests of orthodoxy and in self-defence against charges of Arianism and Manicheism, did not hesitate to tamper with the text, even where genuine. Thus in St. John i. the Romance version had ' *The Son* was in the beginning,' and in v. 51 ' The Son of the Virgin,' for ' the Son of Man,' and so throughout all the Dublin, Zurich,

[1] Gasquet ' Roger Bacon and the Vulgate ' in his ' Monastic Life in the Middle Ages.' One instance may be given. ' Qui me confusus fuerit . . . confundebitur', for ' Qui me confessus fuerit. . . . confitebitur ' (St. Mark. viii. 38.)

[2] Dr. Gilly ' Romant Version of the Gospel according to St. John.' Scrivener, *Cod. Bez.*, p. viii.

Grenoble and Paris MSS. in every corresponding place. The same feature is found in some of the earliest treatises said to be Waldensian.

In spite of these defects the sword which the zeal, the wisdom and the sacrifice of Peter Waldo put into the hands of his co-religionists was a far finer weapon than that wielded by the Church ; and their familiarity with it which personal study of the vernacular made possible and their eagerness at whatever cost to obtain copies [1] gave them the advantage in debate.

[1] v p. 207.

INDEX

A

Agen, 64, 118, 142, 156, 161, 163

Albi, 1, 7, 8, 13, 62, 118, 122, 124, 142, 145, 161, 180f, 192, 194f, 197, 211ff

Albi, Bishop of, 13, 76, 161, 162, 163, 187f, 195, 197, 203, 214 (*v.* also Councils).

Alexander III, 8, 184.

———— IV, 162, 185

Alfonse, 147, 161

Alise, Countess de Montfort, 69, 96, 101, 156, 160, 161, 182, 195, 202

Amauri, C. de Montfort, 28, 101, 105, 108ff

Arnauld of Citeaux, 15, 18, 38, 40, 46, 48, 52, 55, 58, 60, 61, 70, 71, 73ff, 81, 84, 94, 105, 109, 125

Arnauld, William, 124, 143ff, 151, 191, 192.

Auch, Archbishop of, 14, 103

Autéri, James, 205, 207

———— Peter, 192, 204ff

———— Robert, 197, 205

Avignon, 95, 112, 162

Avignonet, 128, 145, 151

B

Baldwin (Catharist), 22

———— Count, 59, 65, 79

Beaucaire, 42, 95, 96

Benedict XII (Fournier), 162, 213

Bernard de Caux, 155, 160, 179, 186, 190

Bernard de Clairvaux, 3, 4, 132

———— Simorra, 23

———— Gui, 164, 186, 190, 204, 206, 208

Béziers, 7, 22, 51f, 56, 122, 139, 197, 198

Béziers, Bishop of, 15, 51, 102, 126

Béziers, Viscount of, 7, 9, 12, 48, 51ff, 55, 62, 86, 115 (*v.* also Councils)

Bologna, 37, 207

C

Cahors, 75, 118, 145

Carcassonne, 7, 23, 51, 53, 55, 66, 76, 98, 108, 124, 142, 167, 175, 182, 183, 186f, 197, 198, 206ff, 210ff, 215

Carcassonne, Bishop of, 16, 64, 72, 161, 169, 175, 197

Casseneuil, 28, 34, 51

Castelnau, 66 (*v.* also Peter de C.)

Castres, 7, 23, 67, 204, 214f

Causia, 80

Chrysogonus, Peter, 5f

Clement IV, 159, 185, 200

———— V, 202f

Comminges, C. de, 66, 75, 81, 119, 124

Confiscation, 57, 72, 90, 105, 129, 147, 162, 166, 167, 189, 190, 193ff, 201, 205

Consolamentum, 11, 149, 198, 205

Cordes, 68, 180, 181, 183, 197, 203, 212, 215

Councils—

———— Albi, 161, 165, 170, 174

———— Avignonet, 58

———— Béziers, 167, 174, 179, 182

———— Lateran II, 4

———— ———— III, 8

———— ———— IV, 29f, 84ff

———— — Lavour, 76

———— — L'isle, 161

———— — Lombers, 5

———— — Lyons, 202

———— — Montpellier, 10, 21, 81, 110

———— Narbonne, 63, 115, 153, 168, 174, 182, 190